REQUIREMENTS ENGINEERING

REQUIREMENTS ENGINEERING

A Good Practice Guide

Ian Sommerville and
Pete Sawyer
Lancaster University

JOHN WILEY & SONS

Chichester · New York · Weinheim · Brisbane · Singapore · Toronto

Other Wiley Editorial Offices

John Wiley & Sons, Inc., 605 Third Avenue,
New York, NY 10158-0012, USA

VCH Verlagsgesellschaft mbH, Pappelallee 3,
D-69569 Weinheim, Germany

Jacaranda Wiley Ltd, 33 Park Road, Milton,
Queensland 4064, Australia

John Wiley & Sons (Canada) Ltd, 22 Worcester Road,
Rexdale, Ontario M9W IL1, Canada

John Wiley & Sons (Asia) Pte Ltd, 2 Clementi Loop #02-01,
Jin Xing Distripark, Singapore 129809

British Library Cataloguing in Publication Data

A catalogue record for this book is available from the British Library

ISBN 0 471 97444 7

Typeset in 11/13 Melior by Acorn Bookwork, Salisbury
Printed and bound in Great Britain by Bookcraft (Bath) Ltd
This book is printed on acid-free paper responsibly manufactured from sustain-
able forestation, for which at least two trees are planted for each one used for
paper production.

Contents

Preface   vii

1 Introduction   1

2 Practical Process Improvement   15

3 The Requirements Document   37

4 Requirements Elicitation   63

5 Requirements Analysis and Negotiation   111

6 Describing Requirements   141

7 System Modelling   161

8 Requirements Validation   189

9 Requirements Management   215

10 Requirements Engineering for Critical Systems   255

11 System Modelling with Structured Methods   299

12 Formal Specification   331

13 Viewpoints   359

Index   389

Preface

A recent European survey showed that the principal problem areas in software development and production are the requirements specification and the management of customer requirements. There is no doubt that this is equally true in other parts of the world. Improving the processes of discovering, documenting and managing system requirements is critical for future business success.

The aim of this book is to give you advice which can help you improve your requirements engineering process. By improving these processes, you will create descriptions of system requirements which are easier to understand and contain fewer errors and inconsistencies. You will also have more effective procedures for managing changes to these requirements and assessing the impact and costs of these changes.

This book has something to say to everyone who is involved in either software or systems requirements engineering or who have to wrestle with the problems caused by poor system requirements. It is particularly relevant for systems engineers and their managers and for everyone involved in organisational process improvement programmes. It doesn't focus on any specific application domain but we have paid particular attention to the problems of requirements engineering for critical systems. Requirements engineering is a relatively new name and systems analysis is more or less the same thing. If you think of yourself as a systems analyst, you'll find useful advice in the book. We use the term 'engineer' in the book to mean anyone involved in requirements engineering irrespective of their technical background or job title.

We take for granted that you are committed to quality improvement and have good quality management procedures in place. Our suggestions for process improvement are therefore based on changing your process by introducing new or improved practices. We give practical advice on improving your presentation of requirements, your processes for discovering, understanding and analysing requirements and your systems for requirements management.

We have written this handbook because we know that many organisations have problems with discovering, analysing and negotiating requirements for the systems they are developing. Different ways of tackling these problems have been devised but we don't know of any book which collects together this good practice. Existing books on requirements engineering are mostly designed for students who need to develop an awareness of system requirements and the requirements engineering process. They don't say much about practical solutions to requirements engineering problems. We believe that the practical advice which we offer here is more relevant to practitioners who are responsible for system and software requirements engineering.

Standards such as the ISO 9000 standard have emphasised the importance of process definition and standardisation. Surprisingly, however, requirements engineering has been largely neglected in the move towards process definition and standardisation. ISO 9000 says nothing about processes to establish system requirements. The other major influence on software process improvement, namely the Software Engineering Institute's Capability Maturity Model (CMM), simply says that you should manage your requirements but only gives brief guidelines on what this involves. Everything in this book is consistent with both ISO 9000 and the CMM.

The book is organised into three logical parts.

1 An introductory part which discusses the problems of requirements engineering, discusses the requirements engineering process and suggests strategies for process improvement (Chapters 1 and 2).

2 A guidelines part where we make practical suggestions for improving requirements engineering processes. These are based on good requirements engineering practice. The

guidelines are presented in an easy-to-read way without too much jargon or complexity (Chapters 3–10).

3 A number of more detailed chapters where we provide further information to supplement the guidelines on system modelling, formal methods and viewpoint-oriented approaches. You may find this information helpful for implementing some of the guidelines (Chapters 11–13).

We recommend that everyone should read the introductory part then skim through the guidelines to get a general understanding of them. You should think about your process improvement strategies and then return to a more detailed reading of the guidelines which are most relevant to your needs. The material in Part 3 is intended to help implement some of the guidelines and to help you decide if these guidelines are likely to be useful to you. You don't need to read it until you are planning the implementation of the relevant guidelines.

Further Information

To supplement the book, we have established a World-Wide-Web site which includes detailed information which we felt was not appropriate to include in the book. This includes information which changes rapidly and information about systems which seemed interesting but which we didn't know in detail. On the web site, you can find:

1 links to requirements engineering pages elsewhere on the WWW.

2 further information on some of the topics covered in the book such as traceability and process dependability analysis.

3 information about CASE tools to support requirements engineering.

4 contact information for a small number of consultants who provide advice in requirements engineering, process improvement and critical systems.

The URL for the Good Practice Guide web page is:

http://www.comp.lancs.ac.uk/computing/resources/re-gpg/

The REAIMS Project

The guidelines here have been developed as part of the work of a collaborative European project called REAIMS (Project number 8649) whose aim was to develop new techniques and strategies for requirements engineering process improvement, particularly for safety-critical systems. In addition to this handbook, the results of the REAIMS project are:

1 A complementary handbook concerned with general strategies for process improvement. This is entitled 'Process Improvement – A Good Practice Guide'.

2 PREview: this is a viewpoint-oriented method for requirements engineering and process analysis. We describe this approach briefly in Chapter 13.

3 MERE: this is a method for reusing knowledge of previous problems and incidents in the requirements engineering process.

4 PERE: this is a method of process analysis whose aim is to highlight potential process weaknesses where errors may be introduced in the system requirements.

5 FRERE: this is a method concerned with the formal specification and proof of safety-critical software systems.

Information about the REAIMS project including contact information from partners, summaries of the project results and the process improvement good practice guide are available through either the book's web pages or the REAIMS web pages at URL:

http://www.comp.lancs.ac.uk/computing/research/cseg/projects/reaims/

Acknowledgements

We would like to thank all of our partners in the REAIMS project for their support in developing this handbook.

These are GEC-Alsthom Transport, Adelard, Aerospaciale Avions, Aerospaciale Protection Systems (APSYS), Digilog, TUVit and the University of Manchester. We would also like to acknowledge the support of the European Commission for the REAIMS project and to thank the REAIMS reviewing team Andrea Servida, Michael Jackson, Roberto Santoro and Werner Philipp for their advice throughout the project.

Particular thanks to Stephen Shirlaw (GEC-Alsthom), Robin Bloomfield (Adelard) and Jean-Pierre Heckman (Aerospaciale) for their constructive suggestions on how to improve the first draft of the book and to Steve Viller, Tom Rodden, Jacqui Forsyth, Gerald Kotonya and John Bowers (Manchester University) who were part of the Lancaster REAIMS team.

We would also like to thank Watts Humphrey, Peter Wegner, Martyn Ould, Pat Hall, Roel Wieringa and Neil Maiden who reviewed the first draft of the book and provided helpful advice on how it could be improved.

1 Introduction

Summary

This chapter introduces the notion of requirements engineering and requirements engineering process improvement. To simplify the presentation, we have organised it as a set of questions and answers about requirements engineering. The questions which we answer are as follows:

Contents

1.1 How Will This Book Help Me?

1.2 What are Requirements?

1.3 What is Requirements Engineering?

1.4 What is a Requirements Document?

1.5 What is the Best Way to Write Requirements?

1.6 How Detailed Should Requirements Be?

1.7 What is the Difference Between Functional and Non-functional Requirements?

1.8 What are System Stakeholders?

1.9 Does System Size Make a Difference?

1.10 What is a Requirements Engineering Process?

1.11 How do I Recognise Requirements Engineering Process Problems?

1.12 Can You Suggest a Good Requirements Engineering Process?

1.13 Where Does ISO 9000 Fit In?

1.14 Where Can I Find Out More About Requirements Engineering?

The development of computer-based systems has been plagued with problems since the 1960s. Systems may be delivered late, over budget, they do not do what users really want and they are often never used to their full effectiveness by the people who have paid for them. There is rarely a single reason (or a single solution) for these problems but we know that a major contributory factor is problems with system and software requirements.

System requirements define what services the system should provide and set out constraints on the system's operation. Common problems which arise with system requirements are that:

1 the requirements do not reflect the real needs of the customer for the system.

2 requirements are inconsistent and/or incomplete.

3 it is expensive to make changes to requirements after they have been agreed.

4 there are misunderstandings between customers, those developing the system requirements and software engineers developing or maintaining the system.

We are convinced that the best way to reduce these problems is to improve the processes of discovering, understanding, negotiating, describing, validating and managing system requirements. We believe that the best way to do this is in a *gradual* way where you introduce new or improved procedures over a period of time. We do not suggest rapid process change. No-one knows enough about requirements engineering processes to assess if some radically different process will be effective. We think that the business risks of major process re-engineering are simply too high to be acceptable.

The guidelines in this book are therefore intended to support a gradual approach to process improvement. They are based on good requirements engineering practice. They range from very simple guidelines which might be thought of as common sense (but which are easy to overlook) through to suggestions for introducing new methods and techniques to discover and analyse system requirements.

In this introductory chapter, we discuss requirements engineering and the requirements engineering process. To help you understand what the book is about, we have structured this chapter as a list of related questions and answers. This is rather like the increasingly widely used FAQ (frequently asked questions) lists which are used to introduce newcomers to information on the Internet.

We then go on, in Chapter 2, to discuss how to use the book to improve your requirements engineering process. We also introduce the notion of requirements engineering process maturity and suggest how you can assess your maturity level. Detailed good practice guidelines are presented in Chapters 3 to 10 and Chapters 11 to 13 give more detailed information on requirements engineering techniques.

1.1 How Will This Book Help Me?

The book is designed to help you improve your requirements engineering processes. We suggest that you should improve your process by identifying weaknesses then introducing new practices to address these weaknesses. We describe a set of good requirements engineering practices and suggest how you can implement these in your organisation.

To make the description of these good practices easy to read, we have organised them as a set of guidelines (presented in Chapters 3 to 10). Each guideline is presented in a standard way which will help you assess if it is appropriate for your organisation

1 The name of the guideline and a brief guideline description.

2 A set of bullet points setting out the benefits of implementing the guideline.

3 An implementation guide which provides some advice on how to implement the guideline. This is advice *not* instruction. You may have a better way to implement a guideline.

4   A brief assessment of the costs of introducing the guideline in to an organisation, the costs of applying the guideline in requirements engineering processes and problems
which you may encounter when applying the guideline.
Costs are given as low medium or high. Low-cost guidelines should involve less than 10 days of effort to introduce or apply, medium-cost involves 10–100 days of
effort and high-cost involves more than 100 effort-days.

We suggest that you read this chapter and Chapter 2 to
get an overall understanding of the requirements
engineering process and our approach to process improvement. You should then dip into the guideline chapters to
read the specific guidelines which are most relevant to
your problems.

1.2 What are Requirements?

Requirements are defined during the early stages of a
system development as a specification of what should be
implemented. They are descriptions of how the system
should behave, or of a system property or attribute. They
may be a constraint on the development process of the
system. Therefore a requirement might describe:

- a user-level facility (e.g. 'the word processor must include
a spell checking and correction command'),

- a very general system property (e.g. 'the system must
ensure that personal information is never made available
without authorisation'),

- a specific constraint on the system (e.g. 'the sensor must
be polled 10 times per second'),

- a constraint on the development of the system (e.g. 'the
system must be developed using Ada').

Some people suggest that requirements should always be
statements of *what* a system should do rather than a
statement of *how* it should do it. This is an attractive idea
but it is too simplistic in practice.

1   The readers of a document are often practical engineers
who can relate to implementation descriptions much

better than they can understand very abstract problem statements. You have to write requirements which are understandable to the likely readers of the document.

2 In almost all cases, the system being specified is only one of several systems in an environment. To be compatible with its environment, and to conform to standards and with organisational concerns, you may have to specify implementation policies which constrain the options of the system designers.

Requirements therefore invariably contain a mixture of problem information, statements of system behaviour and properties and design and manufacturing constraints.

1.3 What is Requirements Engineering?

Requirements engineering is a relatively new term which has been invented to cover all of the activities involved in discovering, documenting, and maintaining a set of requirements for a computer-based system. The use of the term 'engineering' implies that systematic and repeatable techniques should be used to ensure that system requirements are complete, consistent, relevant, etc. The term 'requirements engineering' has come from a systems engineering background; if you are from a commercial systems background, you can think of requirements engineering as more or less the same thing as systems analysis.

Most of the guidelines in the book apply to system requirements engineering. That is, they apply to systems implemented as software, hardware, or by the people involved with the system. However, in some cases, the guidelines only really make sense when applied to software requirements. This is normally obvious from the guideline text.

1.4 What is a Requirements Document?

The requirements document is an official statement of the system requirements for customers, end-users and software developers. Depending on the organisation, the requirements document may have different names such as the 'functional specification', 'the requirements definition', 'the software requirements specification (SRS)', 'the safety/reliability plan', etc. We use the term 'requirements document' in this book to cover all of these.

1.5 What is the Best Way to Write Requirements?

There is no best way to write requirements. It depends on normal organisational practice and the notations which are used by writers and readers of the requirements. Requirements may be stated in a language which reflects the background of the requirement source. If the source is an engineer, it may be written in engineering terms; if the source is a manager, it will be written in natural language. Most requirements are written as natural language sentences supplemented with diagrams and tables of detailed information. We make no assumptions in this book about how you write requirements nor are we trying to sell any particular notation for requirements specification.

1.6 How Detailed Should Requirements Be?

There is no simple answer to this question. Different organisations think of requirements in different ways and write them at different levels of detail. A requirement for controlling a motor may include details of the specific control signals to be used; a requirement for managing customer information might simply state the information to be provided. The system designer decides how to organise and present this information.

The level of detail that you need largely depends on the normal practice in your organisation, whether or not the requirements document will be the basis of a contract for software development and the type of system which is being developed. If you are developing a product which you both specify and implement, you may produce a fairly general specification. You will add details to this as the system development proceeds. On the other hand, if you are contracting the system development to another company, you need a much more detailed specification which defines what they must implement.

In some organisations, requirements are first expressed as an informal high-level description which is then developed into a more detailed specification. The abstract requirements are the requirements of the stakeholders of the system and the detailed requirements are a system specification.

1 *Stakeholder requirements* (sometimes called user requirements). These are requirements which are written from the point-of-view of system stakeholders. They are not usually expressed in great detail. They are described in natural language, informal diagrams or using some notation which is appropriate to the problem being solved (e.g. mathematical equations for a control system).

2 *System requirements.* These are more detailed specifications of requirements which may be expressed as an abstract model of the system. This may be a mathematical model or may be based on graphical notations such as data-flow diagrams, object class hierarchies, etc. These models are always annotated with natural language descriptions.
It is generally true that system requirements are more detailed than stakeholder requirements. However, there are exceptions to this and, in both cases, requirements may be stated in a detailed or in an abstract way or anywhere in between.

1.7   What is the Difference Between Functional and Non-functional Requirements?

Very roughly, functional requirements describe what the system should do and non-functional requirements place constraints on how these functional requirements are implemented. A functional requirement might state that a system must provide some facility for authenticating the identity of a system user; a non-functional requirement might state that the authentication process should be completed in four seconds or less.

However, it is not always as simple as this. The same functional authentication requirement could have a supplementary requirement which stated that a specific signature verification system (which was known to work in less than four seconds) should be used for authentication. This could be interpreted as either a functional requirement or a non-functional requirement according to the above definition. High-level non-functional requirements are often decomposed into functional system requirements.

1.8 What are System Stakeholders?

System stakeholders are people who will be affected by the system and who have a direct or indirect influence on the system requirements. This includes end-users of the system, managers and others involved in the organisational processes influenced by the system, engineers responsible for the system development and maintenance, customers of the organisation who will use the system to provide some services, external bodies such as regulators or certification authorities, etc.

For example, say an automated railway signalling system is to be developed. Possible stakeholders are:

- operators responsible for running the signalling system
- train crew
- railway managers
- passengers
- equipment installation and maintenance engineers
- safety certification authorities

We recommend that you draw up an explicit list of stakeholders at an early stage in your requirements engineering process.

1.9   Does System Size Make a Difference?

System size makes a tremendous difference. The problems of requirements engineering increase exponentially with the size of the system. Some military systems are gigantic; for such a case a requirements document is organised into several volumes with thousands of individual requirements. Almost everything (CASE tools, databases, organisational processes) starts to break down when it has to deal with the amount of information which is involved in something like this.

Requirements engineering for these huge systems often requires special-purpose notations, tools and techniques. These are too specialised to discuss here. The guidelines suggested in this book are intended to be helpful for all types of system requirements engineering but we know that some of them break down when applied to very large systems. In particular, techniques which involve cross-comparisons of requirements simply do not work when there are too many requirements. The information management problem is so great that the guidelines cannot be applied.

1.10   What is a Requirements Engineering Process?

A requirements engineering process is a structured set of activities which are followed to derive, validate and maintain a systems requirements document. A complete process description should include what activities are carried out, the structuring or schedule of these activities, who is responsible for each activity, the inputs and outputs to/from the activity and the tools used to support requirements engineering.

Very few organisations have an explicitly-defined and standardized requirements engineering process. They simply define the result of the process, namely the requirements document. The people involved in the process are responsible for deciding what to do and when to do it, what information they need, what tools they should use, etc.

We are convinced that you will benefit by defining a requirements engineering process which is appropriate to your organisation. A good process description will provide guidance to the people involved and will reduce the probability that activities will be forgotten about or carried out in a perfunctory way.

1.11   How Do I Recognise Requirements Engineering Process Problems?

You can recognise requirements engineering process problems through either information about the process or information about the product. If you answer 'yes' to some or all of the following questions, there is almost certainly scope for requirements engineering process improvements.

1   Is your requirements engineering process usually over-budget and/or does it take longer than predicted?

2   Do people involved in requirements engineering complain that they do not have enough time or resources to do their job properly?

3   Are there complaints about the understandability or the completeness of the requirements documents which you produce?

4   Do system designers complain of rework resulting from requirements errors?

5   Do customers for your systems fail to use all of the system capabilities?

6   Is there a very high volume of change requests immediately after a system is delivered to customers?

7   Does it take a very long time to agree on system changes resulting from new requirements?

If you have answered 'no' to all these questions, you can stop reading now. You do not need the advice in this book.

1.12   Can You Suggest a Good Requirements Engineering Process?

We cannot do this without knowing about your organisation, your systems engineering and software development processes and the type of software which you develop. There are many possible ways to organise requirements engineering processes and they do not transfer well from one organisation to another. To define a good requirements engineering process, you need to involve people from your organisation who are actually involved in requirements engineering. You may have to get outside help from consultants, as they can take a more objective perspective than those involved in the process.

Most of the standards which have been developed for requirements engineering are concerned with process outputs such as the structure of requirements documents. Within general software engineering standards such as the US DoD standard 2167A, there is some mention of requirements engineering activities but nothing like a standard process description.

However, we would normally expect a good requirements engineering process to include the following activities.

1 *Requirements elicitation.* The system requirements are discovered through consultation with stakeholders, from system documents, domain knowledge and market studies.

2 *Requirements analysis and negotiation.* The requirements are analysed in detail, and should be some formal negotiation process involving different stakeholders to decide on which requirements are to be accepted.

3 *Requirements validation.* These should be a careful check of the requirements for consistency and completeness.

To support these activities, a requirements management process should be introduced to manage changes to the requirements.

1.13   Where Does ISO 9000 Fit In?

ISO 9000 is a standard for quality management processes and variants of this standard have been developed for software engineering. Many organisations have invested a lot of effort in improving their quality management and are now 'ISO 9000 certified'. This has led to significant improvements in quality management across many business sectors. However, ISO 9000 says nothing about requirements engineering. Therefore, there has been a natural tendency in business to focus on ISO 9000 activities at the expense of other processes even if these other processes are known to be a problem.

Approaches to process improvement which are embodied in standards such as ISO 9000 concentrate on process management and process improvement through the development and application of management procedures. They emphasise that you should define processes and put procedures in place to ensure that people follow these defined processes. They do not specify what these processes should be.

We take a complementary approach and discuss process activities rather than process management. Our view is that processes are improved by including particular good practices in your defined processes. All our suggestions are conformant with existing standards. They can be introduced without compromising any ISO 9000 certification which you have.

1.14   Where Can I Find Out More About Requirements Engineering?

There are a number of books on requirements engineering which may help you understand requirements engineering and how to improve your requirements engineering process. However, you should be warned that these books seem mostly to talk about problems rather than solutions.

1   *Software Requirements: Objects, Functions and States* (A. Davis, Prentice-Hall, 1993). This is probably the best

known book in this area. Its orientation is towards the use of structured methods for requirements engineering. It is quite long (500+ pages) and of most interest to practitioners who already have well-developed requirements engineering practices. It is very good on system modelling but weak on areas such as requirements validation and management.

2 *System Requirements Engineering* (P. Loucopoulos and V. Karakostas, McGraw-Hill, 1995). A short textbook which presents an overview of requirements engineering intended for students taking courses in this topic. It touches on lots of topics but provides little detail about any of them. It mostly describes problems and current research in this area rather than practical requirements engineering solutions.

3 *Exploring Requirements: Quality before Design* (D. C. Gause and G. M. Weinberg, Dorset House, 1989). This is an anecdotal book about requirements. It is easy to read and includes a lot of good practical advice. Its focus is on non-technical issues.

4 *Requirements and Specifications: A Lexicon of Software Practice, Principles and Prejudices* (M. Jackson, Addison Wesley, 1995). An interesting selection of short pieces on requirements and specifications. Readable and wise but not intended as a process improvement guide. It covers both technical and non-technical issues.

5 *Requirements Engineering: Frameworks for Understanding* (R. J. Wieringa, Wiley, 1996). A book for students which is mostly concerned with structured methods for modelling information systems. It covers modelling techniques such as data-flow diagrams and entity-relation modelling. It does not cover more general issues of requirements engineering and management.

6 *System and Software Requirements Engineering* (R. H. Thayer and M. Dorfman, IEEE Computer Society Press, 1990). An excellent tutorial volume of research papers in requirements engineering. A new edition is planned for 1997.

7 *Standards, Guidelines and Examples on System and Soft-*

ware Requirements Engineering (M. Dorfman and R. H. Thayer, IEEE Computer Society Press, 1990). This is a comprehensive set of standards which are relevant to requirements engineering.

8 A very comprehensive list of CASE tools, including tools for supporting the requirements engineering process, is available through the World-Wide-Web at URL http://www.qucis.queensu.ca:1999/Software-Engineering/tools.html

Another good site for CASE tool information is at URL http://stfc.comp.polyu.edu.hk/STFC/SoftFactory/database/tools.html

9 Techniques which are designed to help with requirements engineering process improvement have been developed in the REAIMS project and are available through the World-Wide-Web at URL:

http://www.comp.lancs.ac.uk/computing/research/cseg/projects/reaims/

2 Practical Process Improvement

Summary

This chapter discusses how to use the guidelines in this book as part of a practical programme of requirements engineering process improvement. We introduce the idea of process maturity and propose a requirements engineering process maturity model. We discuss the planning of process improvements, describe how to assess your current process and how to use the guidelines suggested in Chapters 3–10 for process improvement. We suggest the 'top ten' guidelines which we believe every organisation should implement, and provide a checklist of guidelines for process assessment.

Contents

2.1   Process Maturity

2.2   Process Assessment

2.3   Process Improvement

2.4   Top Ten Guidelines

2.5   Guideline Lists

Getting started with process improvement is a daunting task. There are always other deadlines to be met, crises which arise and which have to be dealt with, budget and staffing problems, re-organisations, etc. We believe that practical process improvement must recognise these realities. It is not realistic to expect you to invest a lot of time and money in 'improvements' whose value is difficult to assess. Revolutionary approaches to process improvement cost too much and are far too risky for most organisations.

Rather, we are believers in an evolutionary approach to process improvement. A continuous improvement cycle through a series of small steps is required. Small-scale improvements with a high benefit/cost ratio should be introduced before expensive new techniques. These new techniques may involve high training and adaptation costs and, perhaps, organisational changes.

It is not sensible to take a casual or unstructured approach to process improvement. Process improvement is sometimes seen simply as the introduction of new methods or techniques. Because these are more advanced technically than existing methods, you might think that these will necessarily lead to process improvements. A good example of this was the widespread investment in CASE technology in the late 1980s and early 1990s. Many organisations bought CASE tools then found that they had no significant effect on the productivity or quality of their products. The CASE tools changed the process but did not address the real problems faced by these organisations. In many cases, these were problems with the system requirements.

There are four questions which should be answered when you are planning process improvements:

1   *What are the problems with our current processes?* These may be identifiable problems such as late delivery of products, budget over-runs, poor quality products, etc. They may be less tangible problems such as poor staff morale, a reluctance for people to take responsibility or a meeting-dominated process where people spend too much time in meetings. Alternatively, the key problems might be pro-

blems of process understanding – no-one actually knows what processes are followed.

2   *What are our improvement goals?* These should normally be related to the identified problems. For example, if you have quality management problems, your goal may be to improve your quality management procedures to ISO 9000 certification standard. If you have problems with budget over-runs, your goal may be to reduce the amount of rework which is required in a process. It is important that your goals should be realistic. There is no point in setting unrealisable goals or having unrealistic expectations about the benefits of new techniques or methods.

3   *How can we introduce process improvements to achieve these goals?* The set of guidelines in this book are intended to help you with this decision. They suggest specific improvements (some small-scale, others large-scale) which can be applied in a range of different organisations.

4   *How should improvements be controlled and managed?* You need to establish procedures to collect feedback on improvements which may be either quantitative measurements of the process or informal comments on the improvements. You should also ensure that action is taken in response to this feedback to correct any identified problems.

A complementary issue is how to decide upon and manage process improvements. Effective process improvement cannot be achieved by management instruction. The people involved in the processes must be committed to the improvement goals and must be involved in the practical implementation of process change. You must be willing to establish a process improvement group of some kind, which should largely consist of people with practical process experience. The responsibility of the group is to analyse processes, and plan and implement process change.

   The process improvement approach which we propose is based on the iterative application of the guidelines

Guideline type	Description	Costs
Basic	Relatively simple guidelines which provide a framework for a repeatable requirements engineering process where you can estimate the cost, time and resources needed for requirements engineering.	Basic guidelines are usually relatively cheap to introduce and use. You should introduce these first.
Intermediate	More complex guidelines which lead to a defined requirements engineering process. These guidelines are mostly concerned with the introduction of systematic and structured methods into the RE process.	These usually cost more and take more time to introduce than basic guidelines.
Advanced	These are intended to support the continuous improvement of your RE process. They include guidelines for technically advanced methods and guidelines for organisational change.	Costs vary. Some advanced guidelines, based on advanced technology, are expensive. Others are relatively cheap but may require organisational change.

Figure 2.1   Guideline classification

which we suggest. We cannot specify exactly which guidelines should be applied in which order. Different organisations have different priorities for improvement, different problems and different organisational structures. Therefore, each organisation must choose and prioritise the most appropriate guidelines for its needs.

The guidelines which we suggest range from simple 'common-sense' to guidelines which propose the introduction of complex new methods. Clearly, all the guidelines are not applicable to all organisations. You must pick and choose according to your problems, goals and available budget. To help you make this choice, we have classified the guidelines into basic, intermediate and advanced guidelines as described in Figure 2.1.

As a general rule, the level of a guideline is an indicator of the likely cost of introducing that guideline. However, this is not always true. Some basic guidelines are concerned with the definition of standards and these are relatively expensive to implement. Some advanced guidelines are relatively cheap to implement if you have already implemented basic database technology for requirements management.

You can find out more about practical process improvement from the REAIMS process improvement guide. This explains, in more detail, the three-level model of requirements engineering process maturity which we briefly describe in this chapter, suggests different ways to tackle process improvement, and provides information about process analysis and modelling techniques. It is available, free of charge, through the REAIMS Web pages whose URL is given in the Preface.

2.1 Process Maturity

The idea of 'process maturity' came about through the work of the US Department of Defense's Software Engineering Institute. They developed a method of assessing the capabilities of companies bidding for defence contracts and this has become known as the 'Capability Maturity Model' (CMM). This model rates organisations on a scale from 1 to 5. The higher the rating, the higher the maturity of the organisation. The assumption is that the more mature the process used to develop software, the better the software systems will be.

The basis idea underlying the CMM approach is that organisations should assess their maturity then introduce process changes which will enable them to progress up the maturity 'ladder' in a five stage process. The steps in this maturity ladder are shown in Figure 2.2.

The five levels in the SEI's capability maturity model are as follows.

1 *Initial level.* Organisations have an undisciplined process and it is left to individuals to decide how to manage the process and which development techniques to use.

2 *Repeatable level.* Organisations have basic cost and schedule management procedures in place. They are likely to be able to make consistent budget and schedule predictions for projects in the same application areas.

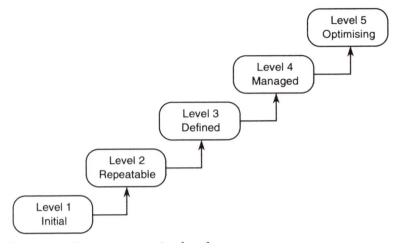

Figure 2.2 Process maturity levels

3 *Defined level.* The software process for both management and engineering activities is documented, standardized and integrated into a standard software process for the organisation.

4 *Managed level.* Detailed measurements of both process and product quality are collected and used to control the process.

5 *Optimizing level.* The organisation has a continuous process improvement strategy, based on objective measurements, in place.

At each of these levels, a set of 'Key Practices' has been defined*. Once all of the practices at one level have been introduced in an organisation, it has reached that level of maturity and moves up to the next level. Examples of practices include requirements management (repeatable level), configuration management (repeatable level), peer reviews (defined level), quantitative and process management (managed level).

The Capability Maturity Model: Guidelines for Improving the Software Process, Carnegie Mellon University – Software Engineering Institute, Addison Wesley, 1995.

The SEI's Capability Maturity Model has been very influential and has spawned other models (such as the Bootstrap model) of process maturity and process improvements. Many organisations are assessing their processes using the CMM and have the declared objective to move to a given level of maturity (usually either 2 or 3) within some defined timescale. Experience has shown that moving from one level to another takes several years in most organisations. As yet, few organisations have reached the higher levels of the model.

2.1.1 Requirements engineering process maturity

The CMM is focused on software development and does not cover the requirements engineering process, so we have created a comparable model of requirements engineering process maturity. Requirements engineering process maturity is the extent to which an organisation has a *defined* requirements engineering process based on good requirements engineering practices. An organisation with a mature RE process will have this process explicitly defined. It will use appropriate methods and techniques for requirements engineering, will have defined standards for requirements documents, requirements descriptions, etc. The organisation may use automated tools to support process activities. It will have management policies and procedures in place to ensure that the process is followed and may use process measurements to collect information about the process to help assess the value of process changes.

The SEI's Capability Maturity Model is mostly concerned with the management of software development processes and does not cover system requirements engineering. Our requirements process maturity model is a three-level model. The first two levels are roughly comparable to the first two levels of the SEI model. The third level encompasses all of the higher levels in that model. This is illustrated in Figure 2.3.

1 *Level 1 – Initial level.* Level 1 organisations do not have a defined requirements engineering process and often suffer from the problems discussed above. They do not use

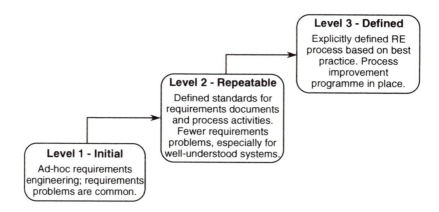

Figure 2.3 Requirements engineering process maturity levels

advanced methods to support their requirements engineering processes. They often fail to produce good quality requirement documents on time and within budget. They are dependent on the skills and experience of individual engineers for requirements elicitation, analysis and validation.

2 *Level 2 – Repeatable level.* Level 2 organisations have defined standards for requirements documents and requirements descriptions and have introduced policies and procedures for requirements management. They may use some advanced tools and techniques in their requirements engineering processes. Their requirements documents are more likely to be of a consistently high quality and to be produced on schedule.

3 *Level 3 – Defined level.* Level 3 organisations have a defined requirements engineering process model based on good practices and techniques. They have an active process improvement programme in place and can make objective assessments of the value of new methods and techniques.

These are rough classifications which are convenient for discussing the guidelines which we propose. In general, level 1 organisations should focus in introducing the basic guidelines which we suggest; level 2 organisations should have implemented most of the basic guidelines and are in a position to implement the intermediate guidelines; level 3 organisations should have implemented almost all basic guidelines and all appropriate intermediate guidelines. They may improve their process by introducing the advanced guidelines which we suggest.

The effectiveness of the particular suggestions which we make is partially dependent on the level of process maturity. Organisations which do not have a controlled and defined requirements engineering process may experience problems if they wish to introduce technically advanced methods such as formal specification of systems. It is not necessary to implement all basic and intermediate guidelines before advanced guidelines. However, if you want to introduce advanced methods with an uncontrolled process, you must expect this to take additional time and money; you may also find that the payoff from these methods is less than expected.

Some organisations will find it cost-effective to try to increase their level of process maturity; others will find it best to stay at a particular level and to improve their processes within that level. It depends on the type, the complexity and the size of the systems which you produce. The larger and more complex the system, the more benefits you are likely to gain by increasing your level of process maturity.

The requirements engineering process maturity level is only one of the factors which affects the quality of the final requirements document. Other important factors are the abilities and experience of the people involved in·the process, the novelty, difficulty and size of the problem and the time and resources available. Immature organisations can and do produce good quality requirements documents. However, they may not be able to do so consistently or when working under tight deadlines.

Mature organisations should normally produce good quality documents on time and within budget. It does not mean that they will never have requirements engineering problems. New systems, particularly, are always likely to be difficult to specify. However, a mature organisation should have processes and procedures in place which give them the best chance of solving unforeseen requirements problems.

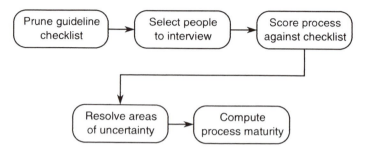

Figure 2.4 Process maturity assessment

2.2   Process Assessment

The first stage in process improvement is to assess your existing process. This will reveal how well your process is defined and the areas of weakness in your process. To do so, we recommend that you use the guideline checklist given later in this chapter. Starting with the basic guidelines, you should assess your current requirements engineering practice and check off the guidelines against it. The activities involved in carrying out an assessment are shown in Figure 2.4.

Against each guideline, you should make one of the following assessments.

1 *Standardized.* This means that the guideline describes a process or practice that has a documented standard in your organisation and which is followed and checked as part of your quality management process.

2 *Normal use.* This means that the guideline is widely followed in your organisation but is not mandatory.

3 *Used at discretion of project manager.* This means that some project managers may have introduced the guideline but it is not universally used.

4 *Never.* This means that the guideline is never or very rarely applied.

The stages in the assessment process have been designed to minimise the costs of carrying out an assessment.

1 *Prune guideline checklist.* This activity is intended to identify, very quickly, guidelines which you never use. You should do this from your own knowledge and by consulting with an experienced requirements engineer.

2 *Select people to interview.* In large organisations, different projects may use different practices. You should identify a range of people across the organisation to interview for the maturity assessment.

3 *Score practices against checklist.* This initial scoring should be 'quick and dirty', and based on brief guideline descriptions. If there is some doubt about whether or not a guideline has been adopted, you should leave this for later consideration.

4 *Resolve areas of uncertainty.* This is likely to be the most time-consuming stage where you may need to use the guideline descriptions here to discover if a guideline is used. You need also make some decision at this stage about practices which are used by some people in the organisation but not by others.

5 *Compute process maturity.* We describe below how to do this.

A systematic assessment tells you two things about your requirements engineering processes.

1 Particular areas of weakness (e.g. requirements management) where you may wish to focus your improvements.

2 Your level of process maturity. You should score three points for a standardized guideline, two for normal use, one for discretionary use and zero for guidelines which are never used. The higher your score, the fewer weaknesses there are likely to be in your RE process. Figure 2.5 is a rough indicator of the relationships between assessment scores and maturity levels.

Notice that our assessment model allows for flexibility. You do not have to implement all of the basic guidelines to have a mature requirements engineering process. Some guidelines may not be appropriate for your organisation and you will never need to implement them.

Do not despair if your assessment results in a low score for your organisation. Surveys have shown that the

Maturity level	Assessment score
Initial	Less than 55 in the basic guidelines. May have implemented some intermediate guidelines.
Repeatable	Above 55 in the basic guidelines but less than 40 in the intermediate and advanced guidelines.
Defined	More than 85 in the basic guidelines and more than 40 in the intermediate and advanced guidelines.

Figure 2.5 Assessment scores and maturity levels

requirements engineering maturity of almost all organisations is at the initial level. Although most organisations had implemented some basic guidelines, few organisations is implemented all of them. Intermediate practices were only used in a minority of organisations. Advanced practices have been used successfully in pilot projects and have not yet been universally introduced in any organisation.

2.3 Process Improvement

Making changes and introducing new techniques in an organisation is always difficult. You must always leave enough time to implement these new techniques. People who must apply these techniques must be kept fully informed during the introduction process. You should always try to introduce techniques where everyone involved (not just managers) sees some benefit. Some very general suggestions for facilitating process change are as follows

1 *Find an evangelist.* If you can convince someone who is involved in the process of the value of proposed changes, he or she will be the best person to convince other practitioners to accept the changes.

2 *Try changes out on pilot projects.* Do not rush headlong into change. Introduce process changes in pilot projects

and find out the advantages and disadvantages of the change.

3 *Allow enough time to make the change.* When you introduce changes, you must accept that it will take some time to introduce the change. Do not use projects with very tight deadlines as pilot projects.

4 *Respect professional skills.* Do not introduce changes which degrade professional abilities and respect the judgement of professionals involved in requirements engineering. Emphasise that the point of changes is to help people improve the quality of their work.

If you want improvements to be effective, you need to introduce guidelines incrementally and assess the impact of these guidelines before introducing more changes. You must strike a balance between introducing too many new guidelines at once and introducing too few new process changes which have limited effect. The number of guidelines to be introduced at any one time obviously depends on the guideline. For example, it is usually possible to introduce several basic guidelines at the same time. However, you may find it is only possible to introduce intermediate and advanced guidelines one-by-one.

The order in which improvement guidelines are introduced depends on your process and the need for improvements which you have identified. However, if you are starting from a baseline of an unstructured requirements engineering process, we recommend that you should introduce the guidelines in the order shown in Figure 2.6.

Of course, you will not necessarily implement all of the guidelines in these sections before moving on to the next section. Rather, you have to make a decision about which guidelines are likely to be the most cost-effective for you. This must be based on:

1 knowledge of your requirements engineering process and your process maturity level

2 your budget and timescale for improvements

3 the people involved in implementing the requirements engineering process improvements.

Guidelines	Rationale
Guidelines related to the requirements document (Chapter 3)	Establishing a standard, accepted document structure which is easy to maintain is, we believe, the essential first step for better requirements engineering processes.
Guidelines related to requirements management (Chapter 9)	You must be able to manage changes to your requirements and assess the impact of these changes.
Guidelines related to requirements description (Chapter 6)	These allow you to establish a standard way of describing requirements so that you simplify requirements understanding and open up possibilities for requirements reuse across different projects.
Guidelines related to requirements validation (Chapter 8)	Problems with requirements validation are very common as, typically, requirements engineering processes run out of budget or schedule before extensive validation has been completed. The guidelines here should reduce the costs of validation and so allow you to spend more time on the validation process.

Figure 2.6　Guideline implementation priority

Once you have implemented guidelines for these activities, you can then move onto guidelines in other areas such as requirements elicitation, system modelling, etc. There is no ideal ordering for these and you must use your judgement about which guidelines are likely to be most cost-effective.

2.3.1　Improvement costs

To implement process improvements, you need a small dedicated team who plan and introduce these improvements. You must allow several months to assess your existing process and plan an initial set of improvements. The improvement team should consult widely in the organisation and should make sure that project managers understand why improvements are being introduced. The first set of improvements will also take several months to implement but, once the idea of improvement has taken hold, it may be possible to accelerate the process.

We recommend that you should change the membership of the improvement team after the initial set of improvements have been planned. This means that you will have people committed to improvement working on projects in the organisation. You will not have to sell improvement to them.

The costs of improvement are, obviously, the costs of the improvement team plus the initial costs of introducing process change. As improvement is a long-term process, you must budget for several years of improvement effort. Process change costs are harder to estimate but you should certainly allow for several months of additional effort on the part of team members to learn about and use new processes. Of course, once these processes have not introduced, you should start to see a payback from your improvements. However, do not expect short-term savings; process improvement is a long-term commitment. You will only gain the benefits after new processes have come into general use.

You can certainly measure aspects of your process such as the number of requirements change requests and the time required to implement change requests. In the long term, you should see improvements in these figures. However, introducing a measurement programme is itself a costly exercise*. You do not always need quantitative information to judge if something has been successful. You can learn a lot about the effectiveness of process change simply by talking to people involved in the process. If guidelines do not work for you, do not be afraid to discard them.

2.3.2 CASE tool use

Some of the guidelines suggested here require the use of CASE tools for their support and others can be implemented more efficiently if you use appropriate tools. We have not associated specific tools with guidelines and we do not recommend tools from any particular tool vendor. In most cases, there are various alternative tools which

---

*For practical advice on introducing process measurement, see *A quantitative approach to software management* by K. Pulford, A. Kuntzmann-Combelles and S. Shirlaw (Addison Wesley, 1995).

may be used and you must make your own selection of what is appropriate for your organisation. We provide some information about tool suppliers on the book's Web page.

Tool selection depends on a variety of factors: as follows.

1 The tools which are already in use in your organisation and the computers used by your requirements engineers. Obviously, any new tools have to be compatible with these existing systems.

2 Your tool budget and, critically, your training budget. If you intend to introduce new tools, you must train people in their use.

3 The size of the systems which you specify. The larger the system, the more you need specialised tools for information management.

4 The specific guidelines which you wish to implement. Some require significant tool support, others, very little.

5 The stability of the companies supplying the tools. Specialised requirements engineering tools are often produced by small companies which have spun-off from some larger organisation. These companies may be unstable and you may not wish to risk buying from them.

It is important not to be seduced by some of the more extravagant claims made by CASE tool vendors. Experience has shown that the introduction and use of CASE tools is expensive; there are real benefits but it takes several years to have a positive return on investment. In some cases, particularly where large volumes of information must be handled, there is no alternative to specific CASE tools. In other situations, it may be more cost-effective to adapt general-purpose programs such as word processors and spreadsheets for requirements engineering process support.

2.4   Top Ten Guidelines

The importance of the different guidelines depends on your organisation and the type of systems which you

Guideline	Description	Page
3.1	Define a standard document structure	41
3.8	Make the document easy to change	60
9.1	Uniquely identify each requirement	218
9.2	Define policies for requirements management	221
6.1	Define standard templates for requirements description	144
6.2	Use language simply, consistently and concisely	147
8.2	Organise formal requirements inspections	195
8.4	Define validation checklists	200
5.2	Use checklists for requirements analysis	117
5.4	Plan for conflicts and conflict resolution	125

Figure 2.7   Top ten guidelines

develop. However, we think that there are some basic guidelines which are so important that they should be implemented in all organisations. We recommend that you start your process improvement programme by implementing the guidelines shown in Figure 2.7.

All of these guidelines may be introduced into organisations at any level of requirements engineering process maturity. They are cost-effective practices which we believe should be part of all requirements engineering processes.

2.5   Guideline Lists

As discussed above, we recommend that organisations at the initial level in the RE process maturity model should focus on basic guidelines, level 2 organisations, at the repeatable level, should move onto intermediate guidelines and that you should not normally introduce the advanced guidelines until you have reached the defined level in RE process maturity. The guideline checklists below are arranged according to our classification of the guideline type. Remember, however, that you should interpret our classification flexibly. If a guideline seems right for your organisation, you should implement it irrespective of your maturity level.

, The checklists include:

1   the guideline number; guideline 2.3 (say) is the third guideline in Chapter 2

2   a brief, meaningful statement of the guideline

3   an assessment of the stage of the RE process where the guideline is most applicable

4   a column headed 'Usage' which you can use as part of your process assessment. You should fill this in as 'S' (standardized), 'N' (normal), 'D' (discretionary) or '–' (never).

2.5.1   Basic guidelines

	Guideline	Applicability	Usage
3.1	Define a standard document structure	Requirements document	
3.2	Explain how to use the document	Requirements document	
3.3	Include a summary of the requirements	Requirements document	
3.4	Make a business case for the system	Requirements document	
3.5	Define specialised terms	Requirements document	
3.6	Lay out the document for readability	Requirements document	
3.7	Help readers find information	Requirements document	
3.8	Make the document easy to change	Requirements document	
4.1	Assess system feasibility	Requirements elicitation	

	Guideline	Applicability	Usage
4.2	Be sensitive to organisational and political considerations	Requirements elicitation	
4.3	Identify and consult system stakeholders	Requirements elicitation	
4.4	Record requirements sources	Requirements elicitation	
4.5	Define the system's operating environment	Requirements elicitation	
4.6	Use business concerns to drive requirements elicitation	Requirements elicitation	
5.1	Define system boundaries	Requirements analysis and negotiation	
5.2	Use checklists for requirements analysis	Requirements analysis and negotiation	
5.3	Provide software to support negotiations	Requirements analysis and negotiation	
5.4	Plan for conflicts and conflict resolution	Requirements analysis and negotiation	
5.5	Prioritise requirements	Requirements analysis and negotiation	
6.1	Define standard templates for describing requirements	Describing requirements	
6.2	Use language simply and concisely	Describing requirements	
6.3	Use diagrams appropriately	Describing requirements	
6.4	Supplement natural language with other descriptions of requirements	Describing requirements	
7.1	Develop complementary system models	System modelling	
7.2	Model the system's environment	System modelling	
7.3	Model the system architecture	System modelling	
8.1	Check that the requirements document meets your standards	Requirements validation	

	Guideline	Applicability	Usage
8.2	Organise formal requirements inspections	Requirements validation	
8.3	Use multi-disciplinary teams to review requirements	Requirements validation	
8.4	Define validation checklists	Requirements validation	
9.1	Uniquely identify each requirement	Requirements management	
9.2	Define policies for requirements management	Requirements management	
9.3	Define traceability policies	Requirements management	
9.4	Maintain a traceability manual	Requirements management	
10.1	Create safety requirement checklists	Requirements engineering for critical systems	
10.2	Involve external reviewers in the validation process	Requirements engineering for critical systems	

2.5.2 Intermediate guidelines

	Guideline	Applicability	Usage
4.7	Look for domain constraints	Requirements elicitation	
4.8	Record requirements rationale	Requirements elicitation	
4.9	Collect requirements from multiple viewpoints	Requirements elicitation	
4.10	Prototype poorly understood requirements	Requirements elicitation	
4.11	Use scenarios to elicit requirements	Requirements elicitation	
4.12	Define operational processes	Requirements elicitation	
5.6	Classify requirements using a multi-dimensional approach	Requirements analysis and negotiation	
5.7	Use interaction matrices to find conflicts and overlaps	Requirements analysis and negotiation	

	Guideline	Applicability	Usage
6.5	Specify requirements quantitatively	Describing requirements	
7.4	Use structured methods for system modelling	System modelling	
7.5	Use a data dictionary	System modelling	
7.6	Document the links between stakeholder requirements and system models	System modelling	
8.5	Use prototyping to animate requirements	Requirements validation	
8.6	Write a draft user manual	Requirements validation	
8.7	Propose requirements test cases	Requirements validation	
9.5	Use a database to manage requirements	Requirements management	
9.6	Define change management policies	Requirements management	
9.7	Identify global system requirements	Requirements management	
10.3	Identify and analyse hazards	Requirements engineering for critical systems	
10.4	Derive safety requirements from hazard analysis	Requirements engineering for critical systems	
10.5	Cross-check operational and functional requirements against safety requirements	Requirements engineering for critical systems	

2.5.3 Advanced guidelines

	Guideline	Applicability	Usage
4.13	Reuse requirements	Requirements elicitation	
5.8	Assess requirements risks	Requirements analysis and negotiation	

	Guideline	Applicability	Usage
8.8	Paraphrase system models	Requirements validation	
9.8	Identify volatile requirements	Requirements management	
9.9	Record rejected requirements	Requirements management	
10.6	Specify systems using formal specification	Requirements engineering for critical systems	
10.7	Collect incident experience	Requirements engineering for critical systems	
10.8	Learn from incident experience	Requirements engineering for critical systems	
10.9	Establish an organisational safety culture	Requirements engineering for critical systems	

3 The Requirements Document

Summary

The requirements document is used to communicate system requirements to customers, system users, managers and system developers. This chapter suggests how you can improve the structure and organisation of this document. We suggest the following guidelines for the requirements document:

Guidelines

3.1 Define a Standard Document Structure.

3.2 How To Use The Document.

3.3 Include a Summary of the Requirements.

3.4 Make a Business Case for the System.

3.5 Define Specialised Terms.

3.6 Lay Out the Document for Readability.

3.7 Help Readers Find Information.

3.8 Make the Document Easy to Change.

The requirements document is an official statement of the system requirements for customers, end-users and software developers. Depending on the organisation, the requirements document may have different names such as the 'functional specification', 'the requirements definition', 'the software requirements specification (SRS)', 'the safety/quality plan', etc. These documents are all basically similar. They specify what services the system should provide, system properties such as reliability, efficiency, etc. and the constraints on the operation and (sometimes) the development of the system.

The objective of this chapter is to present a set of guidelines which will help you improve the quality of your requirements documents. Improving requirements documents is just as important as putting new process activities in place. Good quality requirements documents present a clear and consistent specification of the system to be implemented. They are readily understandable by a range of different readers. They are as concise as possible and are designed so that changes may be made without too much expense.

The requirements document may be used for reference by a number of different people.

1 System customers who specify the requirements and who read the requirements document to check that it is an acceptable expression of their needs. They also use the document when specifying changes to the requirements while the system is being developed or after it has gone into operation.

2 Managers responsible for planning, costing and scheduling the system development. In some cases, these estimates are the basis for a bid to develop the system. In all cases, the requirements document is used as an input to the project planning process after system development is underway.

3 System engineers responsible for designing and implementing the system. They use the requirements document to understand what is to be developed.

4 System test engineers who use the document to derive

tests which verify that the developed system meets the requirements.

5 System maintenance staff who maintain and modify the system after it has gone into use. They use the document to understand the initial system characteristics and the relationships between different parts of the system.

The software requirements document is not a design document. Ideally, it should focus on what the system should do without specifying *how* it should be done. In principle, it should not include requirements which constrain the design of the system. In reality, this is virtually impossible. There is not a clear boundary between specification and design. The specification may have to be structured to reflect the architectural design of the system; design and implementation constraints may be specific requirements; designs may have to be reused and it may be almost impossible to express some requirements without referring to a design model.

Different types of organisation produce different types of requirements document. In some cases, the requirements document is a fairly short, abstract description of the system. In other cases, it is a very detailed specification of system functionality. These differences reflect the fact that there are really two types of requirements.

1 Stakeholder requirements which are abstract requirements describing the system services which people need to use the system and to integrate it with their business processes. These are sometimes called user requirements. As requirements may not just come from end-users of the system, we prefer the more general name. Requirements on the development process which must be used for the system may also be stakeholder requirements.

2 System requirements which are a detailed specification of the system facilities which should be implemented and the constraints on that implementation. This description may be the basis of a contract for the system development so it should be a complete description of the behaviour of the system.

In some organisations, stakeholder requirements and

system requirements will be produced separately. The stakeholder requirements will be developed first then, after these have been agreed, a more detailed system-level requirements specification will be produced. In other cases, there will only be a single requirements document which includes both stakeholder and system requirements.

Where an organisation is responsible for both writing requirements and producing the system, a detailed requirements specification may not be necessary. Microsoft adopts this approach where it produces an outline specification and develops the specification at the same time as the system. This allows scope for change in response to new requirements, market pressure and technical problems which arise. It is important, however, to have some kind of specification, otherwise project management and planning is impossible.

3.1   Define a Standard Document Structure

Key benefit	Higher quality, lower cost requirements documents
Costs of introduction	Moderate–high
Costs of application	Low
Guideline type	Basic

Requirements documents should have a common structure which should be defined as a company standard and should be checked as part of the document quality assurance process. A standard document structure should encapsulate what your organisation thinks is the best way to organise a requirements document. Because of the diversity of different types of system which may be developed, you may need to have variants from a single standard depending on the type of system and the expected readership of the document.

Benefits

- A standard format for requirements documents means that readers can use their knowledge of previous documents when reading a new requirements document. They can find information more easily and understand the relationships between different parts of the document.

- The standard document format acts as a checklist for writers of requirements documents and reduces the chances of them accidentally omitting information. Similarly, document reviewers can use the standard to check if sections have been left out of the document and as a driver of the reviewing process.

- Software can be developed to support the production of requirements documents conforming to the common standard.

Implementation

If a standard is to be useful, it must reflect the best practice in your organisation for requirements documents. You should examine the structure of several existing requirements documents to find common characteristics. You should also discuss, with document users, what they like and dislike about these existing documents and what they think have been omitted from these documents.

The best document structure for your needs depends on custom and practice in your organisation, the type of system being developed and the organisational system development processes. We can not tell you the best structure for you but, in developing a structure, you may find it helpful to use some published standard as a starting point.

A number of different large organisations such as the US Department of Defense and the IEEE have defined their own standard for requirements documents. Probably the most accessible of these standards is the IEEE/ANSI 830-1993 standard which suggests the following structure for requirements documents.

1 Introduction
   1.1 Purpose of the requirements document
   1.2 Scope of the product
   1.3 Definitions, acronyms and abbreviations
   1.4 References
   1.5 Overview of the remainder of the document

2 General description
   2.1 Product perspective
   2.2 Product functions
   2.3 User characteristics
   2.4 General constraints
   2.5 Assumptions and dependencies

3 Specific requirements covering functional, non-functional and interface requirements. These should document external interfaces, functionality, performance requirements, logical database requirements, design constraints, system attributes and quality characteristics.

Appendices

Index

This is a generic document structure and organisations should adapt it to their own specific needs. Irrespective of its organisation, the standard should define the information which you would expect to find in a requirements document. This may include the following.

1 An overview of the system and the benefits of developing the system.

2 A glossary explaining the technical terms used.

3 A definition of the services or functional requirements of the system.

4 A definition of system properties or non-functional requirements such as reliability, safety, etc.

5 Constraints on the operation of the system and the system development process.

6 A definition of the system's operating environment and likely changes to that environment.

7 Detailed system specifications expressed as system models (see Chapter 7) showing the relationships between system components. These may include data processing models, data structure models, etc. You should only include them if you need to produce a very detailed requirements document.

A requirements document standard must allow for differences between systems. You should be able to omit parts of the document and to add new sections. Part of your standard should therefore be an introductory page which explains allowed variances from the defined standard.

To allow for variants, you may find it helpful to define the standard as a list of stable and variant parts. Stable parts are those chapters (such as an introduction and a glossary) which should appear in all requirements documents. Variant parts are those chapters which may but need not be included and whose contents may vary depending on the system being specified.

If organisations do not already have a standard, we recommend that this should be one of the first guidelines implemented. Of course, as good practices are introduced, the standard may have to be revised to take account of the organisation's increasing level of requirements engineering process maturity.

An extensive summary of requirements standards is given in *Standards, Guidelines and Examples on System and Software Requirements Engineering* (M. Dorfman and R. H. Thayer, IEEE Press, 1990).

Costs and problems

Setting up any kind of standard is not cheap. It may take several months of effort to analyse and understand the existing documents and to extract an appropriate standard from them. In large organisations especially, you must also allow for a long period of consultation before the standard can be agreed. Once a standard has been established, it should be reviewed periodically and updated when necessary. This is relatively inexpensive, assuming that the standard does not have to be radically changed.

Once you have established a standard and requirements engineers have become familiar with it, the costs of actually applying the standard are low. You need some quality checks to assure conformance, but apart from that, using the standard should not significantly increase the costs of producing a requirements document.

Some people, particularly software developers, are sometimes resistant to standards. They argue against a standard on the grounds that it will reduce the flexibility and, potentially, increase the costs of producing the requirements document. Apart from the fact that this is a pretty dubious argument, you should always remember, that the document is likely to be read more often than it is written. Any increased costs in writing the document are likely to be offset by lower costs in document reading.

3.2   Explain How To Use The Document

Key benefit	Less reading time required to understand the requirements document
Costs of introduction	Very low
Costs of application	Very low
Guideline type	Basic

You should always include a section in the introduction to a document which explains how it should be used. This should be addressed to different types of readers such as end-users, engineers implementing the system, managers planning the system development, etc. It should explain what sections are most appropriate for each class of reader and the technical background required to understand them.

Benefits

- If you describe how to read the document in an effective way, readers will spend less time reading and understanding the system requirements and will probably be less frustrated by problems which arise. The costs associated with reading the document will be reduced.

- If you tell readers what they need to know in order to understand a document it helps them judge whether any problems of comprehensibility are a result of their lack of technical background or whether it is due to badly-expressed requirements.

Implementation

This section should be called 'How to use this document' and should be part of the introductory chapter in the requirements document. You should include at least the following information in this section.

1   The different types of reader that the document is aimed
    at. If readers need specialised knowledge to understand
    the system requirements, you may want to warn potential
    readers of sections which they may find hard to under-
    stand.

2   The technical background required to understand the
    document in general and any specialist technical knowl-
    edge which is required for specific sections.

3   Pointers to overview sections which may be read to give a
    general understanding of the requirements before con-
    sidering the detailed specification.

4   Sections of the document which are intended for a spe-
    cific type of reader and which may be skipped by other
    readers. You should suggest sections which may be skip-
    ped on a first reading if the intention is to develop a gen-
    eral understanding of the system.

5   Order dependencies which describe the order in which
    sections should be read. You may also explain which sec-
    tions of the document are independent and which may be
    read without reference to other sections.

Costs and problems

There are no significant costs associated with introducing
or applying this guideline. To introduce the guideline
simply involves specifying that this section is an essential
part of all requirements documents. The section on how
to use the document should be short and succinct and
should not take more than an hour to write.

The principal problem in applying the guideline is that
you may find it difficult to identify the technical
background required to understand each part of the
document. If you are very familiar with the document,
you may also find it difficult to identify the best order for
reading it.

3.3   **Include a Summary of the Requirements**

Key benefit	More understandable requirements document
Costs of introduction	Very low
Costs of application	Low
Guideline type	Basic

You should always include an overview section in the requirements document which summarises the purpose of the system and principal system requirements

Benefits

- It is much easier for readers to comprehend system requirements if they have a broad picture of what they are trying to understand. Summarising the requirements allows requirements to make forward references to other requirements without confusing the reader.

- Creating a summary focuses attention on the critical requirements and can help establish the priorities of the requirements.

- The summary acts as a map of the requirements in the document and may help readers find specific requirements of interest to them.

Implementation

Requirements summaries can be written in a number of different ways.

1 The most important requirements may be presented in a numbered list.

2 Based on some classification structure, the different requirements may be presented in a table. You can see an example of this type of overview in the guideline tables which have been included in Chapter 2 of this book.

3 A graphical view of the requirements can be produced with each principal requirement shown as a node in a diagram. Graphical views are particularly useful when you need to show relationships between requirements or groups of requirements.

It is usually best to organise the summary on a per chapter basis so that the reader can see what requirements are presented in each chapter of the document. The summary should also briefly define the standard presentation style which you use for requirements description (see **Guideline 6.1**, *Define standard templates for describing requirements*).

Costs and problems

There are no significant costs in introducing this guideline. The costs of implementing the guideline are the time required to produce a summary of the requirements document. This obviously depends on the size of the document. If the summariser already understands the requirements, it should not normally take more than a few days of effort.

There are two problems which you may face in implementing this requirement. If you have a very large number of requirements, you may find it difficult to present a coherent requirements overview. There is no easy solution to this problem. Large numbers of requirements are always a problem. However, the larger the requirements document, the more an overview is needed so we believe that it is worthwhile to invest effort in producing this summary.

The other problem you may face is that requirements engineers do not see this as a critical part of the requirements document. When working to tight deadlines, they may argue that this section could be left out of the document. To counter this, you should ensure that the overview section is defined as part of the document standard and that it is checked as part of the quality assurance process.

3.4   Make a Business Case for the System

Key benefit	Provides a rationale for the system requirements
Costs of introduction	Very low
Costs of application	Very low
Guideline type	Basic

The requirements document should always include a section explaining why the system is required and how it will contribute to the overall business objectives of the organisation buying the system.

Benefits

- When proposals for requirements change are made, you can use the business case for the system to assess whether or not the proposed changes are sensible. Of course, the business case itself may change and then you may have to address whether or not the specified system is still required.

- The case for the system helps readers of the document understand why particular requirements have been included. This is particularly helpful when requirements change proposals are made. At this stage, the original reason for including a particular requirement may have been forgotten and readers may be able to infer the rationale from the business case.

Implementation

The case for a system should be made as a separate section of the introduction to the requirements document. In that section, the business objectives which have led to the need for the computer-based system should be summarised. You should then include a rationale which explains how the system will contribute to these objectives of the organisation. This should relate the facilities provided by the system to the business objectives.

In this section, you should also, if possible, predict possible business changes and how these will affect the system. This may help system designers organise the system so that it is more resilient to change.

Costs and problems

There are no significant costs involved in introducing or applying this guideline. The major problem which you may encounter is that many organisations do not have explicit business objectives which may be included in this section. Different senior managers may, in fact, have different objectives and decisions on buying systems may depend on whoever wields the most political power in the organisation.

3.5   Define Specialised Terms

Key benefit	Avoids misunderstandings among requirements document readers and writers
Costs of introduction	Low
Costs of application	Low–moderate
Guideline type	Basic

Specialised terms used in the requirements document should be defined in a glossary. A glossary defines terms which are specific to an application domain (e.g. if the system is concerned with banking, it would include terms such as 'account', 'balance', etc.) and terms which are used in a specialised way. For example, the term 'printer' in the context of this document may not just mean normal printing devices connected to a computer but also a microfilm writer.

Benefits

- Problems with terminology are perhaps the most common sources of confusion in requirements documents. Different readers from different backgrounds are likely to understand the same term in different ways and hence misunderstand parts of the document.

- If the document is written by several people then it is likely that they will also use the same term in different ways as the document is being written. They can use the glossary as a shared reference manual which helps avoid this problem.

- Application domains always have their own jargon which is only understandable by readers who are expert in that domain. Requirements documents are used by a wide class of readers so it is important to explain the meaning of this jargon to readers who are not domain experts.

Implementation

The best way to produce a glossary is to start with a standard glossary then modify it for each new requirements document. The existing glossary serves as a reference for writers. When a new term, which is not in the glossary, is discovered it can be defined and added to a project-specific glossary. The project-specific glossary and the standard glossary are merged to produce the final glossary for the requirements document.

When a new glossary is produced, you should review it to see if it includes terms which you should add to your standard glossary. You must be careful about this. Some terminology may be project-specific rather than common to an application domain or organisation. You need to have a review process for glossary modifications to ensure that it is appropriate to add them to the standard glossary.

As you re-use the glossary in more and more systems, you will find that it grows and includes all organisation and domain-specific terminology. However, there will almost always be project-specific terms which have to be added for individual requirements documents.

If you do not have an existing company glossary, the simplest way to produce one is to start with an existing requirements document, make a list of the technical terms used in that document then define each of these. Circulate the list for comment, then amend it accordingly to create the first version of the standard glossary.

You may find it helpful to highlight the terms which are included in the glossary when they are used in the body of the requirements document. This indicates to readers that these terms have a formal definition. You may highlight terms by writing them in italic or upper-case text or by some form of bracketing such as %pressure%. We prefer to use italic or upper-case text as this is more readable.

Costs and problems?

Producing and maintaining a glossary is not cheap but the returns are usually worth the costs involved. If you do not have a glossary to start with, the initial glossary production is likely to involve at least one to two person-months of effort plus the effort required to review the terminology. It will probably take at least four months in calendar time and perhaps much longer to agree on an initial set of terms. You have to consult with many different people in the organisation to ensure that important terms have not been left out and to agree on meanings for commonly used terms.

Once an initial version of the glossary has been produced, the costs of maintaining this are the costs of one person spending some time as a glossary manager and the small effort costs involved in reviewing and agreeing new terminology to be added to the glossary.

A problem which may arise is that some staff may be reluctant to explicitly define their terminology. Specialist terminology represents their professional expertise which they wish to maintain. They may feel that others do not need to know their terminology and that they wish to maintain the mystique associated with their profession.

In such cases, you have to make clear that you are not trying to undermine or de-skill them but that you need knowledge of the terminology to reduce the long-term problems of requirements understanding. Rather, the role of the glossary is to help them to communicate more effectively and to help engineers from all disciplines do their job in a better way.

3.6 Lay Out the Document for Readability

Key benefit	Requirements documents are easier to read
Costs of introduction	Low
Costs of application	Low
Guideline type	Basic

The layout of the requirements document should be designed so that it is easy to read. People find densely packed information and cluttered text confusing and hard-to-read.

Benefits

- Requirements documents are read much more often than they are written so producing readable documents is generally cost-effective. You are likely to read a document more quickly and make fewer mistakes if the document is easy to read rather than a dense mass of complex text.

- When documents are readable, reviewers find it easier to discover problems in the document; users of the document who are looking for specific information will spend less time looking for this information.

Implementation

You should define a set of layout guidelines as part of the standard for requirements documents and you should check compliance during the document quality assurance process. These guidelines should be implemented as standard styles in your word processing system and used by all document writers.

You can use the following advice as a starting point for your own organisational layout guidelines.

1 Use wide margins so that text lines are not too long. Psychological research has shown that long lines are more

difficult to read than short lines. Unless you arrange your document in columns, you should not right justify the lines in the document as, again, research has found that documents with a ragged right margin are easier to read (yes, we know the text in this book is right justified; publishers think it looks neater). Wide margins have the additional advantage that readers can make their own document annotations.

2 Use section and sub-section headings with a consistent style for sections and sub-sections. Leave white space around the section and sub-section headings.

3 Use emphasis sparingly and consistently. You can emphasise information by using a bold or italic font or by underlining it. Once you have decided what should be emphasised, always use the same emphasis technique for the same type of information.

4 Use tables, bulleted or numbered lists to present sets of related information items rather than list them within a sentence.

5 Where a number of items of information have to be presented with some stable and some variant parts, use a table to show commonalities and differences.

6 Separate equations from the text using white space and present them using a different font.

7 If you are describing a sequence of events or a sequential process, use diagrams to show the steps in the process. However, you should also provide explanations of the diagrams as people from different backgrounds sometimes interpret diagrams in different ways.

8 Do not use complex diagrams. Complex diagrams become very confusing and you should normally have less than 12 elements in a diagram. It is much better to use several simpler diagrams than a single complex diagram.

Your organisational guidelines for requirements document layout should be presented as part of your document standards.

Costs and problems

To introduce this guideline, you should organise a short training session in writing readable documents. This should last two or three hours and you can organise it using in-house writers or external consultants. The only costs of applying the guideline are the costs of checking your documents against your readability guidelines and making changes where problems are discovered.

However, you will probably find that it takes a considerable time to convince people to lay out documents for readability. Unfortunately, the basic writing training which people have at school is mostly geared towards the production of essays where information is presented as paragraphs of text. It takes quite some time to convert from this style of writing to the more structured style required to produce good technical documents.

3.7   Help Readers Find Information

Key benefit	Makes the document more usable as a system reference
Costs of introduction	Very low
Costs of application	Low–moderate
Guideline type	Basic

A requirements document is a reference document which is valuable throughout the lifetime of the system. You should use normal documentary facilities such as a contents list and an index to help readers find the information which they require.

Benefits

- Indexes and contents lists make it much easier to use the requirements specification as a reference document. They help you find related information and make it easier to assess the impact of changes to a document.

- An index helps readers review the document. Specialists can check the contents and the index for terms which they would expect to find in the document. If these are missing, either there is a problem with the index or there are omissions in the requirements.

Implementation

The simplest way to generate indexes and contents lists is to use the automatic facilities which are included with most word-processing systems. Contents are produced by identifying chapter, section and sub-section headings. You then tell the system to create a contents list and it will automatically find marked headings and their associated page numbers and list these in a separate section.

Document indexes can also be produced by most word processing systems. This is a two-stage process.

1 The terms which are to appear in the index are marked in the text. This may either be done by the writer as the text is prepared or it may be a post-processing step after the text has been written and reviewed. If you write the document and mark index terms as you write, it is fairly cheap. However, if you index the finished document separately this is a more expensive process.

2 The automatic facilities in the word processing system are used to create the index. The system finds the marked terms and their page numbers.

For the majority of requirements documents, this is usually more cost-effective than manual index creation. However, manually created indexes are usually better than automatically created indexes. People can recognise words and phrases of similar meaning and index them under the same heading. They can discover compound terms for indexing as they can see that phrases such as 'the creation of an index' and 'index creation' are really the same thing.

Creating an index manually involves an indexer reading the text and using a highlighter pen to identify index terms. These are then created and a further pass through the document made to add page numbers. Some pruning of terms is usually also carried out at this stage. The indexer should have technical knowledge of the system so that he or she can identify related terminology.

Costs and problems

Introducing this guideline simply involves including it in your document standard and, very quickly, showing engineers how to create indexes. Creating a contents list automatically is a cheap and simple process which only requires the assignment of consistent styles to chapter and section headings. Automatic index creation is a little more complex but also a relatively cheap process. If the writers of the document create index terms as they go along, they only have to remember to mark the required terms using the word processor's facilities. If the index is created as a post-processing step, the time required is roughly the time required to read the document. As the indexer may also be responsible for reviewing the draft document, this can be done as part of your normal quality assurance process.

The costs of creating a manual index are usually higher. Not only must the document be read through and the list of index terms created manually, the indexer must spend some time thinking about how to relate terms. If the indexer is familiar with the document, our experience is that it is possible to index about 200 pages per day. However, if the indexer does not know the document well, at least twice that amount of time must be allowed.

Indexes and contents lists use the document page numbers so it is important that pagination is the same in all copies of the document. Sometimes page numbering problems arise if the document is distributed in electronic form and printed on different types of printer. Different printers use slightly different font sets so that text layout varies from machine to machine. You should always designate one copy of the document as the master as far as indexing is concerned, and photocopy this, rather than expecting people to print the document from a machine-readable version.

3.8 Make the Document Easy to Change

Key benefit	Reduced costs of changing requirements
Costs of introduction	Low
Costs of application	Very low
Guideline type	Basic

Requirements documents should be written and produced so that they can be modified by users of the document. It should not be necessary to re-issue a completely new document every time a change is made to it.

Benefits

- Producing and distributing a new requirements document is both expensive and time-consuming as it involves writing, reviewing, printing and distributing the revised document.

- If the document is not easy to change, the costs of making changes may mean that changes are batched until there are enough of them to justify a new version of the document. This means that errors will go uncorrected and users may be misled by the document.

Implementation

We recommend that you combine the implementation of this guideline with **Guideline 3.6** which gives advice on producing readable documents. These guidelines reinforce each other and both require some changes to be made in normal writing practice. You may find it helpful to define a short style guide which explains how to lay out requirements documents and how to organise the requirements document so that it can be changed.

Modifications become a problem when changes to one part of a document affect other parts of the document. Therefore, when developing requirements documents, you should try to ensure that the different sections of the document are loosely rather than tightly integrated. You should try to minimise explicit relationships between the different parts of the document and design the document in such a way that parts of it may be selectively replaced.

There are some general techniques which may be used to improve the modifiability of a requirements document.

- Produce documents in loose-leaf binders rather than in bound versions. Users may then selectively replace parts of the document. This may not always be possible where documents are externally distributed, but for internal use loose-leaf versions should be maintained.

- Many word processors allow the automatic insertion of change bars to indicate that text has been changed. Where appropriate you should use this facility. However, the problem is that automatic change bars do not distinguish between significant changes and minor changes which do not affect the meaning of a document (e.g. to fix a spelling mistake or remove superfluous white space).

- When writing documents, avoid references to other page numbers in the document. These page numbers will change as the document is modified.

- Ensure that all figures and tables are labelled and always refer to them by that label rather than, for example, 'the table below'.

- Keep chapters short so that entire chapters may be replaced by document users.

- Start new chapters on separate pages. This means that the chapter may be replaced without disrupting the remainder of the document.

- Always number pages relative to chapters, i.e. the first page in chapter 2 is 2.1, the eighth page of chapter 12 is 12.8, etc. Avoid numbers of the form Page X of Y where Y is the total number of document pages. The total page count is liable to change with time.

- If available, use the facilities in your word processor which allow for relative references to figures, tables, etc. (Framemaker is an example of a document processing system with this facility). The word processor automatically updates these references when changes are made. However, if you have already standardized on a word-processing system without such a facility then it is not worth changing to an alternative system.

Costs and problems

The costs of introducing this guideline are very low. You need a brief training session which can be combined with a session on writing readable documents. There are no real costs involved in applying the guideline. Loose-leaf binders are a little more expensive than glued binding but the difference in cost is not significant. The savings in paper and copying costs will outweigh this very quickly.

You may find that people are not used to producing documents in this way and that it is difficult for them to avoid introducing physical dependencies between different parts of the document.

Probably the biggest practical problem is ensuring that readers actually replace sections of the document when new sections are distributed. People are fallible and they are likely to forget to replace outdated sections of the document. We recommend that you include acknowledgement slips with document changes to be returned when changes are made to the document. However, you must accept that some people will return the slips without ever making the change.

You can, however, help detect if a document has not been updated by printing changed sections on different coloured paper and by ensuring that each section has an associated header or footer which includes the date of latest revision. You should keep a list of the revision dates and colours and distribute this periodically so that people can check if they have included the most recent versions of document chapters.

4 Requirements Elicitation

Summary

Requirements elicitation is the process of discovering the requirements for a system by communication with customers, system users and other who have a stake in the system development. It requires application domain and organisational knowledge as well as specific problem knowledge. We suggest the following requirements elicitation guidelines:

Guidelines

4.1 Assess System Feasibility.

4.2 Be Sensitive to Organisational and Political Considerations.

4.3 Identify and Consult System Stakeholders.

4.4 Record Requirements Sources.

4.5 Define the System's Operating Environment.

4.6 Use Business Concerns to Drive Requirements Elicitation.

4.7 Look for Domain Constraints.

4.8 Record Requirements Rationale.

4.9 Collect Requirements From Multiple Viewpoints.

4.10 Prototype Poorly Understood Requirements.

4.11 Use Scenarios to Elicit Requirements.

4.12 Define Operational Processes.

4.13 Reuse Requirements.

Requirements elicitation is the usual name given to activities involved in discovering what requirements the system should provide. Technical software development staff work with customers and system end-users to find out about the application domain, the system services, the required performance of the system, hardware constraints, and so on. This process does not just involve asking people what they want; it requires a careful analysis of the organisation, the application domain and how the system is likely to be used.

Effective requirements elicitation is very important. If the analyst does not discover the customer's real requirements, the delivered system may not be acceptable to customers or end-users. The acceptability of the system depends on how well it meets the customer's needs and supports the work to be automated. It is not always easy to assess this as there may be a wide range of stakeholders who benefit directly or indirectly from the system and who use different criteria to judge the system's acceptability.

The analysts involved in the requirements elicitation process must address the following problems.

1   Stakeholders often do not really know what they want from the computer system except in the most general terms. Even when they have a clear idea of what they would like the system to do, they often find this difficult to articulate. They may make unrealistic demands because they are unaware of the costs of their requests.

2   Customers express requirements in their own terms and with implicit knowledge of their own work. Analysts, who may not have much experience in the customer's domain, must understand these requirements and express them in a way that can be understood by everyone involved in the process.

3   Different stakeholders have different requirements and they may express these in quite different ways. Analysts have to discover all potential sources of requirements and they must expose requirements commonalities and conflicts.

4 Organisational issues and political factors may influence the requirements of the system. These factors may not be obvious to the system end-users. They may come from higher management influencing the system requirements in ways that satisfy their personal agenda. For example, they may wish to move some functions to their department so propose requirements which integrate the support for these functions with support for functions which they already provide.

5 The economic and business environment in which the analysis takes place is dynamic. It inevitably changes during the elicitation process. Hence the importance of particular requirements may change. Requirements may emerge from new stakeholders who were not originally consulted.

To elicit system requirements, you must understand the problem to be solved, the business processes in an organisation, the ways in which the system is likely to be used and the application domain of the system. You need to find out about the system from available documents and discuss with stakeholders the system services which they need and the operational constraints on the system. You must be sympathetic to the concerns of system stakeholders and take the time to discover their real requirements.

4.1   Assess System Feasibility

Key benefit	Reveals if a system is actually needed and technologically realistic
Costs of introduction	Low
Costs of application	Low to moderate
Guideline type	Basic

Before investing effort and incurring expense in discovering system requirements, you should always carry out a feasibility study. This should assess whether or not the system can be implemented given existing technology and whether or not it can be effectively integrated with your current way of working. The feasibility study should also check that the system should provide adequate returns for the investment in its development.

Benefits

- A feasibility study is a low-cost way of avoiding problems. People proposing a system are often unaware of technological limitations. They do not know the consequences of installing the system in its actual working environment. A feasibility study may reveal that the system is unlikely to be used effectively in which case there is little point in developing it.

- To carry out a feasibility study, you need to make the business objectives for the system explicit. The business objectives represent the fundamental reasons for the system development. Requirements which are discovered during the elicitation process must be consistent with these objectives. See **Guideline 3.4**, *Make a business case for the system.*

- The study is likely to reveal initial sources of information about the system which should be consulted during the requirements elicitation.

Implementation

Feasibility studies consist of three phases. These are:

- decide on the information that you need
- gather that information from key information sources
- produce a feasibility report

Firstly, you must identify the critical information which you need about the system and develop a set of questions to discover that information. Examples of these questions might be as follows.

1 Do we really need this system?

2 What would the consequences be if we did not develop this system?

3 In what direct and indirect ways will the system contribute to our business objectives?

4 What critical processes must the system support?

5 What critical processes need *not* be supported by the system?

6 How will the system affect other systems which are already installed?

7 What are the likely technology limitations which we face?

8 Can a useful system be developed for the budget available?

The next stage involves putting these questions to key people in the organisation. Using the questions as a guide, you should identify a small number of people who can give informed answers. These may include managers of departments where the system will be installed, systems engineers and technical experts such as system managers who can answer questions about the technology available.

The final stage involves collating the answers to these questions and preparing a report for management on the system. This should discuss the advantages and disadvantages of developing the system, make recommendations about the type of system which should be developed and should (perhaps) establish an initial set of high-level requirements and constraints. This report is used to decide whether or not to go further in the system development.

Costs and problems

This guideline can be introduced relatively cheaply, as feasibility studies do not require specialised training. You can limit the costs of feasibility studies by establishing a budget for the study and collecting information until that budget is exhausted. Even a one-day study is likely to reveal useful information and is better than nothing. In general, however, for a completely new, medium-sized software system, you should budget for at least 6–10 days of effort to carry out the feasibility study and allow about a calendar month for it to be completed. For systems which are intended to replace existing systems, the feasibility study should require less effort and calendar time.

Apart from the possibility that the feasibility study will miss information and hence give misleading results, there are two possible problems which can arise.

1 *User uncertainty.* The feasibility study may disturb end-users of the system as they find out about the possibility of the system but are unsure about how it will affect their work. You need to address this problem by openness and telling people as much as you know about the system, emphasising its positive benefits to the organisation.

2 *Premature commitment.* If the people involved in the feasibility study are committed to the idea of the system, they may not be wholly objective in carrying out the study. They may find good arguments for the system but miss problems which are likely to arise. You can avoid this difficulty by bringing in outsiders (e.g. consultants) to conduct the study but this will increase the expense. Not only will costs be higher but they will have to spend time understanding your organisation before the work can begin.

4.2 Be Sensitive to Organisational and Political Considerations

Key benefit	Helps you understand why some requirements are suggested
Costs of introduction	Low
Costs of application	Very low
Guideline type	Basic

When eliciting requirements, you must be sensitive to organisational and political factors which influence requirements sources and which may conceal the real system requirements from you.

Benefits

- If you understand organisational politics, you are more likely to be able to understand the real rationale for some requirements and to assess whether or not a proposed requirement has been influenced by hidden organisational or political considerations.

- If you do not take organisational and political considerations into account, you may miss important sources of information about the system requirements.

Implementation

The successful application of this guideline is dependent on the sensitivity of the analysts involved in the elicitation process. Some people seem to have a natural awareness of political considerations; others have a more technical focus and find it difficult to relate to intangible organisational politics. People who come from inside an organisation are more likely to understand these considerations than external consultants but they are also more likely to be biased by them.

When eliciting requirements, there are a number of

things you should watch for as these suggest organisational and political influences on the requirements.

1 *Conflicting goals.* Do not assume that all people in the organisation have common goals or that their most significant goals are the stated business goals. Try to find out personal goals, as these may reveal hidden agendas when requirements are proposed.

2 *Loss or transfer of responsibility.* Try to understand the power structure in an organisation. One reason for developing the software may be to alter this in some way by transferring responsibilities from one part of the organisation to another. Those who will lose responsibility may suggest requirements which are impossible or very expensive to implement.

3 *The organisational culture.* If there is a competitive culture in an organisation with each department competing against others, you will find that requirements from different departments may be designed to give them some kind of competitive edge.

4 *Management attitudes and the morale of the organisation.* If the organisation has gone through a period where jobs have been lost, people in the organisation may be hostile to management. They may be unwilling to participate in the requirements engineering process and find excuses not to get involved.

5 *Departmental differences.* If you notice marked differences between one department in an organisation and most other departments, this suggests a different culture in that department. Requirements from there are likely to be influenced by that culture.

Costs and problems

The costs of introducing this guideline are generally low. You may simply suggest to analysts that they must be aware of organisational and political considerations (costing nothing), you may organise short internal training courses or you may use external consultants who offer courses in topics such as organisational psychology etc.

The problem with using consultants is that their advice is likely to be very general; they may help to make people aware of the problems but are unlikely to train people how to discover them. If possible, it is best to organise training using internal staff who have experience of organisational influences on requirements. They can therefore base their courses on examples which people can relate to.

The problem of applying this guideline during elicitation is that many people in the organisation will not wish to reveal their real reasons for requirements and, sometimes, may actively work to undermine the requirements elicitation process. They deliberately conceal political and organisational information from the analyst. Sometimes people can gain more from system failure than success and you should not always assume that they have the same goals as those people who are committed to the system.

4.3   Identify and Consult System Stakeholders

Key benefit	Discovery of all likely sources of requirements
Costs of introduction	Very low
Costs of application	Low
Guideline type	Basic

A system stakeholder is anyone who benefits in a direct or indirect way from the system which is being developed. Examples of stakeholders are end-users of the system, managers, customers, system developers, etc. As part of the requirements elicitation process, you should explicitly identify all potential stakeholders and consult them to discover if they have specific requirements or if they impose specific constraints on the system.

Benefits

- If you do not consider everyone who is likely to be affected by the introduction of a system, you are likely to miss important requirements. The system may have to be reworked to include these at a later stage or, in the worst case, may never be used.

- If you use a viewpoint-oriented approach to structure the requirements elicitation process, identification of stakeholders can help you discover viewpoints for structuring the system requirements (see **Guideline 4.9**, *Collect requirements from multiple viewpoints*).

- Identifying stakeholders and discussing the system with them makes people feel that they are part of the requirements elicitation process. They are more likely to be sympathetic to the introduction of the system and to volunteer information about their requirements.

Implementation

Stakeholders in the system may be identified using the following checklist:

1 by discovering the potential end-users of the system

2 by considering descriptions of the business processes which the system is intended to support and the people involved in these processes

3 by initial discussions with organisational management where you ask who will be affected by the introduction of the system

4 by considering the customers of the organisation who will use the system

5 by considering engineers and maintenance staff responsible for developing and maintaining the system

6 by considering external bodies such as regulators and certification authorities who may wish to place requirements on the system

It does not necessarily follow that all of these will be stakeholders but your initial stakeholder identification should consider all of them as possibilities. We recommend that you design your documentation so that you make an explicit list of stakeholders which includes brief reasons why their requirements are likely to be important.

The stakeholders in a system should always be explicitly identified in the requirements document and, if appropriate, information should be maintained which links specific requirements to the stakeholders who proposed these requirements. If a viewpoint-oriented approach is used, stakeholders may be associated with specific viewpoints and may be considered as sources of requirements.

Costs and problems

There are no significant costs in introducing this guideline. Analysts readily understand the need for this and are unlikely to raise any objections to it. To apply the guideline, there is a small additional cost in initially identifying and listing stakeholders. There are, of course, costs incurred when consulting stakeholders but these should not be additional to your current informal consultation costs.

The major problem which you are likely to encounter is identifying a complete set of system stakeholders. The stake which people have in a system is not always obvious and you need to consult widely in an organisation to find all possible stakeholders.

4.4 Record Requirements Sources

Key benefit	Requirements traceability from original sources
Costs of introduction	Low
Costs of application	Low
Guideline type	Basic

The source of requirements is a link to the information on which the requirement is based. When you document a requirement, you should record the source or sources who have expressed the requirement. A requirements source can be any stakeholder or group who have suggested requirements. Other possible sources are organisational quality standards, technical documentation, incident reports, or other requirements.

Benefits

- A major cost factor in analysing and changing requirements is the cost of consultation with requirements sources. This can be minimised if you do not have to spend too much time finding out who to consult. With available source information, you know immediately what people and documents must be consulted.

- The source information can help you understand why the requirement exists. For example, if the source is a safety standard, you are given the clue that the requirement is likely to be safety-related in some way.

Implementation

You should design your requirements collection form so that there is a field which can record the source of the requirement. As the requirements are collected, note the source immediately. Do not wait until later or you will forget where the information came from. If you store your requirements in a database (see **Guideline 9.5**, *Use a* *database to manage requirements*), make sure that your database definition includes a field for noting source information.

You can record requirements sources along with each individual requirement or with a group of related requirements. There are advantages and disadvantages with each approach.

1 Assigning sources to each requirement improves requirements traceability. In principle at least, you can go back directly to a source when the requirement is to be changed. However, it is sometimes the case that a requirement does not come from a single source but is an interpretation of information from several sources. Furthermore, people change jobs. If you record the source as a named person, they often will not be available for future consultation.

2 If you associate source information with a group of requirements (e.g. requirements organised in a viewpoint) it is easier to cope with source changes. In this case, the source information usually consists of several stakeholders or documents. When requirements are changed at a later date, it is likely that some of the members of this group will be available.

If you note requirements sources as the name of the person who provided the requirement you should also record their role in the organisation. If you need to re-consult the source, you might find that the individual is no longer available. If you know their role, you may be able to consult their replacement. If you note the source as a document, make sure that copies of the source document are kept in some known location so that they are available for future consultation.

Several people may suggest the same requirement or the requirement may be a result of information taken from several different documents. You should record all sources but you should designate one of these as the principal source. This is the first contact point in any consultation. Make sure that you allow for multiple sources in your form and database definition.

Costs and problems

The costs of introducing this guideline are very low, as it simply involves defining or re-defining your requirements collection form with a field for collecting source information. Applying this guideline adds no significant overhead to the requirements elicitation process as you record source information at the same time as you collect the requirements.

There are unlikely to be significant problems in implementing this guideline unless you use an existing, inflexible database structure for requirements which does not include a field for source details and which cannot easily be modified to include this information. The principal problem which is likely to arise is getting analysts to remember to record source information when it is collected. If they do not do so and they try to reconstruct the source information later, mistakes are bound to happen.

4.5   Define the System's Operating Environment

Key benefit	Fewer installation problems for delivered systems
Costs of introduction	Low
Costs of application	Low
Guideline type	Basic

The operating environment of a system consists of the host computer, which is the platform for the software which is being specified, and other hardware and software systems which will interact with the system. During the requirements elicitation process, you should define that environment and how it might change over the lifetime of the system.

Benefits

- Many system installation problems arise because of unexpected interactions with other installed systems. If you understand and define the environment in advance, you can anticipate and avoid some of these problems.

- Defining the environment helps reveal system requirements for interaction with these other systems or, sometimes, compatibility requirements where the new system and existing systems have to run on the same platform.

Implementation

When defining the operating environment of a system, you should always collect the following information.

1 *Platform information.* If the system software is to run on an existing computer, you should specify the characteristics of that machine, the operating system which will be installed and the libraries of software which may be used. It is particularly important to specify the versions of the

operating system and libraries which will be used. Many compatibility problems arise because assumptions made during elicitation about which versions of software systems are installed on the operating environment are often outdated when the system is installed.

2 *Interface information.* If the system interacts directly with existing systems such as databases, you should discover and specify the interface provided by these system. Conforming to this interface is an inter-operability requirement for the system being specified.

3 *Software dependencies.* Your system may rely on other software systems to provide functionality even although it is not directly interfaced to them. For example, you may assume that there is some word processor system available. If specific systems are required, you should specify which versions of these systems should be installed on the system platform.

You may also need to collect other information, depending on the type of system which you are specifying. An example is information on the physical layout of the place where the system is to be installed. This may be necessary because of limited space available for the system equipment.

The operating environment should be defined as a separate chapter in the requirements document. This should include an environmental model showing the different systems and their relationships, detailed descriptions of the systems and specifications of system interfaces. In that chapter, you should include predictions of possible changes to the operating environment over the lifetime of the system. **Guideline 7.2**, *Model the system's environment*, discusses this in more detail.

Costs and problems

This guideline simply suggests that you should be systematic in doing something which you must already do as part of your system development process. There should be no significant additional costs in introducing and applying this guideline.

A major problem which you are likely to face is environmental instability. The rate of change of hardware and software is now so high that it is likely that the operational environment of the system will change during the development process. The environment may be changed without considering the effects on new systems under development. Although you should try to predict changes, it is almost certain that unpredicted changes of some type will occur.

Changes to versions of software (e.g. Windows 3.1 is replaced by Windows 95) are common. The consequences of these changes are difficult to anticipate and they often cause tremendous problems because of version incompatibilities. You should regularly check that your environmental assumptions are still valid and should inform system managers of your environmental requirements.

You can avoid change to some extent by deliberately freezing the operational environment but this is usually only possible when the system is a stand-alone system and no other software runs on the same platform. Even in such situations, it is possible that the interfaces of other systems will change so there will still be some environmental instability.

4.6 Use Business Concerns to Drive Requirements Elicitation

Key benefit	Requirements are focused on core business needs
Costs of introduction	Low (but require senior management involvement)
Costs of application	Low
Guideline type	Basic

Business concerns are abstract high-level goals which must be satisfied if a system is to make a contribution to the organisation which is paying for it. You should identify and write down these goals and use them as drivers of the requirements elicitation. Business concerns are more general than the specific business case for the system which should be included in the requirements document (see **Guideline 3.4**, *Make a business case for the system*).

Benefits

- If a system is to be useful, it must contribute to the key concerns of the business. If these concerns are identified and used as drivers of the requirements elicitation process, you can be more confident that the system will meet real organisation needs and will actually be useful.

- Making the business concerns explicit helps to focus and clarify these goals. Explicit business concerns help people make decisions about their work and how it contributes to overall business goals.

Implementation

By discussions with senior management, from the business case for the system and from a general understanding of the work of the organisation, you should identify critical business concerns such as customer service, system reliability, safety and cost. It is important not to have too many of these concerns, We recommend that there should be five or less, otherwise costs and information management problems can increase significantly.

Each of these concerns should then be decomposed into more detailed sub-concerns which may then be further decomposed. Eventually, concerns should be decomposed to a set of questions associated with the sub-concern. These questions may then be put to system stakeholders to discover requirements related to these goals and to check that their requirements are consistent with the business concerns.

For example, say a concern was customer service. This could be decomposed into goals such as 'faster response to customer queries', 'lower costs for customers', 'fewer complaints from customers', etc. Eventually, you might decompose these into questions which are asked during the requirements elicitation process. For example, if we take the concern 'faster response to customer queries' we might get questions such as:

- what factors affect the response time to customer queries?

- is hardware/database performance a significant issue in response times?

- do particular questions require a series of interactions with the system?

- would suggested requirements have a positive/negative effect on customer response time?

The method of viewpoint-oriented requirements elicitation which we discuss in Chapter 13 uses this approach. It proposes that the requirements elicitation should be driven by a set of concerns which are derived from key business goals. These concerns are used to generate a checklist of questions which are put to potential sources of requirements during the elicitation process.

If you develop safety-critical systems, the concerns can be safety and availability. Using the concerns to derive the system requirements should simplify the production of the safety case for the system.

Costs and problems

The costs of introducing this guideline are the consultation costs involved in talking to senior management about what they see as critical business goals. The costs of implementing the guideline involve decomposing the goals to a set of questions which can be put to requirements sources. Once you understand the business goals, it should be possible to do this in 1 or 2 days of work (assuming that you do not have too many goals).

The problems which are likely to arise in implementing this guideline are difficulties of decomposing concerns into practical sub-concerns and the fact that concerns may change in response to external influences such as competition, legislation, etc. Although it is easy to define abstract concerns such as 'cost reduction', 'quality improvement', etc., it is more difficult to establish exactly what these mean in an organisation. These difficulties are made worse by the fact that the time of senior management is very limited and it may not be possible to have extensive discussions with them on the business concerns. There is also a tendency for senior management to have unrealistic expectations of the system. Using your knowledge of what is realistically possible, you have to work with management to define their concerns.

4.7   Look for Domain Constraints

Key benefit	Domain constraints often lead to critical requirements identi- fication
Costs of introduction	Low
Costs of application	Moderate
Guideline type	Intermediate

Domain constraints are system requirements which come from the application domain of the system. For example, in a banking system there may be accounting regulations which must be followed; in a train control system, the braking capabilities of a train must be taken into account. You should study the domain and understand these constraints as part of the requirements elicitation process.

Benefits

- Domain constraints generate system requirements and place limitations on other requirements. If you do not take domain considerations into account, there may be insuperable legal, organisational or physical obstacles to implementing the proposed requirements. Many systems have failed because they did not take real-world limita- tions into account.

- By recording domain constraints, you can avoid the expense of re-collecting this information when further systems are developed.

- For legal or organisational reasons (e.g. conformance with health and safety regulations or company security policy) you may have to demonstrate that the system meets given domain constraints.

Implementation

You should interview domain experts to find out what problems are likely to arise and what must be taken into account when developing the system. This should not be a one-off process. As you improve your understanding of the system requirements, you should discuss your revised understanding with domain experts. This will check if your knowledge is consistent with domain constraints and if further domain considerations must be taken into account.

Domain requirements and constraints are likely to fall into two categories.

1 Overall constraints which apply to all other requirements. You must check that other requirements do not conflict with these constraints.

2 Specific requirements derived from domain considerations. These are likely to come from regulations and policies such as safety legislation and company security policies. They will result in specific requirements such as 'A log of all transactions must be maintained'.

You need a fairly flexible standard for domain information as there are many types of domain information which may be relevant. Domain information which you might record includes the following.

1 An informal statement of the domain knowledge. For example, you might record that the parameters affecting the braking characteristics of trains include the brake system specification, the train velocity and mass, the type of track on which the train is running, weather conditions, the acceptable level of deceleration, etc.

2 More formal descriptions of the domain knowledge. For example, in the brake system specification, you might include a formula to compute the normal braking distance of a train.

3 The types of system where this domain knowledge is applicable and, if necessary, exceptions.

4 Knowledge classification terms such as *safety*, *performance*, etc., which may be used for information retrieval.

5 The sources of the domain information.

Domain information is an important organisational

resource so it should not simply be considered as information which is specific to one project. You should try to record domain information in a standard way in a 'domain handbook' which can be used by different teams in the organisation. This handbook can be a paper document but we recommend that you collect the information electronically and make it widely available in the organisation. A good way of doing this is to make it accessible on an Intranet where organisational information may be accessed using Internet tools such as World-Wide-Web browsers.

Costs and problems

The costs of introducing this guideline are the costs of defining a standard way of recording domain information. We recommend that you use a simple form with fields for different types of domain knowledge. These costs should be fairly low.

When applying the guideline, you must allow sufficient time to discover appropriate domain experts and to consult with them about the system. If you enter domain information in a database, you must define a database schema and there will clearly be data entry and validation costs associated with this. You will also need to write documentation for requirements engineers which explains how to discover and retrieve information from this database.

A major problem which is likely to arise is the unavailability of these domain experts when you need them. They are busy people and will undoubtedly have many other things to do. You may also find that there are problems in retrieving information which has been collected in previous projects irrespective of whether or not this has been collected in a database.

4.8   Record Requirements Rationale

Key benefit	Improves requirements understanding
Costs of introduction	Low
Costs of application	Low–moderate
Guideline type	Intermediate

The rationale of a requirement is information which summarises the reasons why that requirement has been specified. It justifies the requirement in terms of the problem which the system is designed to solve. The rationale is derived from a source, so it can come from a person, a group or a document.

Benefits

- The rationale associated with a requirement is a link between the problem and the requirements for the proposed problem solution. The rationale makes it easier for readers to understand the requirement and to assess the impact of changes to the requirement.

- Problem experts can use the rationale to check if the requirement is consistent with the problem being solved. If the rationale description includes a description of alternatives and arguments for each of them, the rationale information may predict future requirements changes.

Implementation

A simple model of requirements rationale can be recorded by designing your requirements collection form so that there is a field which can record the rationale of the requirement. As you discover requirements either from documentation, as a result of analysis of other requirements, or from system stakeholders, you should briefly note the rationale for including that requirement in that field. This could be a link to a domain handbook as suggested in **Guideline 4.7**. Rationale should normally be recorded as a simple natural language explanation although, sometimes, you may need to include domain-specific notations.

If you manage your requirements in a database, you need to ensure that your database definition makes provision for recording rationale and that the rationale information is entered along with the requirement.

More complex approaches to rationale recording can be derived based on the use of hypertext systems for supporting formal argumentation. We provide information about software products of this type in the book's Web pages. This system allows requirements to be recorded and arguments for and against these requirements to be linked to them. This may then be used during requirements negotiation to decide whether or not a requirement is to be accepted and if requirement changes should be made.

Costs and problems

Introducing this guideline is not expensive if you record rationale in an informal way. You simply need to ensure that your requirements standard has a field for recording rationale. If you record your requirements in a database, you need to make sure that you have a field in your database records for rationale. The costs of applying the guideline include the costs of the time needed to elicit the rationale from people who understand the problem and the application domain and to understand that rationale.

The costs of introducing and using a more structured rationale model with explicit comparison of alternatives is significantly higher. You need to invest in a hypertext system or a special-purpose support tool for this method. There are also significant training costs. Experience in industrial experiments has shown that many engineers find it difficult to organise their thoughts into formal arguments.

There are two main problems which you might encounter when introducing this guideline.

1   *Misleading rationale.* Some requirements sources may be unwilling to reveal the true rationale for some requirement. This is usually because they have some personal goals for the system (e.g. 'increase the size of my department') which they are unwilling to make public.

2   *Conflicting rationale.* Different requirements sources may suggest the same or similar requirements for completely different reasons. Sometimes this reveals a misunderstanding of the requirement but, if this is not the case, you should record both reasons and identify the source of the requirements rationale.

4.9 Collect Requirements From Multiple Viewpoints

Key benefit	Better requirements coverage
Costs of introduction	Moderate–high
Costs of application	Moderate
Guideline type	Intermediate

There are many different influences on the requirements for a computer-based system. These include end-users of the system who are involved in the processes which the system is designed to support, managers and others in the organisation whose work is indirectly affected by the system, and customers of the organisation buying the system.

All of these and more are potential sources of system requirements and they have their own *viewpoint* on the services that the system should provide and the ways in which it should be provided. You should recognise this diversity and collect requirements from these multiple viewpoints.

Benefits

- If your requirements are collected from a single view-point, you are unlikely to meet the needs of other stake-holders in the system. These will often be influential (e.g. managers) and this failure will mean that the system is not used.

- Collecting requirements from multiple viewpoints is a useful way of prioritising requirements. Requirements which all viewpoints suggest should probably have a high priority.

- You can use the identified viewpoints to help organise the process of requirements elicitation and to structure the requirements document. Different analysts can concurrently collect information from different viewpoints.

Implementation

A number of viewpoint-oriented requirements elicitation and analysis methods have been proposed. Some of these methods are suitable for requirements elicitation; others are more suited to managing system models developed from different viewpoints. However, a problem with these approaches is that they are difficult to introduce alongside existing methods of requirements elicitation and systems design.

The PREview (Process and Requirements Engineering viewpoints) approach which we describe in Chapter 13 can be introduced into existing requirements engineering processes without radical change. You can use it with your existing notations. You can introduce it in an incremental way alongside your existing requirements engineering methods.

PREview is based around 3 types of viewpoint:

- *interactor viewpoints* associated with people or equipment which interact with the system

- *stakeholder viewpoints* associated with people who benefit, in some way, from the system and

- *domain viewpoints* which are associated with domain information.

You can use any type of notation to describe the requirements derived from these viewpoints; PREview does not have its own built-in notations.

Applying this technique involves a number of steps.

1 You must identify the principal concerns of the organisation for the system being specified. Concerns reflect business goals such as faster time to delivery or the production of safety and reliable systems.

2 You then identify viewpoints and viewpoint sources. There may be as few as two or as many as eight or nine viewpoints. Normally, we recommend four or five viewpoints for medium-sized systems. The association of sources with viewpoints reflects **Guideline 4.4**.

3 You elicit requirements from viewpoint sources using the

concerns as a driver and a checklist for this elicitation. This reflects **Guideline 4.6**.

4   After requirements have been made available, you should cross-check these across viewpoints for conflicts and inconsistencies. We suggest an approach as described in **Guideline 5.4**, *Plan for conflicts and conflict resolution*.

5   Finally, you integrate the requirements from the different viewpoints to produce a requirements document.

Chapter 13 covers the PREview approach in more detail. We describe the steps in the method and illustrate this with an example of a safety-critical system. Other viewpoint-oriented methods are discussed in the January 1996 issue of the *Software Engineering Journal* (published by the British Computer Society and the Institute of Electrical Engineers). The introduction to this special issue on viewpoint-oriented approaches describes the ideas of viewpoints and the articles describe several viewpoint-oriented approaches.

Costs and problems

Introducing a viewpoint-oriented approach is quite expensive. Costs include:

1   training costs for some viewpoint-oriented method

2   costs of adapting or procuring software support for the method; viewpoint-oriented analysis tends to generate a lot of information and some automated way to manage this information is essential

3   costs of integrating information from these different viewpoints into a single requirements document.

Viewpoint-oriented analysis usually requires more effort and calendar time that an unstructured, informal approach to requirements elicitation. However, we are convinced that you will recover this time later in the system development, as rework caused by requirements problems will be reduced.

Good requirements analysts appreciate that there are many different perspectives on a system and they try to identify these perspectives and collect information from them. They implicitly identify viewpoints. A viewpoint-oriented approach to elicitation, therefore, really just involves making this an explicit process. Consequently, applying this guideline need not necessarily involve a significant increase in requirements engineering process costs.

We recommend that viewpoint-oriented elicitation should firstly be introduced using a relatively small pilot project. This will help discover what viewpoints are likely to be significant for an organisation and will allow a specific elicitation process to be developed. Possible problems which may arise when implementing this guideline are problems of identifying the right viewpoints and collating information from these different viewpoints. These are the same problems that you find with any method. As requirements engineers gain experience with the approach, the problems become less significant.

4.10   Prototype Poorly Understood Requirements

Key benefit	Better understanding of the real needs of system users
Costs of introduction	Moderate
Costs of application	Low–high
Guideline type	Intermediate

A prototype is a demonstration system which shows end-users and system stakeholders what facilities the system can provide. If you have vague or poorly understood requirements, you should consider developing a prototype system which simulates the behaviour of system software and hardware. End-users can experiment with this to refine their ideas about the system requirements.

Benefits

- Prototyping makes the real meaning of requirements easier to understand. If stakeholders do not fully understand the system requirements, they may agree to a requirements specification which does not reflect their real needs. The ultimate system which is developed is likely to be unsuitable.

- Prototyping is the only effective way of developing system user interfaces. If a prototype has been developed as part of the requirements process, this can reduce later development costs for the system.

- The prototype system may help establish the overall feasibility and usefulness of the system before high development costs are incurred.

- For some types of system, which are primarily software, the final system can sometimes be developed by modifying and adding facilities to the prototype. This means that a limited but usable system may be available relatively quickly.

Implementation

There are three possible approaches to system proto-typing:

1 paper prototyping where a mock-up of the system is developed and used for system experiments

2 'Wizard of Oz' prototyping where a person simulates the responses of the system in response to some user inputs

3 automated prototyping where a fourth generation language or other rapid development environment is used to develop an executable prototype.

Paper prototyping is a cheap and surprisingly effective approach to prototype development. It is most suitable for establishing end-user requirements for software systems. Paper versions of the screens which might be presented to the end-user are drawn and various usage scenarios are planned. Analysts and end-users work through these scenarios to find users reactions to the system, the information they require and how they would normally interact with the system.

'Wizard of Oz' prototyping is also relatively cheap as it does not require much software to be developed. The user interacts with what appears to be the system but his or her inputs are actually channelled to a person who simulates the responses of the system. This approach is particularly useful when a new system has to be developed based on an existing interface. Users are familiar with the interface and can see the interactions between it and the system functionality simulated by the 'Wizard of Oz'.

Developing an executable prototype of the system is a more expensive option. It involves writing software to simulate the functionality of the system to be delivered. It is very important that the prototype should be developed quickly and this means that you should use very high level languages and support environments for prototype development. Depending on the class of system you might use any of the following.

1 Fourth generation languages based around database systems. These are good for prototyping applications which involve information management. However, they do have restrictions which are inherent in the interaction facilities which they provide. You must develop your prototype within these limitations and this may mean that some facilities (e.g. navigation around a database by using a graphical visualisation of the data) may be impossible.

2 Very high-level languages such as Visual Basic or Small-talk. These are general purpose programming language which usually come with a powerful development environment and access to a range of reusable objects. These allow applications to be developed quickly and with more flexibility than is usually provided with 4GLs.

3 Internet-based prototyping solutions based on World-Wide-Web browsers and languages such as Java. Here, you have a ready-made user interface. You add functionality to it by associating segments of Java programs with the information to be displayed. These segments (called applets) are executed automatically when the page is loaded into the browser. This approach is a fast way of developing user interface prototypes but you must accept the inherent restrictions imposed by the browser. At the time of writing, this approach seems to have a lot of potential but is still immature.

Prototyping interactive systems is much easier than proto-typing real-time systems. Most prototype systems are not designed for efficient hardware interaction so you may not be able to access the sensors and actuators which will be used in the final system.

Some requirements are practically impossible to prototype. This is particularly true for 'whole system' requirements which reflect general objectives such as system usability, reliability, etc. In general, because the performance, efficiency, reliability, etc., of a prototype is quite different from a finished system, you can only use prototypes to discover the functional requirements for a system.

You can find a good description of paper prototyping in *Usability Engineering* (J. Nielsen, Addison Wesley, 1993). Approaches to executable prototyping are summarised in *Software Engineering*, 5th edition (Ian Sommerville, Addison Wesley, 1996).

Costs and problems

Paper prototyping is relatively cheap to apply but you must expect some costs in introducing this approach as specialist expertise is required. Currently, there are few organisations which can provide training and consultancy in this area. You must be prepared to invest time and effort in experimentation and working out the best way for your organisation to use the approach. The time required to develop a paper prototype can range from a few hours to a few days.

If you do not have a prototyping environment, there are fairly high costs involved in introducing executable proto-typing. Although the software costs are relatively low, there are significant training costs involved for prototype developers. The development costs for the prototype depend on the type of system. Modern prototyping facil-ities provide a basic development framework such as a database, an interaction model, etc. If this can be used as a basis for your system then it may be possible to develop a prototype for a moderate cost. However, if the framework is inadequate and you need to develop a lot of basic functionality before any useful experimentation is possible, then prototyping costs will be high.

There are various problems which can arise with proto-typing. You must accept that, for the initial prototypes, the development time will be extended as developers learn the most effective ways to use the system. If you want to employ prototyping specialists, you may find that there is a lack of skilled people with experience in this area.

In some circumstances, the time-to-market for new systems will be increased. The final system should be better but you may feel that this does not compensate for the delays in system delivery. Some requirements (such as real-time requirements) are difficult or impossible to prototype and, sometimes, a prototype gives a false picture of the final system. This is especially true when you use the built-in facilities of some prototyping system which cannot be replicated cost-effectively in conventional programming languages.

A 'problem' with using a prototyping approach for requirements elicitation is that you may be pressurised by customers to continue development of the prototype to produce the final system. There are some situations where this may be the right thing to do but, for systems which will have a long-lifetime, delivering the prototype instead of throwing it away and starting again can lead to increased long-term costs and system inflexibility.

The reason for this is that prototypes tend to be unstructured and rapid development is given priority over long-term maintainability. The consequence of using a prototype rather than re-developing a system is therefore increased system maintenance costs and (almost certainly) a shorter overall system lifetime. Where time to market is of the utmost priority, there may be a good case for development based on evolutionary prototyping but we do not generally recommend this approach for large, long-lifetime systems.

4.11   Use Scenarios to Elicit Requirements

Key benefit	Users find it easy to under stand scenarios and to describe associated requirements
Costs of introduction	Fairly high
Costs of application	Low
Guideline type	Intermediate

Scenarios are examples of interaction sessions which are concerned with a single type of interaction between an end-user and the system. End-users simulate their interaction using the scenario. They explain to the requirements engineering team what they are doing and the information which they require from the system.

Benefits

- Scenarios are based on actual or predicted system interactions and end-users usually find it easier to relate to these rather than a statement of the functionality to be provided by the system.

- Developing a set of scenarios for end-users is itself a useful exercise for elicitation, as it exposes the range of possible system interactions and reveals system facilities which may be required.

Implementation

Scenarios can be thought of as stories which explain how the system is used. They are primarily useful for adding detail to an outline requirements description. Once you have a basic idea of the facilities that a system should provide, you can develop usage scenarios around these facilities. You can identify scenarios by initial discussions with stakeholders who interact with the system. For complex systems, a fairly large number (tens or hundreds) of scenarios will usually be required.

Scenarios can have different forms but they should at least include the following information:

1 a description of the state of the system before entering the scenario

2 the normal flow of events in the scenario

3 exceptions to the normal flow of events

4 information about other activities which might be going on at the same time

5 a description of the system after completion of the scenario

It usually takes three or four pages to describe each scenario. The description should be supplemented with tables, flowcharts, etc. It takes some time to develop each scenario but, in many cases, parts of other scenarios can be reused.

Applying a scenario involves the requirements engineer and the system end-user working through the scenario together with the engineer taking notes of the user's comments, problems and suggestions. The end-user simulates the use of the system, following the scenario and points out areas where the scenario is incorrect, simplistic, variable, etc. The requirements engineer may ask questions at various points. He or she may ask questions concerned with current user actions, how tasks are carried out, who is involved in tasks, and what would happen if some alternative approach was taken.

If a prototype of a system is available, this can be used to walk through scenarios with end-users. The requirements engineer sits with the end-user in front of the prototype and walks through the scenarios. However, you do not need a system prototype for scenario-based elicitation.

Walking through a scenario with end-users helps you understand what they need from a system. You must then translate this into system requirements, perhaps by integrating information from different scenario walkthroughs. After the scenario has been tested, it should be modified to reflect the lessons learned.

Scenarios (called *use-cases*) are a basic part of some object-oriented analysis methods. You can find out more about this in *Object-oriented Software Engineering* (I. Jacobson *et al.*, Addison Wesley, 1992). Good, simple examples of scenarios are available in 'Inquiry-based Requirements Analysis' (C. Potts *et al.*, *IEEE Software*, 11 (2), March 1994)

Costs and problems

The costs of introducing this guideline are the costs of training people to write scenarios. As this is an intuitive process, some people may be able to teach themselves to do this. However, in other cases, you will need some external training in scenario development.

The cost of developing scenarios depends on the experience of the engineers involved in the process. You should normally allow at least one day to develop each scenario. In an experiment with this method it was found that 88 scenarios were needed to describe interaction with a medical system. Clearly, several months of effort may therefore be needed for developing scenarios for a complex system. However, scenario-based elicitation does not require significantly more effort that other approaches to elicitation for systems of a comparable size. Once a set of scenarios is available, it can be used and adapted for different systems, thus reducing the time required for scenario development.

You may find problems in involving end-users in the process. This approach requires end-users to spend a lot of time interacting with requirements engineers. These users may not be able to take enough time away from their normal job to work through scenarios. You may also find that the end-users who wish to be involved are interested in the computer system and the automation of their work. Their interactions may not be typical of normal users and may suggest requirements which are not strictly necessary.

4.12   Define Operational Processes

Key benefit	Reveals process requirements and requirements constraints
Costs of introduction	Fairly high
Costs of application	Moderate
Guideline type	Intermediate

The objective of developing a computer-based system is often to support some business processes such as producing customer reports or technical activities such as navigating an aircraft. You should analyse, understand and document these processes as part of the requirements elicitation process.

Benefits

- An explicit description of the process which the computer-based system is intended to support is likely to reveal support requirements for the system and constraints which will affect how the system may be used.

- Defining the processes means identifying the roles of the people involved in these processes. This may be a useful way of discovering *system stakeholders* who can provide requirements for the system.

Implementation

Process description is a surprisingly complex activity. There are two possible situations which must be covered.

1 The system being specified is intended to support a completely new activity and there is no existing process which may be studied. In this case, you have to propose an operational process which may be used.

2 The system is intended to support an existing operational process and will either replace an existing computer-based system or will automate part of the process which

is carried out manually. In this case, you can study and document the existing process which is used.

In the first case, you must consider how the new process will interact with existing processes which must also be carried out. For example, assume that the new system is intended to be installed in a service environment with significant customer interaction. If you define an operational process which cannot cope with interruptions from customers, you are likely to find that the system cannot be used in practice.

Where the operational process already exists, you can study this process and derive a model of it. Although you may have created process models as part of your quality management standards, in reality the actual processes followed are likely to be more complex than these standards suggest. We recommend that you should use a combination of techniques to understand processes.

1 *Interviewing.* You should talk to the people involved in the process to discover what they do. If available, you can use an existing process description to structure the interview and you can add details to the description. You are likely to find that there are several viewpoints on the process and that there will be significant variability in the description.

2 *Observation.* Once you have a basic understanding of the process, you can spend time observing the process participants in action to see what they are doing. This is a standard technique of social analysis called ethnography. The advantage of an observation-based approach is that you can discover unconscious actions which people may not think are important and you can also see if social interactions between the people involved in the process are important. For example, strategies for coping with high workloads may have evolved where people help each other. These are often not included in standard process descriptions but it is important that new computer-based systems do not make them impossible to use.

There is no standard way to define processes and we recommend that you use simple diagrams and explanatory text. You should normally try to define the activities involved, the roles of the people responsible for carrying out these activities, the activity inputs and outputs. These can be included in three complementary types of description:

- workflow descriptions which show how work is passed from one activity to another

- role descriptions which show the roles of the different people involved in the process and describe the interactions between these roles

- shared artefact descriptions which show how different people use shared artefacts, such as documents, in different ways.

A method of process analysis which takes into account the viewpoints of different people involved in the process has been developed. This is part of the PREview approach to viewpoint-oriented requirements elicitation described in Chapter 13. The process analysis component of PREview assumes that different people see processes in different ways and that we can only develop a complete understanding of these processes by amalgamating all of these views. The book's Web pages include further information about the use of PREview for process analysis.

Costs and problems

There are significant costs involved in introducing this guideline. Requirements engineers must understand the principles of process analysis and, perhaps, be involved in some formal training in this area. Decisions need to be made on the best way of describing processes and maintaining these descriptions.

Studying and documenting processes is also a fairly expensive activity. If you use interviews and observations to understand the process, you must allow several days to understand and document each process. It is also important to allow time for process validation where the process analyst goes back to the people involved in the process to check his or her process description.

Problems which you are likely to encounter are as follows.

1 *Simplistic analysis.* Processes are often complex and sometimes a simplistic analysis of a process suggests invalid requirements. When you derive requirements from the process study, you must ask the people involved in the process to check that you have understood it properly and that the requirements are actually valid.

2 *Participant resistance.* The people involved in processes may be jealous of their skills in carrying out these processes and may not want to explain the process to outsiders. This is particularly likely if they think that the new system represents some threat to their job and that they may either be replaced or de-skilled by the computer system.

4.13   Reuse Requirements

Key benefit	Lower cost, faster elicitation of requirements
Costs of introduction	Moderate–high
Costs of application	Moderate
Guideline type	Advanced

When developing the requirements for a new system, you should, as far as possible, reuse requirements from other systems which have been developed in the same application area.

Benefits

- Requirements reuse saves money and time. Reusing existing requirements means that you need to spend less effort and time in eliciting, analysing and validating requirements. Experience has shown that for similar systems, up to 80% of the requirements may be more or less the same. Accurate predictions of savings are difficult to make but if requirements are reused across several systems, significant gains are likely.

- Reuse reduces risks. If you use requirements which have already been implemented in other systems, you reduce the risks of producing requirements which are difficult to implement or which interact in undesirable ways with other requirements.

- Requirements reuse may lead to design, code and test reuse thus further reducing life-cycle costs for your system.

Implementation

Requirements may either be reused directly or indirectly in the requirements elicitation process. Direct reuse means that a requirement from one system is taken as a requirement for some other system with minimal change; indirect reuse means using existing requirements in the elicitation process to prompt users for their specific requirements.

It is usually much simpler to implement indirect requirements reuse, so we recommend that you try indirect reuse before attempting any direct reuse of requirements. People find it much easier to suggest requirements when they have an existing requirement to criticise and add to. You can therefore ask them to define their requirements in terms of modifications to the existing requirement. The steps involved in indirect reuse are as follows.

1   Identify requirements which are likely to be close to or overlap with the stakeholder requirements for the system being studied.

2   Present these requirements to the stakeholder and explain what they mean.

3   Ask him/her to explain where these requirements would be suitable and where they would be unsuitable. Find out if they would be acceptable although not ideal if implemented without change.

4   Rewrite the requirement according to the suggestions made and repeat the process until the stakeholder is satisfied.

This approach can be combined very effectively with scenario-based elicitation (**Guideline 4.11**) where the existing requirements are used to define the scenarios to be explored by the end-user and the requirements engineer. You can also, of course, reuse scenarios as we have already suggested.

Direct requirements reuse is more difficult. For reasons of commercial confidentiality, it may not be possible to reuse requirements developed for one customer in systems for a different customer. There may be subtle but important domain differences between systems which make direct reuse impossible.

Where there is a close similarity between systems and there are no problems with customer confidentiality, some direct reuse may be possible. A number of steps are involved in this process.

1 Identify common features of the existing system and the system to be developed. You have to find the parts of the system where requirements reuse is likely.

2 Identify requirements in the existing system which are potentially reusable and which are relevant to the identified common features. A reusable requirement must be independent, i.e. it should not be tightly integrated with a group of other requirements. This identification may be difficult because of differences in terminology used in the different systems.

3 Assess these potentially reusable requirements for validity in the system to be developed.

4 Check with users that these requirements actually meet their needs.

This type of reuse is hard to introduce in most organisations. The returns are potentially very high but you must be prepared to spend a good deal of effort and time defining and introducing an effective reuse process. The problems are comparable to those of software reuse. An article by W. Frakes and S. Isoda ('Success Factors for Systematic Reuse', *IEEE Software*, 11 (5), September 1994) is a good description of how reuse may be established in an organisation.

Costs and problems

The costs of introducing this guideline are the costs of defining and implementing an effective reuse process. These depend on your organisational structure, culture and range of disciplines and the type of systems you develop. Experience has shown that introducing software reuse programmes in large organisations require a small team (two or three people) working with developers for several years. The costs of applying this guideline are the costs of finding requirements for reuse in existing systems and assessing their reusability.

There is often resistance to reuse within an organisation because it is easier to quantify its costs than its benefits. There may also be problems of intellectual property rights. It is difficult to define what is meant by the 'ownership' of requirements. It may not be clear if requirements developed in a system paid for by client A are owned by that client or by the development organisation. If they are owned by client A, can they be reused in another system being developed for client B? The legal situation here is unclear, so you should probably only attempt direct reuse where there is no possible ownership dispute.

5 Requirements Analysis and Negotiation

Summary

After an initial set of requirements has been discovered, you should analyse them for conflicts, overlaps, omissions and inconsistencies. When information from this analysis is available, system stakeholders then negotiate to agree on a set of system requirements. Conflicts must be resolved and requirements prioritised. We suggest the following analysis and negotiation guidelines:

Guidelines

5.1 Define System Boundaries.

5.2 Use Checklists for Requirements Analysis.

5.3 Provide Software to Support Negotiations.

5.4 Plan for Conflicts and Conflict Resolution.

5.5 Prioritise Requirements.

5.6 Classify Requirements Using a Multi-dimensional Approach.

5.7 Use Interaction Matrices to Find Conflicts and Overlaps.

5.8 Assess Requirements Risks.

The objective of requirements analysis and negotiation is to establish an agreed set of requirements which are complete and consistent. These requirements should be unambiguous so that they can be used as a basis for further system development. During this process, you normally discover missing requirements, requirements conflicts, ambiguous requirements, overlapping requirements and unrealistic requirements. Requirements conflicts have to be resolved and you need to decide if the benefits from requirements justify their costs.

Requirements analysis and elicitation are inextricably interleaved processes. As requirements are discovered during the elicitation process, some analysis is carried out. Problems may be immediately recognised, discussed with the source of the requirements and resolved. You should therefore read this chapter in conjunction with Chapter 4 which covers requirements elicitation. Some of the elicitation techniques discussed there, such as **Guideline 4.11**, *Use scenarios to elicit requirements*, may also be used for requirements analysis. Similarly, some of the guidelines suggested in this chapter may be applied during the elicitation process.

Requirements analysis and negotiation are concerned with the high-level statement of requirements elicited from stakeholders. Requirements engineers and stakeholders negotiate to agree on a definition of the system requirements. In some organisations, these requirements will then be developed in more detail as a system specification or model (see Chapter 7). Developing these models usually reveals further contradictions and incompleteness in the requirements. You then must re-enter the elicitation, analysis and negotiation phases to discuss requirements changes.

The elicitation, analysis and negotiation processes may therefore be thought of as segments in a spiral, as shown in Figure 5.1.

You find out some information about requirements, analyse this, negotiate the results of the analysis then enter another round of the spiral where you repeat these activities. You should keep going round the spiral until you are satisfied with the agreed requirements.

Complex systems have many stakeholders and they are

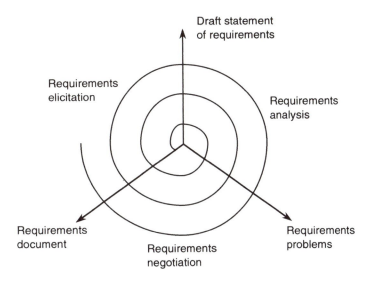

Figure 5.1 The elicitation, analysis and negotiation spiral

bound to have conflicting requirements. The negotiation process is intended to discuss the conflicts in requirements and to find some compromise which satisfies everyone involved. Of course, negotiations are never simply conducted using logical, technical arguments. They are almost always influenced by organisational and political considerations and the personalities of the people involved. You must be aware of these when negotiating requirements and try to avoid making bad technical decisions because of these influences. **Guideline 4.2**, *Be sensitive to organisational and political constraints*, is as applicable to analysis and negotiation as it is to requirements elicitation.

Requirements analysis is an expensive and time-consuming process because skilled and experienced people must spend time reading documents carefully and thinking about the implications of the statements in these documents. People do not all think in the same way and different analysts will tackle the process in different ways. It is not possible to turn requirements analysis and negotiation into a structured, systematic process so the guidelines here describe general principles rather than structured analysis methods.

5.1   Define System Boundaries

Key benefit	Eliminates unnecessary requirements
Costs of introduction	Low
Costs of application	Low
Guideline type	Basic

You should assess the initial set of requirements to define the boundaries of the computer-based system which is to be developed. That is, you should determine which of the requirements are system requirements, which are requirements for the operational processes associated with the system and which requirements should be outside the scope of the system.

Benefits

- Providers of requirements are often unclear about what should and should not be in the system. They may therefore suggest inappropriate requirements. You need this initial partitioning step to eliminate requirements which are clearly outside the scope of the computer-based system so that these requirements do not confuse the later processes of analysis.

Implementation

To implement this guideline, you must examine each requirement and classify it as either a system requirement, a process requirement or a requirement which should be rejected. Individual judgements will vary and different analysts will partition the requirements in different ways. Customers will also have their own ideas about where the system boundaries lie. Therefore, several people should classify the requirements then negotiate which requirements are outside the system boundary.

This process should be carried out as part of the overall analysis of the requirements. The questions in the analysis checklist (**Guideline 5.2**) may help you make decisions about the system boundary. Other questions which might be helpful in making decisions about the system boundary are as follows.

1 *Does a requirement imply the need for some decision-making based on incomplete or unreliable information?* If so, consider making this a process requirement as people are much better than computers at making this kind of decision.

2 *Will the implementation of a requirement need information which is outside the defined database for the system?* If so, you should consider making this a process requirement where the operators of the system are responsible for providing the information. If you do not do this, you need to review the data which should be managed by the system.

3 *Is a requirement concerned with the core functionality of the system?* Most systems are intended to support some critical processes such as command and control for military organisations, controlling aircraft systems for pilots, providing financial information for managers, etc. If the requirement is not concerned with these critical processes, you should consider whether or not it is really needed.

4 *Is a requirement concerned with the functionality or performance of equipment which is external to the system?* In this case, it may be impossible to implement the requirement as you do not have control over that equipment. The requirement is therefore outside the system boundary.

For the requirements which have been associated with the operational process and which have been classified as outside the boundaries of the system, you must prepare technical and/or economic arguments why these have been excluded. These arguments should be based on the defined business objectives of the organisation or on the results of the system feasibility study.

As this guideline requires a complete review of the requirements, it can be combined with more general requirements prioritisation (**Guideline 5.5**) or requirements classification (**Guideline 5.6**).

Costs and problems

In most cases, you will already have some informal process of requirements assessment so the costs of introducing this requirement are simply the costs of defining a checklist and paperwork to formally record decisions. The additional costs of applying the guideline as part of the requirements analysis process are low, as it can be carried out as analysts read the initial statement of requirements.

The most significant problems are the general difficulties of making decisions on the partitioning of requirements and communicating decisions to sources of requirements. Telling stakeholders in the system that their requirements are invalid needs to be done with care and sensitivity. This is particularly true when these stakeholders are system customers or senior management in positions of influence. You may face the problem that they insist that their requirements should be included in the system specification. If they are unwilling to listen to your arguments, you should make clear that significant additional costs are likely to be involved in implementing these requirements.

5.2 Use Checklists for Requirements Analysis

Key benefit	Faster, more complete analysis of requirements
Costs of introduction	Low–moderate
Costs of application	Low
Guideline type	Basic or intermediate

Develop checklists of requirements problems based on your experience and use these in the systematic analysis of requirements. Each requirement should be analysed against this checklist. If any problems are detected, these should be noted with the requirement.

Benefits

- Checklist-based analysis is a focused approach which systematically checks each requirement and speeds up the process of analysis. It reduces the probability of errors in the analysis process and the accidental omission of some requirements.

- Developing a checklist is a way of reusing knowledge of the requirements analysis across projects. The checklists document known problems and hence avoid re-discovering these problems in different projects.

Implementation

A checklist is a list of questions which the analyst uses to assess each requirement. Analysts should check items on this list as they read through the requirements document. When potential problems are discovered, these should be noted either in the margins of the document (if your organisation permits document annotation) or on a separate analysis list.

This analysis list can be implemented as a spreadsheet where the rows are labelled with the requirements identifiers (see **Guideline 9.1**, *Uniquely identify each require-ment*) and the columns are the checklist items. You then fill in the appropriate cell with comments about potential problems.

Checklists are an organisational resource which must evolve with experience of the requirements analysis process. The questions on the checklist should usually be general rather than restrictive. If the questions are too specific, they will be irrelevant for most systems.

You can create an initial checklist based on the questions shown in Figure 5.2.

Checklist item	Description
Premature design	Does the requirement include premature design or implementation information?
Combined requirements	Does the description of a requirement describe a single requirement or could it be broken down into several different requirements?
Unnecessary requirements	Is the requirement 'gold plating'? That is, is the requirement a cosmetic addition to the system which is not really necessary.
Use of non-standard hardware	Does the requirement mean that non-standard hardware or software must be used? To make this decision, you need to know the computer platform requirements (see **Guideline 4.5**, *Define the system's operating environment*).
Conformance with business goals	Is the requirement consistent with the business goals defined in the introduction to the requirements document?
Requirements ambiguity	Is the requirement ambiguous i.e. could it be read in different ways by different people? What are the possible interpretations of the requirement? Ambiguity is not necessarily a bad thing as it allows system designers some freedom. However, it has to be removed at some stage in the development process.
Requirements realism	Is the requirement realistic given the technology which will be used to implement the system?
Requirements testability	Is the requirement testable, that is, is it stated in such a way that test engineers can derive a test which can show if the system meets that requirement?

Figure 5.2 Analysis checklist items

The goal of analysis is to discover requirements problems; it is not a quality management activity (this comes later in the process). Consequently, the checklist should not include general quality questions concerned with conformance to organisational standards, etc.

You should limit the size of checklists to about 10 questions. People can not hold too many items in their head, so long checklists are useless when reading through a document. Furthermore, long checklists inevitably mean that most questions are irrelevant to most requirements and they will be applied in a perfunctory way. If checklists grow too long, you can consider splitting them to create several checklists. Different analysts can work with different checklists, thus giving complete checklist coverage.

Checklists for analysis can be introduced by organisations at any level of requirements engineering process maturity. Organisations at the initial level should develop short and simple generic checklists with questions like those that we suggest here. More mature organisations can use more detailed checklists for requirements checking.

Costs and problems

The principal cost involved in introducing this requirement is drawing up an agreed analysis checklist. You may start with the suggestions here or you may consult experienced analysts for their advice on this. Although it will only take a few days to draw up an initial list, you will also have to spend time in validating the list with people who have been involved in the analysis processes.

Checklist-based analysis may be slightly more expensive and take more time than informal approaches to analyses. However, this type of analysis is likely to discover a greater number of requirements problems and it is easier to check conformance with defined analysis processes.

There are also costs involved in checklist management. You should review the checklist after each analysis to see if any changes are required. When new problems are discovered, checklists should be updated to include questions which reflect these problems. However, checklists are an organisational resource and should not be changed without consultation. New checklist proposals need to be made, reviewed and agreed before new questions are added to the checklist.

There are two potential problems with checklist-based analysis.

1 *Inappropriate checklists.* If the checklist asks the wrong questions, then the resulting information will not be particularly useful. Checklists should be developed from experience and the organisational requirements checklist should be reviewed after each project to decide if changes should be made to it.

2 *Checklist focusing.* This occurs when the analyst uses the checklist exclusively to analyse the requirements and stops thinking about potential problems which are not addressed by the checklist. This is a general problem with any checklist-based approach, particularly if you need to explicitly check off every checklist item. You must emphasise that the checklist is a *guide* for analysts and that they should also think about other requirements problems which it does not cover.

5.3 Provide Software to Support Negotations

Key benefit	Faster resolution of requirements problems
Costs of introduction	Low–moderate
Costs of application	Low–moderate
Guideline type	Basic–intermediate

Encourage the use of electronic systems such as electronic mail to exchange information about requirements and to support the negotiation of agreed requirements. Simple electronic negotiation of requirements using electronic mail and bulletin boards for information exchange can be introduced in organisations at the basic maturity level; more structured approaches based on groupware or conferencing systems are more suited to intermediate maturity level organisations.

Benefits

- Many requirements problems are simply due to a lack of understanding, where one stakeholder does not know or understand how other stakeholders will use the system and the system facilities which they require. Encouraging electronic discussion of the requirements breaks down barriers between stakeholders and makes it easier and faster to arrive at agreements about requirements.

- Electronic information exchange makes it possible for stakeholders who may be in different organisations in different parts of the country to participate in discussions about the requirements.

- It may be possible to reduce the number of requirements negotiation meetings and so reduce travel and effort costs.

- Personality factors are less important in electronic discussions than in face-to-face meetings. Strong personalities cannot impose their views on the requirements. As there is no need for an immediate response, it allows people time to think about problems and issues raised.

Implementation

There are four basic technologies which can be used for the electronic negotiation of requirements.

1   Electronic mail (e-mail) systems where stakeholders exchange messages about the requirements.

2   Bulletin board systems where problems are posted on a common 'bulletin board' which is accessible to all stakeholders. Discussions of these problems may be organised separately using the bulletin board facilities.

3   Shared database systems such as Lotus Notes where a repository of requirements, problems and comments may be accessed by all involved in the process. These systems are based on a central database plus copies of part of this database held on personal machines. The system automatically supports the synchronisation of the central and the local databases.

4   Intranet technologies where Internet software such as World-Wide-Web browsers are used to access an organisation's internal data.

Electronic mail systems are now widely used and are the simplest and cheapest approach to electronic requirements negotiation. Stakeholders are identified as a group and requirements problems and comments mailed to all group members. To use them effectively, you need to make one member of the group a problem manager. The problem manager is responsible for keeping track of the problems raised and circulated by e-mail, the responses to the problems and the agreed solutions. Where necessary, he or she must also prompt people for responses to mail messages.

Bulletin boards usually have a fixed structure consisting of a posting plus an associated discussion thread. Problems are 'posted' to the board and a discussion is based on the problems. They may be linked with electronic mail systems so that posted problems are also circulated by e-mail. These systems allow for a more focused discussion as it is possible to link individual problems with responses to these from different stakeholders. Problems and responses are linked and are visible to all group members. There is less need for problem management, although some moderation to curtail discussions is usually necessary.

Shared database systems or computer conferencing systems can be used in a similar way to bulletin boards. However, they provide more sophisticated data management facilities and can also be used for requirements management (see **Guideline 9.5**, *Use a database to manage requirements*). It is therefore possible to integrate problems and responses with the requirements themselves. Database systems allow for more flexible structures but, of course, these need to be defined in advance.

Intranet systems are a form of shared database system where an organisation uses World-Wide-Web browsers to access a shared database which is structured as a set of hypertext pages. Browsers can be tailored to specific needs by associating scripts with pages which are automatically executed when that page is displayed. Many companies are implementing these systems for organisational data. This approach is relatively low-cost and easy to use and certainly has a lot of potential. However, experience with Intranets is still limited and we can not really comment on their cost-effectiveness at this stage.

You need to be connected to bulletin boards to access the information on them. Shared database systems, however, allow information to be transferred to and from a private database copy held on the user's machine. This simplifies independent working. It is generally easier to integrate work from different people.

Costs and problems

Electronic mail and bulletin board systems are cheap. The costs of shared database and conferencing systems are falling quickly. Capital costs should not therefore be a significant barrier to introducing this type of support.

There may be some training costs involved in teaching people to use bulletin boards or shared databases. Modern versions of these systems have user interfaces which are relatively easy to use so people should be able to use them with only minimal training.

There are some costs involved in managing the electronic discussions. These depend on the number of participants in the discussion and their use of the system. Overall usage costs for electronic communication systems are low although electronic information interchange can result in an information explosion. People can sometimes spend too much time dealing with electronic mail.

If you already have an electronic mail culture in your organisation, the discussion of requirements using e-mail may emerge naturally. Electronic mail is an excellent medium for distributing problem information but it does not support any decision-making capabilities. It also tends to result in information overload where all stakeholders receive all problem and response messages, most of which are of no interest to them. When this happens, people sometimes opt-out of the negotiation process.

The advantage of e-mail is that messages are automatically delivered with no intervention on the part of the receiver. Bulletin boards, intranet and shared database systems have the disadvantage that people must log on to them to find out if there is any information of interest. If they attempt this a few times without finding information, they are likely to lose interest in the system. This is a problem with any new technology and it can only be solved by encouraging use of the system so that benefits are gained by all users.

In some cases, where access to the requirements involves external connections to your computers, you need to be careful about information security and put appropriate safeguards in place.

5.4   Plan for Conflicts and Conflict Resolution

Key benefit	Faster resolution of requirements problems
Costs of introduction	Low
Costs of application	Low
Guideline type	Basic

There will always be conflicts, overlaps and omissions in any set of requirements. You should anticipate these and plan requirements negotiation meetings to discuss the requirements and resolve the problems discovered during the analysis.

Benefits

- Arranging requirements negotiation meetings which concentrate on resolving requirements problems reduces the time required to arrive at an agreed set of requirements.

- The requirements negotiation meeting is an open process in which all stakeholders may be involved. This reduces the probability that critical requirements from some important stakeholder will be missed, and it helps convince stakeholders that their views have been considered.

Implementation

In spite of years of experience, many organisations still do not allow enough time to resolve requirements conflicts. The reason for this is, perhaps, that conflicts are considered as some kind of 'failure' and it is not acceptable to plan for failure. This view is completely wrong. Conflicts are natural and inevitable. They reflect the fact that different stakeholders in the system have different needs and priorities. You cannot produce a system that will completely satisfy everyone. If you do not have open and explicit conflict negotiation, some stakeholders are likely to be disgruntled and hostile to the system.

Meetings are the fastest way to resolve requirements conflicts. Conflict resolution meetings should be solely concerned with resolving outstanding requirements problems. The meeting should be attended by analysts who have discovered requirements conflicts, omissions and overlaps, and system stakeholders who can help resolve the problems which have been discovered. Electronic information exchange is fine for discussing and analysing problems but is a poor substitute for direct discussions when compromises have to be made.

The meeting should discuss those requirements where problems cannot be resolved by informal discussions between stakeholders and analysts. All requirements which are in conflict should be discussed individually. You should not assume that decisions made for one requirement will necessarily apply to related requirements.

The meeting should be conducted in three stages.

1 An information stage where the nature of the problems associated with a requirement is explained.

2 A discussion stage where the stakeholders involved discuss how these problems might be resolved. All stakeholders with an interest in the requirement should be given the opportunity to comment. We recommend putting an explicit limit on the time spent discussing each requirement. If you do not do this, you may have to rush through requirements at the end of the meeting.

3 A resolution stage where actions concerning the requirement are agreed. These actions might be to delete the requirement, to suggest specific modifications to the requirement or to elicit further information about the requirement. If you record requirements rationale, you must remember to modify this to reflect requirements changes made during this meeting.

Meeting participants should be given copies of the results of the analysis (e.g. requirements checklists) and the meeting should be chaired by someone who is not a stakeholder in the system. They should be independent, which makes it easier for them to ensure that the views of all stakeholders are considered.

In our experience, electronic negotiation for conflict resolution takes significantly longer than face to face meetings. However, you should consider it as an option when it is impossible to get all participants together at the same time. Conflict negotiations can be carried out using electronic systems such as bulletin boards or shared databases. We do not recommend electronic mail for this kind of negotiation, as people lose track of discussion threads.

Costs and problems

There are no significant costs involved in introducing this guideline. The costs of applying the guideline are the costs of holding formal negotiation meetings. However, in many cases, these can replace less focused meetings and so will not result in additional costs. The basic problems of introducing this guideline are the same problems that exist for any meeting namely the difficulties of getting all participants in the same place at the same time and the problems which arise from the hidden agendas of some meeting participants.

If people need to travel to the meeting, there is danger that you will try to do too much at a single meeting. Requirements discussed towards the end of the meeting may not be considered as carefully as those discussed early in the meeting. There are various strategies which you can use to avoid this problem.

- Organise a number of short meetings where groups of requirements are considered rather than a single long meeting. This is only practical where everyone involved is located at the same site.

- Identify the most critical or the highest priority requirements and consider any problems with these requirements first. This may mean that you need to do more work preparing the agenda for the meeting but it will ensure that time is available for the most important requirements.

5.5   Prioritise Requirements

Key benefit	Focuses attention on the most important requirements
Costs of introduction	Low
Costs of application	Low
Guideline type	Basic

During the requirements analysis and negotiation process, priorities should be assigned to individual requirements which reflect their importance to stakeholders and to the overall success of the system.

Benefits

- Assigning priorities helps stakeholders to decide on the core requirements for the system. Priorities help focus negotiation meetings and resolve disputes between stakeholders particularly if they are combined with requirements risk analysis (see **Guideline 5.8**).

- The explicit association of requirements priorities helps designers to decide on the system architecture and helps to resolve design conflicts which may arise.

Implementation

Ideally, requirements priorities should be assigned during the requirements elicitation process. When expressing requirements, stakeholders should decide how important they are. However, people find it difficult to assign priorities at this stage because they do not have a complete picture of the system requirements. They usually do not completely understand the implications of the requirements which they propose. Priority assignment is therefore only realistic after a reasonably complete set of requirements has been collected and some preliminary analysis has been carried out. Priorities should be noted in a field on the form used for collecting the requirements.

Priorities should be assigned in discussions between requirements analysts and stakeholders. In many cases, different stakeholders will assign a different priority to the same requirement. This may reflect real needs or may simply reflect different stakeholder perceptions. Try to resolve the differences informally. If this is impossible, the priority conflicts should be discussed and resolved at negotiation meetings.

You should decide on a relatively small number of priority classifications such as 'essential', meaning that it must be included in the system, 'useful' meaning that the system will be less effective without it, and 'desirable' meaning that the facility is not a core system facility but makes the system more attractive to users in some way (e.g. by providing a graphical interface).

Costs and problems

There should be no significant costs in introducing and applying this guideline. You need to spend some time discussing priorities with stakeholders but this should not add appreciably to the time needed for requirements analysis.

The principal problem which can arise in priority assignment is unreal priority assignments from some stakeholders. They may simply say that all the requirements of interest to them are 'essential' and therefore subvert the priority assignment system. This causes particular difficulties if the stakeholders are customers or senior managers in positions of authority.

You can only really counter this by making logical and economic arguments against it. You can ask 'what if' questions such as

- 'what if it doubled the cost of the system to implement this requirement', or

- 'what if this requirement meant that requirements from XX could not be implemented'.

These can help communicate the consequences of thoughtless priority assignment. It is very rare indeed to find that all the requirements proposed are actually essential.

5.6   Classify Requirements Using a Multi-dimensional Approach

Key benefit	Helps discover requirements overlaps and conflicts
Costs of introduction	Low–moderate
Costs of application	Moderate
Guideline type	Intermediate

You should classify your requirements so that you can identify related requirements. You should not necessarily put individual requirements into a single class but should derive several different ways of classifying your requirements for analysis. This is called multi-dimensional classification. Each requirement may therefore fall into a number of different classes.

Benefits

- Classifying requirements is a basis for discovering commonalities and unexpected relationships between them. Conflicts and overlaps are most likely between requirements in the same class. Sometimes you find that requirements are so similar that they can be combined.

- Classifying requirements improves the traceability of the requirements document. When changes are made to requirements in some class, it may be helpful to consider if other requirements in the same class are affected by the change.

- Classification can help you find missing requirements. If you find that there are no requirements in some class which is part of your normal classification scheme, this may mean that important requirements have been left out.

Implementation

The simplest way to classify requirements is to use what is called a faceted approach. You identify a number of dimensions or facets and identify keywords which describe each of these.

For example, possible keywords which you might use to classify requirements are as folows.

1 *System.* This should be applied to requirements which affect the entire system such as performance or reliability requirements (See **Guideline 9.7**, *Identify global system requirements*).

2 *User interface.* This should be applied to requirements which are concerned with user interaction. More detailed classifications may also be used such as 'user input', 'data presentation', 'error indication', etc.

3 *Database.* This should be applied to requirements which are concerned with the data managed by the system.

4 *Communications.* This should be requirements which are concerned with the external communication facilities in the system. Again, it may be broken down into more detailed classifications reflecting, perhaps, the data communications equipment.

5 *Security.* This should be applied to requirements which are likely to have security implications.

These are possible examples and you must devise the most relevant classifications for the requirements which you are classifying. We recommend that you should have no more than five or six classifications. If you have more than this, classes tend to be too narrow. You will find that you only have a few requirements in each class.

After deciding on an initial set of classification terms, you should then go through the requirements, associating one or more of these keywords with each of them. You can classify the requirements using as many of the keywords as is necessary. Therefore, a requirement which states that 'A graphical user interface to the account data should be provided' would be classified as 'User interface', 'Database' and 'Security'.

Once requirements have been classified, you extract groups of requirements with the same classification terms for comparison and analysis. To do this, you need to use some software which will allow you to tag each requirement with its classification terms and then construct a request to the system to find all requirements with a given tag. This is possible if you use a word processor system to manage your requirements, but it is simpler if requirements are managed in a database (see **Guideline 9.5**, *Use a database to manage requirements*).

Costs and problems

Introducing this guideline is straightforward and not expensive. You will need a short training session that illustrates how requirements can be classified and how this allows groups of related requirements to be compared. The costs of applying this guideline are the costs of defining a classification scheme for a particular set of requirements and assigning classifications to each requirement. The initial definition of a classification scheme should be made using some kind of brainstorming approach. You can often reuse classification schemes across systems in the same application domain.

Classifying the requirements involves an analyst checking each requirement and assigning the classification terms to it. This can be done as part of the normal analysis process as the requirements are being checked. However, you usually need to go through the requirements several times to complete the classification. You will probably need to modify your initial classification scheme as you develop a better understanding of the requirements. Therefore, requirements which have already been classified may need to be re-classified to reflect your new scheme.

A problem, of course, is that requirements do not always fit neatly into classes and it is difficult to decide which classifications to assign. Remember, however, that this classification scheme is intended to help you analyse requirements; it is not like a library scheme that is used to find information. If it is not clear which class a requirement falls into, you lose nothing by assigning it to all possible classes.

If you have very large numbers of requirements, you can apply this guideline hierarchically. That is, you can identify an initial set of classes and apply these to the requirements to create principal groupings. For each principal group of requirements you can then devise more detailed classifications and apply these to that group. These classifications can be different for each principal group. This allows you to break down a large set of requirements into groups of manageable size.

5.7 Use Interaction Matrices to Find Conflicts and Overlaps

Key benefit	Reveals requirements conflicts and overlaps
Costs of introduction	Low
Costs of application	Moderate–high
Guideline type	Intermediate

An interaction matrix is a matrix where the rows and columns are labelled with requirements identifiers. The elements of the matrix are filled in with a value which indicates whether or not requirements conflict, overlap or are independent. Interaction matrices are similar to traceability matrices as described in **Guideline 9.3**, *Define traceability policies*.

Benefits

- This is a systematic approach to checking requirements which ensures that the interactions between all requirements in the system or in an identified class of requirements are considered.

- The interaction matrix is a useful input to the negotiation, as it is a clear summary of requirements which may cause problems and whose final form may need to be negotiated.

Implementation

The simplest way to construct an interaction matrix is to use a spreadsheet program and to label the rows and the columns of the spreadsheet with the requirement identifiers (see **Guideline 9.1**, *Uniquely identify each requirement*). Each requirement is then considered and compared with other requirements. You can then fill in values in the spreadsheet cells as follows.

- For requirements which conflict, fill in a 1.

- For requirements which overlap, fill in a 1000.

- For requirements which are independent, fill in a 0.

If you cannot decide whether requirements conflict, you should assume that a conflict exists. If you assume a conflict where none exists then it is usually fairly cheap to fix this problem; it can be much more expensive to resolve undetected conflicts.

The advantage of using numeric values is that you can then sum each row and column to find the number of conflicts (i.e. the remainder when the total is divided by 1000) and the number of overlaps (the total divided by 1000). Requirements which have high values for one or both of these figures should be carefully examined as part of the analysis process. A large number of conflicts or overlaps means that any changes to that requirement will probably have a major impact on the rest of the system.

This technique only works when you have a relatively small number of requirements, as it requires each requirement to be compared with every other requirement in the system. The upper size limit is probably about 200 requirements. It can be applied to small systems or to related groups of requirements in a viewpoint or in the same class. We therefore recommend that this guideline should be implemented at the same time or after you have introduced some requirements classification scheme.

This approach to analysis has been included in the PREview method (Chapter 13) which is a viewpoint-based method of requirements elicitation and analysis. In that method, the requirements from different viewpoints are compared for conflicts and overlaps. You can also use it in conjunction with requirements classification to compare requirements in the same or related classes.

A similar approach to this is used in the QFD (quality–function–deployment) model when considering quality attributes of a system. The application of QFD in software development is described in an article ('Quality Function Deployment: Usage in Software Development'), published in the January 1996 issue of the Communications of the ACM.

Costs and problems

This approach is easy to understand and relatively cheap to introduce into a requirements analysis process. It is an effective and systematic way to discover requirements conflicts and commonalities but it is fairly expensive to implement. Assuming that you use a standard spreadsheet program for the analysis, you need to set up the matrices, then compare each requirement with every other requirement to fill in the cell values.

The major problem with this method is that it is only really suitable for analysing relatively small numbers of requirements. It does not scale up because the number of analyses to be carried out is a function of the square of the number of requirements. You need to limit the number of requirements analysed in this way, either to requirements in a particular class or to the requirements for critical sub-systems.

5.8   Assess Requirements Risks

Key benefit	Identification of problem requirements
Costs of introduction	Moderate
Costs of application	Moderate
Guideline type	Advanced

For each requirement or set of related requirements, carry out a risk analysis in which you suggest possible problems which may arise in the implementation of that requirement, the probability of these problems arising and the effects which these problems would have.

Benefits

- Explicit risk assessment is a means of identifying requirements which are likely to cause particular difficulties to the system developers. If these can be identified at this stage, it may be possible to modify the requirement to reduce the risks to the development process.

- Assigning risks to requirements often reveals that insufficient information about the requirement is available and that further details should be discovered from requirement stakeholders.

Implementation

Risk analysis is a difficult process and there is no general method which is applicable to all types of requirement. You need to involve experienced people to be involved in the analysis process. They use their judgement to decide on the requirements risk.

Risk analysis is particularly important for new systems, where there are unknown factors involved. In these cases, requirements risk analysis helps avoid downstream development problems. Requirements which have high risks associated with them are the most likely to cause development difficulties. Identifying these risks at an early stage means that you can look for more information to reduce the risks before the requirements are finalised.

The types of risk which you should consider are as follows.

1 *Performance risks.* Implementing the requirement may adversely affect the overall performance of the system.

2 *Safety and security risks.* Implementing the requirement may cause problems in meeting overall system requirements for safety and security.

3 *Process risks.* Implementing a requirement may require changes to the normal development process, such as the introduction of mathematical specifications and proof (for a safety requirement) or the use of unfamiliar prototyping systems (for a user interface requirement).

4 *Implementation technology risks.* Implementing a requirement may require the use of unfamiliar implementation technology, such as AI techniques, the use of N-version programming for fault tolerance, etc.

5 *Database risks.* Implementing a requirement may involve non-standard data which is not available in an existing system database.

6 *Schedule risks.* Implementing a requirement may be technically difficult and may threaten the planned development schedule for the system.

7 *External risks.* Implementing a requirement involves external contractors.

8 *Stability risks.* The requirement may be volatile and subject to evolution during the development process.

You need to decide on the appropriate risks for each system being specified and assess each requirement against these risks. Risk assessment is imprecise so you should not use a numeric assessment scheme for risks. Rather, you should assess risks using 'fuzzy' categories such as 'high', 'medium' or 'low'.

Costs and problems

The costs of introducing this guideline are the costs of identifying the types of risk which are most applicable to your organisation and the costs of devising some systematic approach to risk assessment. It is fairly expensive to apply this guideline, as risk assessment is technically difficult. Experienced people must be involved in the process and must spend time weighing up the risks of each requirement. The time required should be proportional to the number of requirements.

As requirements risk assessment is not widely practised, the principal problem that you will find in implementing this guideline is the lack of people with risk assessment experience. In time, however, the problem will become less serious as people gain risk assessment experience.

6 Describing Requirements

Summary

Descriptions of individual requirements should be concise, understandable and unambiguous. In this chapter, we focus on how to write these descriptions rather than what should be in these descriptions. The guidelines which we suggest are:

Guidelines

6.1 Define Standard Templates for Describing Requirements.

6.2 Use Language Simply, Consistently and Concisely.

6.3 Use Diagrams Appropriately.

6.4 Supplement Natural Language With Other Descriptions of Requirements.

6.5 Specify Requirements Quantitatively.

In most organisations, system requirements are written as paragraphs of natural language (English, French, Japanese, etc.), supplemented by diagrams and equations. Natural language is the only notation that we have which is generally understandable by all potential readers of the requirements for a system. Natural language can be ambiguous, surprisingly opaque and is often misunderstood. Nevertheless, everyone can read natural language, so requirements will continue to be written in this way for the foreseeable future.

Natural language can be used to describe requirements clearly. All too often, however, natural language requirements are difficult to understand. Common problems are that:

- the requirements are written using complex conditional clauses (if A then if B then if C. . .) which are confusing

- terminology is used in a sloppy and inconsistent way

- the writers of the requirement assume that the reader has specific knowledge of the domain or the system and they leave essential information out of the requirements document.

These problems make it difficult to check the set of requirements for errors and omissions. Different interpretations of the requirements may lead to contractual disagreements between the customer and the system engineering contractor.

We do not think that these problems can be solved by introducing new languages for writing requirements. Good writing is all that is needed to write good requirements. Well-written requirements include all necessary information. They are succinct and are easy to understand. They use language that is as simple as possible. Technical terms are used in a consistent way and only when necessary.

We are convinced that, irrespective of the level of detail in your requirements description, there are three essential things that you must bear in mind when considering how to improve your requirements descriptions.

1   Requirements are read more often than they are written. Investing effort in writing requirements which are easy to read and understand is almost always cost-effective.

2   Readers of requirements come from diverse backgrounds. If you are a requirements writer, you should not assume that readers have the same background and knowledge as you.

3   Writing clearly and concisely is not easy. If you do not allow sufficient time for requirements descriptions to be drafted, reviewed and improved, you will inevitably end up with poorly written specifications.

Different organisations write requirements at different levels of abstraction from deliberately vague product specifications to detailed and precise descriptions of all aspects of a system. You must decide for yourself on the level of detail that you need. This depends on the type of requirements (stakeholder, system or process requirements), customer expectations, your organisational procedures, and external standards or regulations which you may have to follow. All we can do here is give you general advice which can be applied irrespective of the detail of the requirements.

6.1   Define Standard Templates for Describing Requirements

Key benefit	Requirements are presented in a consistent way so are more understandable
Costs of introduction	Moderate
Costs of application	Low
Guideline type	Basic

When you are writing detailed system requirements, you should define a set of standard templates which you use for organising the description of these requirements. The template should include fields to collect the detailed information necessary to completely specify the requirement.

Benefits

- Standards make requirements easier to read. Once readers understand a standard, they know what to expect when reading requirements. Their reading time and the likelihood of misunderstanding is reduced.

- Standards make requirements easier to collect. The standard form can be used as a checklist by analysts when collecting requirements from end-users, customers, managers, etc.

- Standards make requirements easier to write. They reduce the chances that important information will be forgotten and make it easier for reviewers to check if information has been left out.

Implementation

To ensure that natural language requirements are readable, you should define some structure for the description of each requirement. This structure should include fields to note the information that you wish to associate with the requirement. For example, if the requirement is a functional requirement, your standard may specify that the inputs, the processing and the outputs must be specified in the requirements definition.

A standard form or template should be defined to record requirements information. These forms should have named fields which remind the analyst which information is to be collected and recorded. These replace unstructured sentences which describe the requirement. This template should be based on the type of system which you are specifying and the specific information needs of your organisation. You will need to define several templates to cater for different types of requirement.

Within your requirements template you may wish to include fields to support other guidelines such as the requirements reference number (**Guideline 9.1**, *Uniquely identify each requirement*), the sources of the requirement (**Guideline 4.4**, *Record requirements sources*) and the rationale for the requirement (**Guideline 4.8**, *Record requirements rationale*).

You should provide word processor templates for these forms to all those who are likely to have to collect requirements. Use your standard word processor for this rather than any special-purpose tool. You can then be sure that the forms can be supported on all computers in your organisation.

However, you should not force analysts to fill in all fields on a form and you should not use special-purpose software which requires the fields in a form to be completed in a particular order. Requirements discovery is a difficult process and different people collect information in different ways. Imposing a single approach is likely to be resisted. Always allow for a 'get out' where analysts may simply note the requirement in any way they wish in some comments field of the form. Predefined forms cannot cover everything and there needs to be some flexibility in your system.

Some readers of requirements simply want a high-level description and do not want to read pages and pages of forms. You should allow for this by including fields on the form which may be extracted (automatically if possible) to create a shorter (perhaps incomplete) description of the requirement. Make sure, however, that you maintain links from this shorter description to the complete requirements specification in the standard template. This will then allow you to generate a new short description when changes to the requirement are agreed.

Costs and problems

If you do not already have standards for presenting requirements, there is a significant cost in introducing this guideline and developing an appropriate standard for your organisation. Although you can use the suggestions here as a basis for your standard, you need to look at your existing requirements to check how many different styles (and hence standards) that you use and to decide what information you need to include in a requirements description.

After designing an initial set of standards you will have to assess them and, almost certainly, modify them after you have experience of their use. If you already have standards, you may wish to think about whether you should modify them to incorporate some of the advice given in this book. Once a set of standard templates has been established, there are few additional costs involved in applying the guideline.

A problem which you may face is resistance from requirements engineers to standards. They may have evolved their own way of working and do not wish to be constrained by a standard way of recording requirements. You should try to avoid this problem by disseminating information about the standard during its development and by involving engineers in the standard development process. They will then feel committed to the standard and therefore more likely to use it.

6.2   Use Language Simply, Consistently and Concisely

Key benefit	Requirements are easier to read and understand
Costs of introduction	Fairly low
Costs of application	Low–moderate
Guideline type	Basic

When you express a requirement in natural language, write your descriptions using simple and concise language. Wherever possible you should avoid complex sentence constructions, long sentences and paragraphs and ambiguous terminology.

Benefits

- When requirements are written using simple language, they are easier to read and understand. The principal costs of requirements engineering are the costs of paying people to read requirements. If you can reduce the time required for requirements reading without losing understanding, you will have an immediate cost saving in your requirements process.

- More people can understand requirements that are written in a simple way. It takes less time to explain the requirements to stakeholders and a wider range of people can participate in the validation of the requirements.

Implementation

Many people find it difficult to write clear and concise natural language. They write long and convoluted sentences and express the requirements in an unnecessarily verbose way. To improve requirements descriptions, we recommend that you should write a short style guide which describes how to use language in writing requirements in your organisation.

This guide must be short and easy to read. Otherwise, people will not have the time or the inclination to read it. Ideally, your style guide should include four or five pages of guidelines with examples of good and bad writing drawn from your own experience.

Some basic writing style guidelines which might be included in your guide are as follows.

1 Keep sentences short. Because of the limitation of our short-term memory, you often need to read long sentences more than once before you can understand them.

2 Never express more that one requirement in a single sentence. Avoid the use of 'and' in sentences. This implies that more than one requirement or concept is being discussed.

3 Avoid the use of jargon, abbreviations and acronyms unless you are completely confident that they will be understood by all readers of your document. Even then be very careful; the same acronym may have different meanings in different domains. For example, the acronym 'ATM' is used in both banking systems and networking application domains. In a requirements document which describes how ATMs (Automatic Teller Machines) should be connected using ATM (Asynchronous Transfer Mode), you can imagine the confusion which could arise.

4 Keep paragraphs short. As a general rule, no paragraph should be made up of more than seven sentences. Again, the reason for this is due to the limits on people's short-term memory.

5 Use lists and tables wherever possible to present information sequences. Lists (like this one) are much easier to understand than sequences which are presented as a single paragraph.

6 Use terminology consistently. Do not use a term to mean one thing in one place in the document and something different somewhere else. This is very difficult to achieve, especially when different people are responsible for writing different parts of the document. Using a data dictionary to define the names of system entities can be helpful here (see **Guideline 7.5**, *Use a data dictionary*).

7 Use words such as 'shall', 'should', 'will' and 'must' in a consistent way with the following meanings:

- 'shall'
  indicates that the requirement is mandatory,

- 'should' indicates that the requirement is desirable but not mandatory

- 'will' indicates something that will be externally provided

- 'must' is best avoided. If used, it should be a synonym for 'shall'.

8 Do not express requirements using nested conditional clauses (i.e. if X then if Y then R1a else if Z then R1b else R1c). These are very easy to misunderstand. If you cannot find a convenient way of expressing a requirement in natural language without nested conditional clauses, use a different notation such as a decision table.

9 Use the active rather than the passive voice, particularly when describing actions taken by people or the system. Unfortunately, most technical writing is written impersonally and many people find it difficult to change to a more personal style.

10 Do not try to express complex relationships in a natural language description. Diagrams are much more effective for this purpose (see the next guideline).

11 Never use anonymous references. When you refer to other requirements, tables or diagrams, give a brief description of what you are referring to, as well as the reference number. If you simply use a reference number, the reader may need to look it up specially to remind themselves what it means.

12 Pay attention to spelling and grammar. Poor spelling and grammar can obscure your meaning. A spelling checker should always be used.

The style guide should be included as part of your standard for specifying requirements. When you organise requirements reviews, you should ask reviewers to comment on the writing style used and to highlight requirements which are particularly difficult to understand.

Costs and problems

The principal costs of introducing this guideline are the writing of a style guide and, if necessary, short training sessions for all involved in the RE process. These should introduce them to the style guide and clear writing style. There is also a slightly increased review cost but this is minimal so long as your style guide is not too long.

Initially, you will probably find that it is quite expensive to introduce this guideline into your requirements engineering process. Surprisingly, perhaps, it takes longer to write requirements simply than in a more complex way. However, as people gain experience with clear writing style, these costs will rapidly decline.

The problem that you are likely to face is that many people from a technical background find it very difficult to write clearly and concisely. Introducing a style guide is all very well but we have a long tradition of writing requirements in an opaque and obscure way and this cannot be changed overnight. Although reviews can highlight significant deviations from the style guides, this will not remove all obscure writing.

6.3   Use Diagrams Appropriately

Key benefit	Diagrams are particularly useful for documenting requirements relationships
Costs of introduction	Low
Costs of application	Low
Guideline type	Basic

You should use diagrams in a requirements description wherever it is necessary to show structural information or to show relationships between information in the requirements description. Diagrams may also be used to summarise numeric information and to describe sequences of events or activities.

Benefits

- Diagrams are far more effective than text for presenting relationships between items of information. Most people find diagrams easier to understand than textual descriptions of structure or relationships.

- Diagrams break up sections of text into smaller, more readable fragments. This means that you get a double bonus from the diagram. Information is presented more comprehensibly and the surrounding text is easier to understand.

- Diagrams from a requirements document may be reused when making requirements presentations to customers.

Implementation

As part of your document style guide, we recommend including a section which describes the circumstances where diagrams are most likely to be helpful. These include the following.

1   Where something (a system, a document, etc.) is made up of a number of modules or components and you wish to illustrate relationships between these components. An example of this is where you use a block diagram to illustrate the overall structure of a system.

2   Where you need to show a set of activities where each activity has a number of inputs and outputs. Diagrams can be used to show the activity sequence and where activities can be carried out in parallel.

3   Where you need to illustrate spatial organisation, for example, of a control panel.

4   Where you wish to show some decomposition structure such as an organisation chart.

A good general rule for drawing diagrams is to keep them as simple as possible. Complex diagrams are often worse than no diagram at all. You should use simple labelled boxes and lines to show structure and relationships. Diagrams should fit onto a single page and should not have 'connectors' to other diagrams. Diagrams should always be labelled with a figure number and a title. The figure number should always be used to refer to the diagram.

You should avoid the use of icons which do not have an obvious meaning. Many people find the commercial 'clip art' pictures provided with word processing packages to be trite and irritating. Unless these are particularly appropriate, these are also best avoided.

If colour or shading is used, it should be used to distinguish different parts of the diagram or for emphasis. Colour should be used sparingly. You should not associate meaning with specific colours as people from different backgrounds may interpret colour in different ways. For example, red may mean 'hot' in some application domains and 'danger' in other domains. You should also remember that about 10% of men are colour-blind.

Some people think that diagrams are always easier to understand than textual presentation. They therefore introduce diagrams everywhere even when the same information could be presented more clearly using a list or a table. You should not introduce diagrams unless they provide meaningful information about structure or relationships. They should not be over-used or used to present information which could be more clearly expressed in some other way.

Costs and problems

The costs of introducing this guideline are minimal. Diagrams can be drawn using facilities which are now embedded in most word-processing systems. More complex drawing packages can be used but these are designed for professional illustrators and sometimes encourage the production of over-complex diagrams. There may be some training costs for people to use the drawing facilities but most packages are intuitive and can be self-taught with little effort. The costs of applying the guideline are the costs of drawing diagrams. These should not usually take much more time than textual requirements description.

While you are unlikely to encounter any user resistance to this guideline, you will probably find that some people are much better than others at expressing their ideas in diagrams. This seems to reflect fundamental differences in thinking and there is not much you can do about this. Some people think in pictures, but people who do not think this way often prefer textual descriptions to diagrams.

6.4   Supplement Natural Language With Other Descriptions of Requirements

Key benefit	More concise, less ambiguous requirements descriptions
Costs of introduction	Very low
Costs of application	Low
Guideline type	Basic

Some requirements are best described using specialised notations, such as mathematical formulae, decision tables, design notations or programming languages, rather than natural language. Although you will almost always want to have some description in natural language, you should supplement this, where appropriate, with more precise descriptions in an appropriate notation.

Benefits

- Specialised notations allow for descriptions whose meaning is less likely to be misinterpreted than a natural language description. The description is often more concise than a corresponding natural language description.

- If the notation used is familiar to application domain experts, they are less likely to make mistakes when specifying their requirements and more likely to find any errors which have been made.

Implementation

Customers and systems engineers have different needs. Customers need to be able to understand the requirements for the system. They need to make an assessment of how this will contribute to their overall organisational objectives, fit into existing working processes and integrate with other systems which are used. Systems engineers need a detailed and unambiguous statement of requirements on which their system design should be based. It should be possible to trace from the requirements to the design through to the system implementation.

It is often hard to meet these conflicting objectives if you only use natural language. You should therefore supplement this with other notations such as the following.

- Decision tables where actions have to be taken depending on a complex set of conditions. Text which includes many conditional clauses is often ambiguous. It is notoriously difficult to read and understand.

- Programming languages or program design languages which may be used where you wish to describe a number of actions which must take place in sequence and where some of these actions are conditional or may be repeated. You may also use language descriptions for detailed interface specification.

- Algebra when you wish to describe how particular numeric values must be transformed by an operation or particular values should be computed.

- Data-flow diagrams where you need to define a sequence of transformations which take place during some end-to-end processing of data.

- Timing diagrams to illustrate time-critical system actions.

- System models such as object models, entity-relation models or finite state models where you need to describe detailed system requirements. System modelling is covered in Chapter 7.

The additional information provided by these notations is usually necessary when the requirements must define detailed information such as a sequence of events which must take place, the interfaces between sub-systems, etc. They are therefore most likely to be used when your requirements document is a detailed functional specification of the system to be implemented.

We do not know of any book where all these notations are described but many of them are covered in *Software Engineering*, 5th edition by Ian Sommerville (Addison Wesley, 1996).

Costs and problems

In most cases, introducing this guideline does not require engineers to learn new notations but to use techniques which they already know. In such cases, there are no introductory costs for this guideline. We advise against introducing new unfamiliar notations as these are likely to cause more problems than they solve. There are obviously some costs in applying the guideline as tables, models, etc., have to be created. Like diagrams, however, these should not normally cost much more than writing the equivalent technical description.

A possible problem may arise if mathematical or unfamiliar notations such as decision tables are used. Some readers of the requirements may think that a requirement is harder to understand because they do not know the notation. They may therefore oppose the use of these notations. This is a particular problem when the people against the idea of specialised notation are managers who can decide whether or not they should be used. To overcome this resistance, you may find it helpful to demonstrate that the more concise notations can be paraphrased in natural language (see **Guideline 8.8**, *Paraphrase system models*).

6.5   Specify Requirements Quantitatively

Key benefit	Unambiguous presentation of requirements
Costs of introduction	Low–moderate
Costs of application	Low–moderate
Guideline type	Intermediate–advanced

Wherever possible, you should specify quantitative values for system requirements. This is most applicable to non-functional requirements. Non-functional requirements are requirements which are concerned with attributes of the system as a whole such as performance, RAM utilisation, physical weight or size, usability, etc. You may be able to specify acceptable ranges or limits for these attribute values.

Benefits

- If you specify these attributes in a way which can be objectively measured, you communicate the requirements precisely to both the specifiers and developers of the system.

- Quantitative requirements serve as a basis for system acceptance tests and you reduce the chances of dispute between customers and developers about whether or not these requirements have been met by the system.

Implementation

To specify system attributes quantitatively, you mustdo the following.

1 Decide on the appropriate metric which may be used to express the attribute. This should depend on the type of attribute but also on the possibility of measuring that value in the developed system. There is no point in specifying something that cannot be measured.

2 Decide on an appropriate value for that attribute. In some cases, this may be simple. For example, for a system which is to be installed on a single board, there will be a limited number of chips and this will limit the RAM size. In other cases, the value must be arrived at after discussion with system stakeholders.

Figure 6.1 shows possible metrics which can be used. Note that we sometimes suggest different metrics for the same attribute. The metric you should use depends on the type of system which you are specifying.

You often need to make a trade-off between the values of different attributes, and between the values required for non-functional attributes and the services the system should provide. For example, you may specify that they system must process N transactions per second and must respond to user requests within M seconds. However, you may find that at maximum load, the processor is fully

System attribute	Metric which can be used
Reliability	Mean time to failure
Reliability	Rate of occurrence of failure
Availability	Probability of failure on demand
Performance	Number of transactions to be processed per second
Performance	Response time to user input
Store utilisation	Maximum size of system in kilobytes
Usability	Time taken to learn 75% of user facilities
Usability	Average number of errors made by users in a given time period
Robustness	Time to re-start after system failure
Integrity	Maximum permitted data loss after system failure

Figure 6.1 Possible metrics for non-functional requirements specification

occupied and it is impossible to meet the response time requirement.

It is important to avoid specifying impossible values or values which cannot be tested. This is a particular problem when specifying system reliability as accurate measurement of reliability usually requires a very extensive period of testing. The higher the reliability required, the longer this period will be, so that there is not time to verify reliability requirements which are too high. For example, if you specify that no more than 1 in 100 000 transactions should fail, then you must test the system for several hundred thousand transactions to check this specification.

Costs and problems

Because of the range of system attributes and the different types of metrics which may be used, it is difficult to make a general statement about the costs and problems of introducing this guideline. If you are using familiar metrics, there will be few costs and problems involved in specifying requirements specification quantitatively. In other cases, you may need to involve external consultants such as reliability consultants to help engineers make quantitative specifications and to organise training sessions on reliability specification.

Once metrics are understood, the costs of applying the guideline in the requirements document are relatively low. However, you will obviously incur validation costs at a later time when you check if the system meets its specification. Collecting quantitative information is likely to be more expensive than informal approaches to validation.

Perhaps the main problem that you will face is a general reluctance of people to commit themselves to a precise system specification. This applies to people specifying the system and those developing the system. Once requirements have been precisely specified, it is more expensive to introduce changes as there is no ambiguity in the requirement. System developers also prefer more ambiguous requirements, as these allow them to argue that they have met the requirement even when the system does not meet customer expectations.

You may also encounter resistance to this guideline from engineers involved in the requirements engineering process. They may not be willing to accept that it is possible to specify requirements quantitatively because it is difficult to design tests to check the specification. You can address both of these problems by introducing quantitative specification slowly and incrementally. You should start with simple attributes which can be easily tested. Once these can be specified and checked, then introduce more complex metrics.

7 System Modelling

Summary

The guidelines in this chapter are concerned with the development of abstract system models which may be part of a detailed system specification. We recommend that essential models, which should always be produced, include a model of the system's environment and a model of the architecture of the system. These high-level models supplement more detailed system models, such as data-flow models, which may be produced when a structured analysis method is used. The guidelines we suggest here are:

Guidelines

7.1   Develop Complementary System Models.

7.2   Model the System's Environment.

7.3   Model the System Architecture.

7.4   Use Structured Methods for System Modelling.

7.5   Use a Data Dictionary.

7.6   Document the Links Between Stakeholder Requirements and System Models.

System models describe a particular aspect of a system, such as the way the system is decomposed into subsystems, the way that data is processed, the structure of the data, etc. They are used in a requirements document to add information to natural language descriptions of the system requirements. They may be developed during the requirements elicitation and analysis to help understand the requirements. Sometimes, they can be considered as a detailed system specification of what is required.

System models supplement natural language descriptions of requirements. The requirements description and the associated system models are usually developed at the same time. The development of one helps with the development of the other as exploring aspects of the requirements through modelling reveals inconsistencies and incompleteness.

In some organisations, it is normal practice to develop very detailed and complete system models as part of the system specification. In others, only abstract high-level models are included. These help the reader understand the requirements but are not themselves detailed system specifications. This depends on where the organisation draws the boundaries between specification and design. For example, where a system is specified and implemented in the same organisation, system modelling may be part of the design process. Where it is normal for design and development to be carried out as separate processes, detailed system models may be needed as a system specification.

In this chapter, we recommend that you should develop a number of system models representing different aspects of the system specification. The models which you need for your system depend on the type of system and the people who will use the models. However, we recommend that two high-level models should always be included in a requirements specification. These are as follows.

1 A model which shows the environment in which the system being specified will operate. This is discussed in **Guideline 7.2**.

2 An architectural model which shows how the system is decomposed into sub-systems. This is discussed in **Guideline 7.3**.

Finally, we must say something about object-oriented modelling as this is now such a hot topic. Object models are simply one kind of system model which integrate, to some extent, information about behaviour and structure. They show the operations on data as well as the logical structure of the data. These models include icons which show object attributes and operations. The models illustrate the relationships between objects such as the 'use/used by' relationship and the inheritance relationship. However, because they are based on independent objects, the models do not give a clear picture of end-to-end processing in a system. Instead, they focus on the system's decomposition into objects. Model readers who are not familiar with object-oriented concepts usually find them difficult to understand.

Developing object models is certainly valuable if you plan to use an object-oriented development process. You can often reuse parts of an object-oriented analysis model in an object-oriented design and translate this directly to code in a language such as C++. However, if you do not develop object-oriented programs, we do not recommend the use of object models. Making the transition from an object-oriented model to a system based on functions is not easy.

7.1   Develop Complementary System Models

Key benefit	Reveals errors and inconsistencies in the specification
Costs of introduction	Low–moderate
Costs of application	Moderate
Guideline type	Basic

It is not possible to include all system specification information in a single model as it would be hopelessly complex and impossible to understand. As part of the system modelling process, therefore, you should create several system models to illustrate different aspects of the system specification.

Benefits

- The process of developing different types of model forces you to make different kinds of analysis of the system requirements. These different types of analysis are likely to reveal different types of problem, omission and inconsistency.

- Different stakeholders are interested in different aspects of the system and can analyse these most effectively when they are presented in a separate model. For example, a database administrator may be particularly interested in the data structures used by the system and the required database organisation.

Implementation

Complementary system models show different aspects of the system specification. System models are usually developed to present either a behavioural view or a structural view of the system specification. A behavioural view models the behaviour of the system in response to stimuli from its environment. These stimuli may be either events (such as the arrival of a message) or input data (such as the availability of a report). A structural model shows how the system or its data are decomposed. You should normally develop at least one behavioural and one structural model.

Examples of the different types of system model which might be produced as part of the analysis process are as follows.

1 *A data-processing model.* Data-flow diagrams may be used to show how data is processed at different stages in the system.

2 *A composition model.* Entity-relation diagrams may be used to show how some entities in the system are composed of other entities.

3 *A classification model.* Object class/inheritance diagrams may be used to show how entities have common characteristics.

4 *A stimulus–response model.* State transition diagrams may be used to show how the system reacts to internal and external events.

5 *A process model.* Process models may be used to show the principal activities and deliverables involved in carrying out some process.

Other types of model such as timing models may also be required for some types of system such as telecommunication systems.

There is no ideal set of system models. The set of models which is best for your application depends on the following things.

1 *The type of information that you need to specify.* The value of system models is that they can add more detailed information to a natural language specification. Models should be developed when detailed specification cannot be left until the system is designed. Therefore, if parts of the system exchange data, you should develop a detailed structural model of that data; if a particular sequence of processes must be followed in response to an input, you should define a data processing model to show that process sequence.

2 *Likely readers of the system models.* Models must be expressed in a notation which is understandable by the people who need to read them. Although a Petri net model may be a good way to show concurrent processing, there is no point in developing this if only a few people in your organisation understand this notation.

3 *Skills of the model developers.* A bad model is probably worse than no model. You should not attempt to develop system models which are outside the experience of your requirements engineers.

4 *The availability of CASE tools.* CASE tools reduce the time and effort needed to produce system models. If you do not have tool support for some types of system modelling notation then you will probably find that it is impractical to develop models in these notations.

System models are usually represented graphically. They show system or problem entities and the relationships between them. Graphical representations are used as these are often easier to understand than textual descriptions and are good for showing relationships between the system entities.

You can use an informal approach to system modelling where you define your own notation (often simple boxes and lines) to describe the system specification. This is particularly appropriate for fairly high-level models in stakeholder specifications. These present a system overview and leave details of the system unspecified. Alternatively, you may use the techniques and tools defined as part of a structured method of analysis for model description (**Guideline 7.4**).

Graphical models often appear to be easy to understand but they do suffer from some problems.

1 Graphical models are imprecise and may be interpreted in different ways by different people.

2 Most graphical notations which are used for system modelling do not include facilities for specifying how exceptions should be handled. Models are a good way of presenting an overall picture of 'normal' operation but graphical models become very cluttered when exception information is included.

3   Graphical notations are not standardised. Readers of one notation may misinterpret diagrams in another notations because they make assumptions about the meanings of graphical symbols.

4   We do not have useful notations for modelling non-functional requirements or relating these non-functional requirements to models which specify the system. Many non-functional requirements apply to the system as a whole rather than to identifiable system components. This is almost impossible to illustrate on a graphical model.

Because of these problems, some people advocate developing system models using formal mathematical notations. These notations are less ambiguous than informal graphical notations so the system models are a precise system specification. As we discuss in **Guideline 10.6**, *Specify systems using formal specifications* and in Chapter 12, this is particularly important for systems which have rigorous reliability, safety or security requirements.

Costs and problems

The costs of introducing this guideline depend on the type of models which you wish to include in your specification. If these are abstract, informal models then the costs are low. If they are based on notations used in some structured method, then some training costs are involved. CASE tools may need to be purchased and these are expensive.

The development and validation of detailed models to specify a system takes a significant amount of time. You must budget for this in your requirements engineering process. However, the models may replace some detailed natural language specifications of the details of the system so, in practice, the extra costs may not be significant.

The main problem with introducing this guideline is

that non-specialists often have problems understanding system models. It is commonly argued that notations such as data-flow diagrams, entity-relation models of data and object descriptions are intuitive and easy to understand. However, our experience is that managers and system end-users without a technical background often find them to be incomprehensible.

Even if they appear to understand the notation, readers often misinterpret the model. In our experience, object models are particularly difficult for people who do not have experience of object-oriented development. The reason for this is that these models present a fragmented view of the system. You therefore must be prepared to spend quite a lot of time with these model readers explaining the specification described in the model to them.

7.2   Model the System's Environment

Key benefit	Documents the external systems whose interfaces must be specified
Costs of introduction	Low
Costs of application	Low
Guideline type	Basic

To help understand the requirements, you should develop one or more models of the system's environment. These should show other automated systems which are interfaced to it and business processes which may use the system.

Benefits

- The environmental model shows external systems whose interfaces may have to be specified, in detail, as part of the requirements or system design documents.

- The environmental model shows what lies outside of the system. It helps the system designer to decide if a requirement can be implemented by using some of the facilities provided in the system's environment.

- The environmental model may help readers understand how the system requirements relate to the business processes supported by the system.

Implementation

The environmental model is a model of the context in which the system is used. It should include the following things.

1 Other systems which are directly interfaced to the system being specified. This includes systems which already exist and planned systems which are being developed at the same time.

2   Other systems (where known) which may co-exist with the system and the possible interactions between them. For example, it may be assumed that an electronic mail system is always available to end-users and that information may be cut and pasted from mail messages into the system.

3   The business processes in which the system is used. This may simply be the name of the process or it could be a detailed process description. This depends on the processes and on the familiarity of the specification readers with these processes.

Normally, environmental models are defined using informal block diagrams. The principal components of the environment are shown in boxes and the main relationships between the system and these components are illustrated as lines linking these boxes. Of course, the boxes and lines need to be annotated with additional information to add detail to the model. If you use a data dictionary, (see **Guideline 7.5**) the names used in the environmental model should be added to it.

When you define business processes as part of the environmental model, you should define the activities involved, their inputs and outputs, the people responsible for these processes and the software which they use for process support.

Environmental models should be one of the first system models which you develop. In some cases, these models may be developed as part of the requirements elicitation process (see **Guidelines 4.5**, *Define the system's operating environment* and **4.12**, *Analyse operational processes*). The environmental model can be used during requirements elicitation and analysis to help decide whether or not a requirement is within the scope of the system (see **Guideline 5.1**, *Define system boundaries*).

The process of producing an environmental model involves the following.

1   *Finding out about the environment by consulting system stakeholders.* This can be a surprisingly difficult and time-consuming task. The people involved in maintaining the system's environment may not be interested in the system being developed; they may not have time to provide the environmental information which you need. Some people may not wish to discuss their work because they are fearful of change and consider the new system to be a threat to them. If the system is a new system, the environment itself may not be well-defined.

2   *Deciding what to include and what to leave out of environmental models.* The environment of a system is usually very complex. There are often subtle, implicit relationships between different parts of that environment. It can be difficult to decide whether or not parts of the environment are relevant for the system being developed. Decisions about the system's environment may not be finalised and the environmental information may be unstable.

3   *Producing an initial environmental model.* The initial model should reflect your understanding of the system's environment. You will almost certainly get this wrong but you need some kind of model to discuss with system stakeholders.

4   *Analysing and refining the model.* Once you have an initial model, you need to go back to the system stakeholders and refine this model. Several iterations may be necessary before you have a complete model of the environment.

The process is iterative and you will probably have to repeat these steps a number of times before the final environmental model is established.

Costs and problems

This is a cheap guideline to introduce, as the production of environmental models is an intuitive process and does not require special training. As the notations used are informal, no special-purpose tools are necessary. The graphics facilities available in most word processors are adequate for producing these models. There are obviously some costs involved in applying the guideline. Drawing the model takes some time and some additional consultations may be required to refine the model. Readers may have to spend a little extra time understanding the model. Overall, however, these costs should be fairly low.

The principal problem which you face in applying this guideline is environmental change. The system's environment is not static and it changes as new processes and systems are introduced, as businesses are re-organised and as business processes evolve. An environmental model produced at an early stage in a requirements engineering process will probably be out-of-date by the end of that process. To keep the environmental model up-to-date, you must review it regularly and incorporate changes to the environment which have occurred.

7.3 Model the System Architecture

Key benefit	Helps partition the system requirements
Costs of introduction	Low–moderate
Costs of application	Low
Guideline type	Basic

You should always develop an architectural model of the system which shows how the system is decomposed into sub-systems. The model should also illustrate sub-systems communication, that is, the direct links between sub-systems.

Benefits

- An architectural model may be used to help partition the system requirements. Many requirements are associated with specific sub-systems and you can organise the description of requirements according to the system model.

- An architectural model presents an overview of the system's functionality. People who know the application domain can, very quickly, get an impression of what the system is supposed to do.

- A model of the system architecture helps the requirements engineer identify requirements which involve more than one sub-system. These requirements are likely to cause problems when changes are made either to the requirements or to the design and they should be avoided wherever possible.

Implementation

Architectural models are usually presented as simple block diagrams showing the main sub-systems and the relationships between them. Main sub-systems are those parts of the system which can exist as independent entities. They take information from and provide information to other sub-systems. For example, a car might have a braking sub-system, a steering sub-system, an engine management sub-system, etc.

Sub-systems are represented as boxes in a block diagram and relationships between the sub-systems as lines joining these boxes. Different types of relationship may exist, e.g. a sub-system may pass information to another sub-system, they may share the same processor, etc. You need to be careful to distinguish between these in your architectural model, perhaps by using different styles of line to link the sub-system boxes. For large systems, each sub-system is itself a substantial system in its own right and you may need to develop separate architectural models of each of these.

Designing the architecture of a system is a creative activity. Requirements analysts and engineers must use their general knowledge of similar systems and architectural patterns to design an appropriate system architecture. There are a number of 'standard' architectural patterns which are commonly used. You may find it helpful to develop architectural models using these patterns. Examples of architectural patterns which have been identified in software systems include:

1 client–server systems where shared system facilities are provided via general-purpose servers, and user facilities are provided on client systems which call on servers when information is required

2 layered systems where system facilities are provided by calling on facilities offered by a lower-level layer

3 repository-based systems where sub-systems communicate through a shared repository

4 pipeline systems where each element in the system carries out some computations and passes on information to another element for further processing.

The characteristic of all of these patterns is some kind of separation between parts of the system. This makes it easier to incorporate system changes as these changes may be confined to one part of the architecture.

You might think that the system architecture is a design issue and that it is premature to model the system architecture as part of the requirements engineering process. We disagree with this.

1 Many system engineering problems have resulted because the requirements as specified could not be mapped onto a coherent system architecture which was resilient to requirements change.

2 For some systems, the system architecture may itself be a requirement. This may be due to organisational policies on hardware utilisation, the need to achieve a given level of system reliability or the constraints imposed by other systems. For example, systems which have high reliability requirements may have to be developed using *N*-version programming and this immediately imposes a system architecture.

You can find out more about architectural modelling in Chapter 13 of *Software Engineering*, 5th edition (Ian Sommerville, Addison Wesley, 1996) and in *Software Architectures: Perspectives on an Emerging Discipline* (D. Garlan and M. Shaw, Prentice-Hall, 1996).

Costs and problems

The costs of introducing this guideline vary from low to moderate depending on your organisation. Architectural models are intuitive and simple notations are used to define system architecture. There is therefore no need for specialised CASE tools to support the guideline. However, you may need to organise a training programme to introduce the notion of architectural modelling and standard architectural patterns which may be used. Once this training programme has been completed, the costs of applying the guideline are simply the small amount of additional time required to produce the architectural models.

The problems which you may face in systems engineering projects is that people from different backgrounds may have a different understanding of what is meant by the system architecture. They may see it in terms of their own specific engineering model rather than an overall model of the system structure. This can only be resolved by ensuring that people from different disciplines are involved in the process of developing and validating the architectural model.

7.4 Use Structured Methods for System Modelling

Key benefit	System models are documented in a standardised way
Costs of introduction	Moderate–high
Costs of application	Moderate
Guideline type	Basic–intermediate

Structured methods are systematic approaches to analysis and design which include notations, guidelines and rules for defining system models and the process used to develop and validate these models. The methods may be applied to construct system models for inclusion in the requirements document.

Benefits

- The use of structured methods results in standard documentation of system models. This makes models easier to understand and maintain.

- Structured methods are usually supported by CASE tools which run on workstations or PCs. These tools include model editors, checkers and data dictionaries and generally reduce the costs of developing complex system models.

- Structured methods of analysis usually have a well-defined transition to system design. Therefore, the costs of designing the system specified in the system model should be reduced.

- The guidance and support provided by structured methods may allow less experienced or less skilled staff to develop good quality system models.

Implementation

Structured methods mostly fall into two categories.

- Procedural methods where the behaviour of the system is represented by functional models of some kind. Data structures are defined using entity-relation models.

- Object-oriented methods where object models which combine structural and behavioural information are produced.

The vast majority of structured methods which are in use are procedural methods. These were developed in the 1970s and came into widespread use during the 1980s. There are many analysts trained in their use and mature toolsets to support these methods. Object-oriented methods are more recent but are becoming increasingly widely accepted, as systems are developed using object-oriented programming languages such as C++. Object-oriented methods are particularly appropriate for modelling interactive systems.

The main components of a structured method are:

1 a set of recommended system models which should be developed and a defined notation which should be used to develop these models

2 a set of model rules which should be applied both to individual models and the overall model formed by integrating the different individual models; these may range from simple rules regarding the use of names to complex properties which complete models should satisfy

3 a set of good practice guidelines for producing high-quality system models

4 a description of the process which should be followed to create a system model using the method

5 reports on the system specification which should be produced during the application of the method

Methods are not universally applicable and different methods are appropriate for different types of system and application domains. For example, methods such as SSADM and Structured Analysis are best for modelling commercial data processing systems, Statecharts for real-time systems, and SDL for telecommunication system modelling. Object-oriented methods such as OMT and Objectory are sometimes claimed to be more universal.

Frankly we are sceptical about this. These methods are still relatively new and we do not have enough experience of their use in large systems to know their limitations.

Many organisations invested heavily in structured methods and associated CASE tools in the 1980s. They anticipated that this would result in significant increases in analyst and designer productivity and system quality. Although some companies reported very significant improvements, the majority of companies found that the benefits of structured methods had been oversold. They now use structured methods where appropriate and do not insist on their use for all projects.

We discuss structured methods in more detail in Chapter 11. For further information, we recommend *Software Requirements: Objects, Functions and States* by A.M. Davis (Prentice-Hall, 1992) and *Requirements Engineering: Frameworks for Understanding* by R. J. Wieringa (Wiley, 1996). A good summary of object-oriented modelling methods is given by G. Wilkie in *Object-oriented Software Engineering* (Addison Wesley, 1993).

Costs and problems

There are significant costs involved in introducing structured methods. These costs include the following.

1   Procurement costs, including the costs of the CASE tools to support the method and, possibly, the purchasing or upgrading of hardware to support these methods. It has been estimated that the four-year costs of CASE tool support including initial hardware and software purchase and maintenance can be as much as $50 000 per user.

2   Consultancy costs involved in selecting the appropriate method for your organisation and the projects where it may be deployed. You are unlikely to have available in-house expertise on available methods.

3   The costs of training engineers to understand the method and its limitations and to use the CASE tool support for the method.

Experienced analysts usually find that it takes more time to develop a system model using a structured method. However, the quality of the developed model may be much higher so this may be offset by reduced costs of model validation. Furthermore, if the analyst does not have much experience of system modelling, the guidance given by the structured method will reduce the time required for system modelling.

Problems which may arise when using structured methods include the following.

1 The model types supported by the method may not include all the models which you think are necessary to describe your system. The supporting tools may not allow other types of model to be generated. Tools vary radically in this respect. Some are flexible and allow new model types to be defined; others have a fixed set of models which cannot be changed or altered in any way.

2 The rules of the structured method which are enforced by the supporting CASE tool may be inappropriate. The method may be designed so that it is never possible to generate a model which is either incomplete or inconsistent according to the method rules. However, the system models developed during requirements engineering may have to be incomplete or inconsistent because of a lack of information or because some model information is irrelevant at this stage and is defined later in the development process. The method rules enforced by the tool may therefore prevent you from developing the most appropriate type of system model.

We do not know of any structured method which provides adequate facilities for modelling user interactions with a system. Procedural methods are not good for modelling interaction. We recommend that if you develop this type of system and you decide to use a structured method that you should use an object-oriented method such as OMT.

7.5   Use a Data Dictionary

Key benefit	Avoids name duplication and misunderstandings
Costs of introduction	Moderate
Costs of application	Low
Guideline type	Intermediate

All names used in a system model should be documented in a data dictionary. A data dictionary is a computer-maintained list of names along with information about these names. This information may include a general description of the entity referenced by that name, a description of its physical structure and its type. It may also include information about where in the system model the name is defined and used, who defined the name, and when it was defined.

Benefits

- Large system models are usually developed by a team of people who have to invent names for the different components in the model. Using a data dictionary makes it easier to ensure consistent name use. Everyone uses the same name for the same thing and names are not duplicated.

- The data dictionary can help maintain traceability between the requirements, the design and the system implementation. You can keep information in the data dictionary which links the names in the model with names of entities used in the system design and the program implementing the system.

Implementation

Data dictionary software is an integral part of many CASE systems. If you use these CASE systems for developing and documenting the system model, the names are automatically entered in the data dictionary and you can check the dictionary when new names have to be invented. However, these systems may make assumptions about what information should be maintained in a data dictionary. They may not allow you to put the information which you need into the dictionary. If you do not use a CASE toolset, data dictionaries are simple to implement using commercial database systems on workstations or PCs.

Each name used should be entered as a record in the data dictionary. At least the following information should be maintained.

1 The defined name of the entity in the model. This should be the key to the data dictionary.

2 Any aliases or alternative versions of the name which are used. It is best to avoid aliases if possible but sometimes you need to use them. For example, if you use versions of Microsoft Windows before Windows 95, your file names are restricted to eight characters. You might have a logical file name used in the system model and an alias for it which conforms to the file system standard.

3 The type of the named entity, e.g. process, object, attribute, etc.

4 A description of the named entity and why it has been introduced in the system model.

5 Any constraints on the named entity which are known. These can relate to the use of the entity, its structural representation, its lifetime, etc.

6 Links to related entities. This improves the traceability of the system. When the meaning of a name has to be changed, the related entities should be checked to see if this change affects them.

The data dictionary is a shared resource so it must be accessible to everyone who is developing or using the system model. This means that one of the following two things must happen:

1 It must be maintained on a server computer which is easily accessible to everyone developing the system

model without having to leave the model development system. This is the approach which we recommend.

2   It must be copied daily from a central system to and from the personal computers of the model developers. This approach may have to be used if your model development tools do not support access to a shared server system or where development is taking place at remote sites connected only by slow communications links. To implement this approach, you need software which will integrate changes to the data dictionary, detect name clashes and report these to model developers. Lotus Notes may be used for this purpose, as it has been designed to support remote working on a shared database.

General purpose database software such as Filemaker Pro or Microsoft Access may be used to implement your data dictionary. These are adequate for small or medium-sized system models. There are also special-purpose data dictionary systems available for mainframe computers. These are often provided with database systems such as ORACLE. They may be appropriate if you use the host database for requirements management. Powerful systems of this type must be used if you have a very large number of names to maintain.

Costs and problems

There is an initial cost involved in setting up the data dictionary, particularly if you do not already use a CASE system or a database with data dictionary facilities. This cost may include the costs of software, the costs of defining the schema for the data dictionary and the costs of training people in its use. The costs of applying the guideline after the data dictionary system has been installed are relatively low. These costs are the extra time required to enter names in the data dictionary, to consult the dictionary and to keep it up-to-date.

The principal problem which you will face is making sure that the data dictionary is used and kept in step with the system models. When analysts are working under pressure to complete a system model, it is easy to forget to consult the data dictionary when adding a new name to find out if it has been used or if an alternative name for the entity exists. The fact that many CASE tools automatically enter names in the data dictionary as soon as they are used helps find name clashes but makes the problem of multiple names for the same thing even worse.

To address this problem, you have to, firstly, make sure that accessing the data dictionary is quick and easy. If it takes more than a few seconds, engineers will invariably put off checking or entering names with the intention of sorting everything out in a single access of the data dictionary. They will then, inevitably, forget to do this. Secondly, you have to appeal to the professionalism of the people involved. If they can be convinced that this is part of good professional behaviour, then they will devise their own processes for ensuring that the data dictionary is used. Thirdly, as part of the review process for system models, you should try to find aliases (alternative names for the same thing) in the data dictionary.

7.6	**Document the Links Between Stakeholder Requirements and System**

Key benefit	Makes it easier to find which requirements and models are affected by change
Costs of introduction	Low
Costs of application	Moderate
Guideline type	Intermediate

You should always document the relationships between the natural language stakeholder requirements and the more detailed models specifying the system.

Benefits

- Linking abstract requirements to system models increases the *traceability* of the system. When user requirements change, it is easier to assess the impact and estimate the costs of the proposed changes.

- The development of a system model often reveals requirements problems. An explicit link between the requirements and the models makes it easier to cross-check models and associated requirements.

- Making an explicit link between the requirements and the system model reduces the chances of specification drift where the specifier, engrossed in the problems of developing a detailed specification, loses sight of the real needs of system stakeholders.

- Readers of the requirements specification can easily find the system models which add detail to natural language requirements.

Implementation

We assume that each requirement and each system model have some kind of unique label which you can use to refer to them. We also assume that the system models can be annotated with the identifiers of requirements which have been specified. The best way to link models and requirements depends on the mapping between them. There are four possible types of mapping.

1 There is a 1:1 relationship between a single abstract requirement and a system model. In this case, the relationship is simple and you need only add a reference in the statement of the requirement to the system model which defines that requirement in detail. A comparable reference back to the requirement may also be included in each model.

2 There is a 1:m relationship between a requirement and a number of system models where one requirement is mapped onto a number of system models. For example, an abstract requirement such as 'the system must provide version control facilities' could map onto a process model explaining the process of creating a new version, a data processing model showing the tools used and an entity-relation model showing the structure of the version database. In this case, the link between the requirement and associated models can be maintained by including a list of model identifiers in the requirement itself.

3 There is an m:1 relationship between abstract requirements and a system model where several requirements are specified in detail using the same system model. This is a more complex situation. You should include references in each requirement to the system model and should include explanatory text with the model explaining how the parts of the model relate to the requirements.

4 There is an m:n relationship between abstract requirements and system models. A requirement is specified in a number of system models which also include information about other system requirements. This is the most common and the most complex situation. You must explain what aspects of each requirement are specified in each system model. With each system model, you should include references to the requirements which it specifies and an associated explanation of what parts of these requirements are covered.

Some large-scale CASE tools are based on a repository of all information about a system. With these tools, you can navigate from individual requirements in a requirements database to the models describing these requirements. This is, perhaps, the ideal way of implementing this guideline. However, tools which provide these facilities are expensive to buy and use and are only cost-effective for large-scale systems. Unless there is a simple mapping from model components to individual requirements, traceability matrices (see Chapter 9) cannot normally be used to document these links.

Some types of system model, such as a model of the system architecture, are not intended to specify requirements in more detail but are included to help partition the requirement or to help the reader gain an overall understanding of the system and its contribution to the organisation's business objectives. You should make clear in the text associated with these models that there is no simple link between them and the statement of requirements.

Costs and problems

There are no significant costs involved in introducing this guideline but quite a lot of time is required in the requirements engineering process to create and maintain the links between the requirements and the more detailed system models.

The major problem which you are likely to face is that the requirements engineers who must develop the links between the models and the requirements do not, in the short term, benefit from this information. Under time pressure, they are likely to give this activity a low priority. You need to tackle this problem by appealing to the professionalism of the engineers involved and by defining process and requirements standards which define what links between requirements and models should be listed and how they should be described. You should check the links between models and requirements during the requirements validation process (see Chapter 8).

8 Requirements Validation

Summary

After the requirements document has been produced, the requirements should be formally validated. This validation process is concerned with checking the requirements for omissions, conflicts and ambiguities and for ensuring that the requirements follow quality standards. The validation guidelines which we suggest are as follows:

Guidelines

8.1 Check that the Requirements Document Meets Your Standards.

8.2 Organise Formal Requirements Inspections.

8.3 Use Multi-disciplinary Teams to Review Requirements.

8.4 Define Validation Checklists.

8.5 Use Prototyping to Animate Requirements.

8.6 Write a Draft User Manual.

8.7 Propose Requirements Test Cases.

8.8 Paraphrase system models.

The objectives of requirements validation are to check the set of requirements which have been defined and to discover possible problems with these requirements. The process should involve system stakeholders, requirements engineers and system designers.

Requirements problems might be:

- lack of conformance to quality standards

- poorly worded requirements which are ambiguous

- requirements conflicts which were not detected during the analysis process.

These problems must be solved before the requirements document is approved. To fix these problems, you usually have to re-enter the earlier process stages of requirements elicitation, analysis and negotiation.

In this book, we make a distinction between requirements analysis and requirements validation and cover them in separate chapters. These activities have much in common, as they involve finding omissions in and conflicts between the system requirements. However, there is an important difference between them.

1 Requirements analysis is concerned with 'raw' requirements as elicited from system stakeholders. The requirements are usually incomplete and are expressed in an informal and unstructured way. There will probably be a mixture of notations to describe the requirements.

2 Requirements validation is concerned with checking a final draft of a requirements document which includes all system requirements and where known incompleteness and inconsistency has been removed. The document and the requirements should follow defined quality standards.

The main problem of requirements validation is that there is nothing against which the system can be validated. A design or a program may be validated using the specification. However, there is no way to demonstrate that a requirements specification is correct. The validation process can only increase your confidence that the specification represents a system which will meet the real needs of the system customer. Specification validation, therefore, really means ensuring that the requirements document represents a clear description of the system for design and implementation. It is your last chance before entering the system development process to check that the requirements are acceptable to all system stakeholders.

Discovering and fixing requirements problems can avoid a lot of expensive rework of the system design and implementation. If you can catch errors and problems at this stage, you can save a lot of money later. A number of studies have shown that errors in delivered software systems which are a consequence of requirements errors may cost up to 100 times as much to repair as programming errors.

Requirements validation is a prolonged process as it involves people reading and thinking about a lengthy document. Meetings may have to be arranged and experiments carried out with prototype systems. There is always a natural tendency to rush the validation process so that system development can begin. However, if you do not allow sufficient time for validation, you will almost certainly end up with requirements problems. You may have to start on the system development, but you must be prepared for rework when these requirements problems emerge.

8.1 Check that the Requirements Document Meets your Standards

Key benefit	Rapid discovery of non-compliance with standards
Costs of introduction	Low
Costs of application	Low
Guideline type	Basic

Before distributing the requirements document for general review, one person should carry out a quick standards check to ensure that the document structure and the defined requirements are consistent with whatever standards have been defined.

Benefits

- This is a cheap way to check standards conformance as you only need one person to carry out this type of check. The requirements document should conform to the defined standard but it is not worth everyone involved in the review process checking the document against the standard and all reporting the same standards deviations.

- Checking against a standard can quickly reveal problems with the requirements. If a requirements document does not conform to defined standards, it may indicate large-scale problems with the requirements specification which require management intervention for their solution.

Implementation

An analyst or an engineer who is familiar with the requirements standards but who has not been involved in the system requirements specification should be responsible for this initial standards check. It is not necessary for the document checker to understand the requirements in detail.

The checker should compare the structure of the

requirement document to the defined standard and should highlight missing or incomplete sections. The search and outline facilities provided with most word-processing systems may be used to find parts of the document and display the document structure. If you have a standard for individual requirements (see **Guideline 6.1**, *Define standard templates for describing requirements*), the checker should also check each requirement for compliance with that standard.

This initial check should also check that all pages in the document are numbered, that all diagrams and figures are labelled, that there are no requirements which are unfinished or labelled 'To be completed' and that all required appendices in the document have been completed.

After this process has been completed, there are two possible options if deviations from the standard are found.

1 Return the document to the requirements engineering team to correct deviations from the standards. This option should be chosen if there is enough time to allow for a re-issue of the document.

2 Note the deviations from the standards and distribute this to document reviewers. This saves the time and cost of creating a new version of the requirements document. However, the deviations from standards may increase the difficulty of the requirements review process. This option should be chosen when there is a tight deadline for the requirements review or when the deviations from the standard are minor, easily correctable and don't affect the understandability of the document.

Costs and problems

The costs of introducing and applying this guideline are low. Once you have defined standards, the only introductory costs are where the checker is not familiar with the standard and has to spend some time understanding this.

This is a very cheap guideline to implement and the return on investment in terms of saved reviewing time is likely to be immediate. Unless the requirements document is very large, this initial check should not take longer than one day. There should be no problems in introducing this practice into the requirements engineering process.

While it is unlikely that you will encounter any problems introducing this guideline, there may be some problems applying the guideline, particularly in small organisations. It may be difficult to find an independant checker to review the document (independence is important because people who know the document read what they think is there not what is actually there) and some people may not be convinced of the value of this type of check.

8.2 Organise Formal Requirements Inspections

Key benefit	Finds a high percentage of requirements problems
Costs of introduction	Moderate
Costs of application	Moderate
Guideline type	Basic

The system requirements should be validated by a group of people who systematically check the requirements, meet to discuss problems with the requirements and agree on how these problems should be fixed.

Benefits

- Formal inspections are a cost-effective way of discovering problems in requirements documents, user documentation, software designs and programs.

- The inspection is a neutral meeting for problem resolution where there should be no blame attached to any problems discovered. Conflicts may therefore be resolved during the inspection without confrontations between stakeholders.

Implementation

The requirements inspection is a formal meeting. It should be chaired by someone who has not been involved in producing the requirements which are being validated. During the meeting, a requirements engineer presents each requirement in turn for comment by the group and identified problems are recorded for later discussion. One member of the group should be assigned the role of scribe to note the identified requirements problems.

A formal requirements inspection should involve a team of inspectors from different backgrounds (see **Guideline 8.3**) who read the requirements document and record problems with the system requirements. The document reviewers may use a checklist (see **Guideline 8.4**) to help focus their attention on particular aspects of the requirements and the requirements document.

Unlike program inspections where errors are simply reported to the program author for correction, requirements inspections involve the group making some decisions on actions to be taken to correct the identified problems. Actions which might be decided for each problem are as follows.

1 *Requirements clarification.* The requirement may be badly expressed or may have accidentally omitted information which has been collected during requirements elicitation. The author should improve the requirement by rewriting it.

2 *Missing information.* Some information is missing from the requirements document. It is the responsibility of the requirements engineers who are revising the document to discover this information from system stakeholders or other requirements sources.

3 *Requirements conflict.* There is a significant conflict between requirements and the stakeholders involved must negotiate to resolve the conflict.

4 *Unrealistic requirement.* The requirement does not appear to be implementable with the technology available or given other constraints on the system. Stakeholders must be consulted to decide whether the requirement should be deleted or modified to make it more realistic.

A good practical book on formal inspection is *Software Inspection*, by T. Gilb and D. Graham (Addison Wesley, 1993). Although this is mostly concerned with program inspections, most of the advice is equally applicable to requirements validation.

Costs and problems

Introducing requirements inspections involves establishing checklists which can drive the inspection (**Guideline 8.4**) and training people in inspection techniques. External consultants will usually need to be involved in this training. If you do not have previous experience with inspections as part of your normal validation process, you should introduce requirements inspections in a pilot project. This should run alongside your normal validation process so will involve significant start-up costs. The pilot project will help you assess whether this approach is cost-effective for your organisation and help you judge the best way to run these formal reviews.

Applying the guidelines involves moderate costs but will result in significant downstream effort saving as rework is reduced. The time taken for an inspection obviously depends on the size of the requirements document. There are published figures available for program inspections (about 125 lines of code per hour can be inspected, with the same time required for preparation) but not for requirements inspections. Our guess is that probably about 40 requirements per hour could be inspected with the same time required for preparation. Therefore, a document with 400 requirements would require a total of 50 person-hours of effort to inspect if a 4 person team were involved.

Inspections require a group of people with different skills and responsibilities to read documents and get together in the same place at the same time to carry out the inspection. As the people involved may work for different organisations or different parts of the same organisation this can be very difficult. It is practically impossible to define participation in requirements inspections as part of their job. You must, initially at least, rely on their goodwill and the goodwill of their managers for inspection participation. Of course, once the value of inspections has been demonstrated, participation is less of a problem but, inevitably, people will have problems fitting inspections into already busy schedules.

8.3   Use Multi-Disciplinary Teams to Review Requirements

Key benefit	Increases the probability of finding requirements problems
Costs of introduction	Low
Costs of application	Low
Guideline type	Basic

The requirements document should be reviewed by a multi-disciplinary team drawn from people with different backgrounds. This should include a system end-user or end-user representative, a customer representative, one or more domain experts, one or more engineers who will be responsible for system design and implementation and one or more requirements engineers. This should apply whether you use formal requirements inspections or a less structured review process.

Benefits

- People from different backgrounds bring different skills, knowledge and experience to the review. It is therefore more probable that requirements problems will be discovered.

- If system stakeholders from different backgrounds are involved in the review process, they feel involved in the requirements engineering process and develop an understanding of the needs of other stakeholders. They are therefore more likely to be sympathetic to changes which affect them, as they will know why these are necessary.

Implementation

You should choose the multi-disciplinary team from the different stakeholders who have been involved in the requirements elicitation. Ideally, you should have customer managers, one or more end-users, application domain experts, members of the requirements engineering team and system developers in the validation team.

If this is not possible, try to ensure that you have at least one domain expert and one possible end-user involved in the process. System developers should get involved at this stage as they may find requirements which are particularly difficult to implement. Spotting these and modifying them before design and implementation can save a lot of effort and expense.

Costs and problems

There should be no additional costs involved in introducing and applying this guideline unless you use external consultants to bring specialised expertise into the review. The major problem is ensuring a broad spectrum of involvement as some people may be unable to take time from their other work to participate in the requirements review. They may already have moved on to other projects. This is particularly likely to be the case for domain experts and customer managers.

8.4   Define Validation Checklists

Key benefit	Helps to focus the validation process
Costs of introduction	Low–moderate
Costs of application	Low
Guideline type	Basic

You should define a checklist or checklists which help to focus the attention of requirements validators on critical attributes of the requirements document. These checklists should identify what readers should look for when they are validating the system requirements.

Benefits

- Checklists add structure to the validation process. It is therefore less likely that readers will forget to check some aspects of the requirements document.

- Checklists help in the introduction of people who are new to requirements validation. The checklist gives them hints about what they should be looking for so that they feel more able to participate in the process. This is particularly important for customer management and end-users who may not have requirements validation experience.

Implementation

The use of checklists for requirements analysis has already been discussed in **Guideline 5.2**, *Use checklists for requirements analysis*, and similar checklists may also be used in the validation process. These checklists are oriented towards individual requirements; validation checklists should also be concerned with the quality properties of the requirements document *as a whole* and with the relationships between individual requirements. This cannot be checked during requirements analysis, as the requirements document is unfinished at that stage.

Questions which might be included in such a checklist should be based on the following general issues.

1 Are the requirements complete, that is, does the checker know of any missing requirements or is there any information missing from individual requirement descriptions?

2 Are the requirements consistent, that is, do the descriptions of different requirements include contradictions?

3 Are the requirements comprehensible, that is, can readers of the document understand what the requirements mean?

4 Are the requirements ambiguous, that is, are there different possible interpretations of the requirements?

5 Is the requirements document structured, that is, are the descriptions of requirements organised so that related requirements are grouped? Would an alternative structure be easier to understand?

6 Are the requirements traceable, that is, are requirements unambiguously identified, do they include links to related requirements and to the reasons why these requirements have been included? See Chapter 9 for guidelines on traceability.

7 Does the requirements document as a whole and do individual requirements conform to defined standards?

Checklists should be expressed in a fairly general way and should be understandable by people such as end-users who are not system experts. As a general rule, checklists should not be too long. Checklists should not normally have more than ten items. If you have more than this, checkers cannot remember all items and must continually re-consult the checklist.

The danger, of course, is that checklist becomes too vague and it is impossible to answer the checklist questions in any useful way. You have to find the right balance between generality and detail. Unlike program inspections, low-level checklists concerned with very specific faults are not so good for requirements inspections because of the differences between the requirements for different types of system.

Checklists can be distributed and simply used as a reminder of what people should look for when reading the requirements document. Alternatively, they can be used more systematically where, for each requirement, an indication is given that the checklist item has been considered. This may be done on paper or you can manage this type of checklist completion by using a simple database or a spreadsheet. The checklist items are shown along the horizontal axis and the requirements along the vertical axis. The checker should fill in each cell with an appropriate comment. You should not force checkers to use an automated approach, as people may read the document in places and at times when they do not have computer access.

Costs and problems

This is not an expensive guideline to implement if you use a fairly general checklist with questions like those listed above. To introduce the guideline, you need to draw up an initial checklist based on the experience of people who have been involved in requirements validation.

If a checklist is simply used as a memory aid, there are no costs involved in applying the guideline. If checkers of the requirements must mark each requirement against the checklists, clearly some additional time is required. This should not be more than one or two minutes per requirement.

In principle, there should be few problems in applying the guideline so long as you have a fairly flexible process which allows people to ignore inappropriate checklist entries. In practice, some requirements analysts may resent the introduction of checklists as they see them as de-skilling the process. You have to emphasise that the checklists are designed to help them and point out that professional judgement must still be used.

8.5 Use Prototyping to Animate Requirements

Key benefit	Demonstrates requirements for validation
Costs of introduction	Moderate–high
Costs of application	Moderate–high
Guideline type	Intermediate

Implement a prototype of the system which can be used for experimentation. Stakeholders can then try out the system to see if it meets their real needs and can make suggestions for improvements to the system. This prototype could be an extension of an earlier prototype developed for requirements elicitation.

Benefits

- People find it very difficult to visualise how a written statement of requirements will translate into an executable software system. If you develop a prototype system to demonstrate requirements which are poorly understood, stakeholders find it easier to discover problems and suggest how the requirements may be improved.

- It may be possible to use the prototype to develop system tests (see **Guideline 8.7**) which can be used later in the system validation process. Executable prototypes can also be used for back-to-back testing with the final system where the same tests are submitted to both prototype and final system and checked for consistency.

- An executable prototype may serve as a stop-gap system which can be delivered if there are delays in implementing the final system.

- Prototype implementation requires careful study of the requirements. This, in itself, often reveals requirements inconsistencies and incompleteness.

Implementation

Prototyping methods for requirements elicitation have already been discussed in **Guideline 4.10**, *Prototype poorly understood requirements*. The prototyping methods covered in that guideline may be used to implement a prototype for requirements validation although paper prototyping is likely to be of fairly limited use. We strongly recommend that, if you develop an automated system prototype, you use it for both initial requirements elicitation and requirements validation.

Prototypes for validation must be more complete than elicitation prototypes. Elicitation prototypes can simply include those requirements which are particularly difficult to describe. They may leave out well-understood requirements. While a validation prototype need not include all system facilities, there must be a sufficient number of facilities implemented in a reasonably efficient and robust way that end-users can make practical use of the system. Otherwise, the validation activity will be unnatural. You also need to ensure that the validation prototype includes installation instructions, instructions on how to recover when things go wrong and some end-user documentation describing how to use the system.

During elicitation, the requirements engineer and the end-user may work together, whereas during validation, end-users are more likely to work alone, experimenting with the prototype. If possible, however, requirements engineers should spend some time observing how end-users make use of the system. This can reveal particular problem areas. You can also see if the end-user has developed coping strategies for dealing with system features which they find useful but which are awkward to use in their current form.

You should design the prototype trials so that they do not take too long. End-users will normally have other things to do apart from experiment with the prototype system. Therefore, the system must be reliable. It should not crash and, if there are facilities missing, you must tell users about these in advance.

Unstructured end-user experimentation with the system is unlikely to provide complete coverage of the system. If possible, you should select end-users who do different jobs so that different areas of system functionality will be covered. You should provide end-users with a problem report form (paper or electronic) that they use to record their problems and what they were doing when these problems were discovered. Ideally, you should use scenarios for validation (see **Guideline 4.11**, *Use scenarios to elicit requirements*) where users work through a defined scenario and discover if it is a correct representation of how they work.

Costs and problems

There are fairly high costs involved in introducing this guideline if you do not have prototyping software and experience of using it. These include the costs of buying the prototyping system and training costs for prototype developers. If you wish to employ prototyping specialists, you may find that there is a lack of skilled people with experience in this area.

The development costs for the prototype depend on the type of system. Modern prototyping facilities provide a basic development framework such as a database and software to define system user interfaces. You may also be able to link in other tools such as word processors and spreadsheets. If this can be used as a basis for your system then prototyping costs will be relatively low. However, if the framework is inadequate and you need to develop a lot of basic functionality before any useful experimentation is possible then prototyping costs will be high.

Some problems with prototyping have already been described in **Guideline 4.10**. A particular problem with prototyping in the validation process is that you may not be able to recruit typical end-users for the prototype trials. Often untypical end-users, who are particularly interested in computer systems, will volunteer for the trials. Their comments may therefore be unreliable, as they may be willing to accept features which other end-users would find unusable, and may suggest system 'gold-plating'. Because they like to experiment with computer systems, they may ask for powerful facilities which are not necessary.

8.6   Write a Draft User Manual

Key benefit	Discovers usability problems in the requirements
Costs of introduction	Low
Costs of application	Moderate
Guideline type	Intermediate

Using the requirements document as a system specification, write an initial draft of the user manual of the system. This should cover all aspects of the system functionality and, where necessary, you should make plausible assumptions about the system user interface.

Benefits

- Writing a user manual during the validation process forces the detailed analysis of requirements and helps reveal problems concerning the actual use of the system. It means that system usability issues are uncovered before system development begins.

- Writing the user manual at this stage may be necessary or useful for users who are experimenting with a system prototype. The document may help clarify user interface design issues, as it can illustrate good interface design and design features which should be avoided.

- The document can be an initial draft for the actual user documentation which is to be produced.

Implementation

A draft user manual should explain the system facilities described in the requirements in terms that end-users can understand. You must explain how these facilities should be used. This complements Guideline 8.5 which suggests the use of prototypes for requirements validation. If you develop a system prototype, then you must also provide some guidance for the people who experiment with that system.

However, even if you do not develop a prototype, you can learn a lot about the requirements by writing a draft user manual. You should write the manual by systematically translating the functionality described in the requirements into descriptions, written in end-user terms, of how to use them. Someone with an overall understanding of the system and experience of writing user manuals should be responsible for this. If they find it difficult to explain a function to end-users or to explain how to express system functionality, this suggests that there is a requirements problem. These problems should be raised and documented using a standard requirements review form.

It is sometimes suggested that the system user manual should actually serve as the requirements document for system implementation. We do not agree with this. The user manual should be solely concerned with end-user interaction with the system rather than other system functionality and required system properties. A lot of system functionality is hidden from the end-user and is not normally described in the user manual.

Costs and problems

There are no significant costs involved in introducing this guideline if you have people available who have previous experience of writing user documentation. The costs of applying the guideline are the costs of actually writing the manual. Documentation is expensive but some of this cost is likely to be recovered if the system is implemented. The draft manual can be a basis for the final user documentation. However, this may not always be possible. The system development may be cancelled or the system may change to such an extent that a completely new user manual must to be written. You must therefore include the cost of writing the draft manual in your validation planning and take any subsequent saving as a bonus.

The principal difficulty with this guideline is finding the time and the people to write the manual. Writing takes a long time and if your schedule is very tight, it may be impossible to implement this guideline. This problem is particularly acute in small companies which rarely have specialist documentation writers.

You may find that technically-skilled people who have experience of both reading requirements and writing end-user documentation are not available. Technical authors may be used to working from finished systems and may not be able to visualise the system from the requirements document. Requirements engineers may not have experience of user documentation; they may also tend to write what they *think* is in the requirements rather than what is actually documented.

8.7 Propose Requirements Test Cases

Key benefit	Reveals ambiguities and inconsistencies in the requirements
Costs of introduction	Low
Costs of application	Moderate
Guideline type	Intermediate

For each requirement, propose one or more possible tests which can be used to check if the system meets that requirement.

Benefits

- Proposing possible tests is an effective way of revealing requirements problems such as incompleteness and ambiguity. If there are difficulties in deriving test cases for a requirement, this implies that there is some kind of requirement problem. There may be missing information in the requirement or the requirement description may not make clear exactly what is required.

- The proposed set of test cases can be used as a basis for test planning and the derivation of actual test cases to be applied to the final system.

Implementation

For each requirement in the requirements document, you should analyse that requirement and define a test which can objectively check if the system satisfies the requirement. The objective of proposing test cases for requirements is to validate the requirement rather than the system. You need not be concerned with practicalities such as testing costs, avoiding redundant tests, detailed test data definition, etc. Therefore, you do not have to propose real tests which will be applied to the final system. You can make any assumptions you wish about the way in which the system satisfies other requirements and the ways in which the test may actually be carried out.

To define the test cases, you can ask the following questions about a requirement.

- What usage scenario might be used to check the requirement? This should define the context in which the test should be applied.

- Does the requirement, on its own, include enough information to allow a test to be defined? If not, what other requirements must be examined to find this information? If you need to look at other requirements, you should record these as there may be dependencies between requirements which are important for traceability (see Chapter 9).

- Is it possible to check the requirement using a single test or are multiple test cases required? If you need several tests, this may mean that there is more than one requirement embedded in a single requirement description.

- Could the requirement be re-stated so that the required test cases are fairly obvious?

You should design a test recording form which you fill in for each requirement checked. This should include at least the following information:

1 the requirement identifier

2 related requirements

3 a brief description of the test which could be applied and why this is an objective requirements test

4 a description of requirements problems which made test definition difficult or impossible

5 recommendations for addressing requirements problems which have been discovered

Test case forms may be implemented as electronic documents and managed in a database with links to the associated requirement (see **Guideline 9.5**, *Use a database to manage requirements*). Ideally, forms should be electronic but you must also allow for hand-written forms and, perhaps, budget for secretarial support to type these forms. Some people find it more convenient to review and check documents away from a computer (e.g. while travelling) and you should accommodate this style of working.

Costs and problems

The initial costs of introducing this guideline are fairly low as it does not require any investment in new methods or technology. You will, however, need a training session to demonstrate the value of writing test cases at this stage. This will involve preparing test cases from an existing document and showing how these can reveal requirements problems. You may wish to involve external consultants in this process.

There are moderate costs involved in applying this guideline. Test cases may take anything from a few minutes to a few hours to design. This systematic approach to validation will take longer than simply reading the requirements and noting possible problems. However, this is compensated for by reduced test planning costs where many test cases may be reused.

You may encounter some resistance to this guideline because requirements engineers see the derivation of test cases to be someone else's responsibility. You need to make clear that they are not defining the actual tests which will be applied to the system. You should emphasise that any errors made in the tests themselves are not important so long as they help the requirements validation process.

8.8   Paraphrase System Models

Key benefit	Allows more stakeholders to participate in requirements validation
Costs of introduction	Moderate–high
Costs of application	Moderate
Guideline type	Advanced

If you have a system model in a graphical or formal notation, you should systematically convert the specification described by the model to a natural language representation.

Benefits

- Some stakeholders, particularly end-users, organisational management and external stakeholders such as regulators are unlikely to have the time to learn the notations used to describe the system model. Paraphrasing these into natural language allows them to understand and comment on the detailed system specification.

- The process of explaining the system model in natural language is an effective way to detect errors, inconsistencies and incompleteness in the model. You can find out what is missing from the model.

Implementation

Converting a system model to natural language text should be done in a systematic way. The actual technique used should depend on the type of system model, but we recommend using some kind of form or table where different components in the model are described in different fields or columns. For example, in a data-flow diagram, you might use a template with the following fields to describe each transformation.

1 *Transformation name.*

2 *Transformation inputs and input sources.* Gives the name of each input to the transformation and lists where that input comes from.

3 *Transformation function.* Explain what the transformation is supposed to do to convert inputs to outputs.

4 *Transformation outputs.* Gives the name of each output and lists where the output goes to.

5 *Control* Any exception or control information which is included in the model

In some cases, it may be possible to partially automate this process. Some CASE tools will generate reports on the system models which can be a starting point for paraphrasing. However, these are normally fairly stilted and you have to modify them to make them more readable and to add information which cannot be automatically derived. You may find that it is actually less effort to ignore the generation facilities and simply work directly from the system model.

It is important to avoid reading information into the model which is not there. Therefore, the paraphraser should not try to interpret the model or provide rationale for model elements. Ideally, the paraphrasers should be familiar with the type of system being specified but should not have been involved in the development of the specification.

If you wish to introduce formal specification techniques (**Guideline 10.6**, *Specify systems using formal specifications*), we strongly recommend that you should implement this guideline. Formal models of systems are usually only accessible to specialists. They must be translated into natural language if you wish end-users and domain experts to be involved in the model validation.

Costs and problems

The introductory costs for this guideline are fairly high. To introduce this guideline, you will need to experiment with the best ways to translate system models into natural language text. Several months may be needed for this. After techniques have been designed, there will be further costs of training people to use them.

This is a fairly expensive guideline to implement, as paraphrasing system models is a time-consuming process. In essence, the system model has to be completely rewritten in a different way. Because of the costs, it may only be cost-effective to implement this guideline if you develop critical systems where it is particularly important that system models are understood by domain experts and end-users.

This is one of the main problems with this guideline. Pressure to continue with the system development may not allow enough time to rewrite the system model. It may also be difficult to find people who know enough about the system to describe it, yet who were not involved in developing the specification in the system model.

9 Requirements Management

Summary

Requirements management is concerned with all of the processes involved in changing system requirements. In this chapter, we suggest guidelines which relate directly to the processes which are part of requirements management and which provide some practical information on techniques used for requirements management. The guidelines that we suggest are:

Guidelines

9.1 Uniquely Identify Each Requirement.

9.2 Define Policies for Requirements Management.

9.3 Define Traceability Policies.

9.4 Maintain a Traceability Manual.

9.5 Use a Database to Manage Requirements.

9.6 Define Change Management Policies.

9.7 Identify Global System Requirements.

9.8 Identify Volatile Requirements.

9.9 Record Rejected Requirements.

During the processes of requirements engineering, system development and operation, new requirements emerge and existing requirements change. These changing requirements must be managed to ensure that the quality of the requirements is maintained. The impact of requirements changes must be understood and requirements changes implemented in a timely and cost-effective way. It is also important to ensure that the requirements keep in step with the operational system. System changes must be reflected as requirements changes and vice-versa.

Requirements management is, therefore, a process which supports other requirements engineering activities and is carried out in parallel with them. A recent European survey of 4000 companies found that the management of customer requirements was one of the principal problem areas in software development and production. These problems were not confined to the management of requirements for external clients. There were also problems of managing requirements change where the system was being specified and developed in the same organisation.

Problems with requirements management often mean that systems whose requirements do not satisfy the customer are delivered. Systems development schedules may be extended and high costs incurred for rework of the design and implementation to accommodate requirements changes. The costs of these problems in the long-term usually outweigh the short-term costs of introducing good requirements management practice.

The principal concerns of requirements management are:

1 managing changes to agreed requirements

2 managing the relationships between requirements

3 managing dependencies between the requirements document and other documents produced during the systems and software engineering process.

Requirements changes may be due to errors and misunderstandings in the requirements engineering process, design or implementation problems. New requirements may emerge as stakeholders develop a deeper understanding of the system. Most commonly, however, requirements change is a result of changing external circumstances. The strategy or priorities of the business buying the system may change as a result of changing economic circumstances or new competitors in its market. New information about the system's environment may become available, e.g. new digital maps for a geographic information system. New laws or regulations may be introduced which require system change.

To manage requirements, you need to maintain requirements *traceability* information. A requirement is traceable if you can discover who suggested the requirement, why the requirement exists, what requirements are related to it and how that requirement relates to other information such as systems designs, implementations and user documentation. Traceability information helps you discover what other requirements might be affected by requirements changes.

Good requirements management practices such as maintaining dependencies between requirements have long-term benefits. These are better customer satisfaction and lower system development costs. These returns are not immediate so requirements management may appear to developers as an overhead. It makes it more difficult for them to make changes to the system on time and within budget. In these circumstances, you must persevere; experience has shown that investment in good requirements management processes is always cost-effective.

9.1   Uniquely Identify Each Requirement

Key benefit	Unambiguous references to specific requirements are possible
Costs of introduction	Very low
Costs of application	Very low
Guideline type	Basic

Each requirement should be assigned a unique identifier or reference number which may be used to refer to that requirement in other parts of the requirements document or in other system documentation.

Benefits

- Unique identifiers may be used to make references to related requirements and to construct *traceability tables* (see **Guideline 9.3**).

- If you store your requirements in a database (see **Guideline 9.5**), the requirement identifier may serve as a primary key which uniquely identifies the requirement in the database. References from one requirement to another in the database may use this primary key.

- Requirements inevitably evolve and you may wish to manage this evolution by using a configuration management system. The requirement reference number can be the basis for linking versions of the requirements which have evolved from the same starting point.

Implementation

The most commonly used approach to requirements identification is to assign numbers depending on the chapter and section of the requirements document where the requirement is included. Therefore, the 6th requirement in the 2nd section in chapter 4 would be 4.2.6.

There are two difficulties with this style of requirements identification. Firstly, when you collect a requirement, you do not know where it will appear in the document so you cannot assign it a number until a version of the requirements document is issued. This means that it is difficult to refer to it in other requirements. Secondly, assigning an identifier based on chapter and section numbers positions the requirement in a classification structure. It suggests that the requirement is most closely related to other requirements with similar identifiers. Document readers may be misled into thinking that there are no other important relationships between that requirement and other requirements elsewhere in the document.

You can address this problem in two ways.

- Some word-processing systems allow for automatic renumbering of paragraphs and the inclusion of cross-references. You can therefore assign a number to a requirement at any time. As you re-organise your document and add new requirements, the system keeps track of the cross-reference and automatically renumbers your requirement depending on its chapter, section and position within the section. This is the solution we recommend if you have the right kind of word processor facilities.

- You can assign an interim identifier to each requirement then replace it with some number when you produce your final document. Rather than a number, you are best to use some mnemonic derived from the contents of the requirement e.g. EFF-1, EFF-2, EFF-3 for requirements which concern the efficiency of the system.

These schemes apply to requirements expressed as text. System models (see Chapter 7) should also be assigned a unique identifier. Parts of a system model such as entities in a diagram do not need to have a globally unique identifier but their names should be unique within the model. They may be referenced by giving the model identifier then the entity name.

Costs and problems

Introducing and implementing this guideline is very cheap. To introduce it, the only costs are the costs of defining a numbering convention. People sometimes like to argue over numbering schemes but reaching agreement on a numbering scheme should not be a significant problem in most organisations. The costs of applying the guideline are the costs of renumbering requirements when changes are made. These are negligible if some automatic renumbering system is available.

9.2   Define Policies for Requirements Management

Key benefit	Provide guidance for all involved in requirements management
Costs of introduction	Moderate
Costs of application	Low
Guideline type	Basic

Requirements management policies define goals for requirements management, the procedures which should be followed and the standards which should be used. These policies should be explicitly defined as part of your quality management system.

Benefits

- Explicit policies tell people involved in the process what they are expected to do and why it should be done. Projects generally manage their requirements in comparable ways so, with explicit policies, there is less dependence on individual knowledge and expertise.

- In order to define policies, you must understand your existing processes for requirements management. This is likely to reveal problem areas which may become the focus of process improvements.

Implementation

Requirements management policies are a basis for the quality management of the system requirements. Policies are not the same as standards but are clearly related to them. Policies, loosely, set out *what* should be done; standards describe *how* the policy should be implemented in a particular situation. Some policies may be reflected in organisational standards but individual project managers are sometimes the best judge of how policies should be implemented.

Organisations should define a general set of requirements management policies. For each project, you must look at this general set of policies and select those which are relevant to that project. They may be amended in some ways to suit the specific needs of the project.

General requirements management policies should include:

1 a set of objectives for the requirements management process and rationale associated with each of these objectives

2 the reports which should be produced to make the requirements engineering process visible and the activities which are expected to produce these reports as deliverables

3 the standards for requirements documents and requirements descriptions which should be used (see **Guideline 3.1**, *Define a standard document structure* and **6.1**, *Define standard templates for describing requirements*)

4 change management and control policies for requirements (see **Guideline 9.6**)

5 requirements review and validation policies

6 relationships between requirements management and other system engineering and project planning activities

7 traceability policies which define what information on dependencies between requirements should be maintained and how this information should be used and managed (see **Guideline 9.3**)

8 criteria when these policies can be ignored; in these situations, managers use their own judgement on how to implement a requirements change.

Of course, it is unrealistic to expect to define and introduce all of these policies at the same time. They should be developed incrementally and updated after you have practical experience of their application in requirements management.

You must build some flexibility into your policies

otherwise they will be unworkable. There is sometimes such an urgent need for system change, that it is impossible to follow through a systematic requirements management policy before implementing that change. You must have some mechanism for managing these exceptions. It should suggest how you maintain the information which can eventually be used to update the requirements which are being managed.

Costs and problems

It may take several months of effort and at least a year of calendar time to establish a coherent set of requirements management policies. You must consult with those involved in the requirements engineering process, propose, review and amend policies then introduce a dissemination and training programme to ensure that people are aware of the policies and know how to apply them.

When policies have been defined, you must check that the procedures and standards implementing these policies are being followed. The costs of applying this guideline are therefore part of your quality assurance costs.

In principle, people will always be supportive of requirements management policies. In practice, however, you may find that they do not give the creation of these policies a high priority. This is particularly likely for those who are not directly involved in requirements engineering. They may feel that this is not their responsibility. However, you must try to involve these people. If you do not, they will, at best, complain that they were not consulted; at worst, they will refuse to accept the policies which have been proposed.

9.3   Define Traceability Policies

Key benefit	Leads to consistent traceability information being maintained for all systems
Costs of introduction	Moderate
Costs of application	Moderate–high
Guideline type	Basic–intermediate

As part of your requirements management policy, you should define what traceability information should be maintained and how this should be represented. Traceability information is information which allows you to find dependencies between requirements, and between the requirements and the system design, components and documentation.

Benefits

- Traceability information is standardised. Those responsible for assessing requirements changes therefore know what information is likely to be available and how it will be represented.

- Traceability policies are a basis for cost and quality control. Collecting and managing traceability information is expensive. Traceability policies mean that you can control these costs by collecting essential traceability information and not collecting large amounts of information which you cannot maintain.

- It may be possible to provide some software support for your defined policies.

Implementation

Traceability policies are written policies which should define the following.

- The traceability information which should be maintained. This is described in more detail below.

- The techniques which may be used for maintaining traceability. This is described in more detail below.

- A description of when the traceability information should be collected during the requirements engineering and system development processes. You should also define the roles of the people, such as the traceability manager, who are responsible for maintaining the traceability information.

- A description of how to handle and document policy exceptions, that is, when time constraints make it impossible to implement the normal traceability policy. Realistically, there will always be occasions where you have to make changes to the requirements or the system without first assessing all change impacts and maintaining traceability information. The policy exceptions should define how these changes should be sanctioned. The traceability policies should also define the process used to ensure that the traceability information is updated after the change has been made.

Traceability policies should be written so that they are independent of any particular system. As part of your quality planning process, you should select the most relevant traceability policies and tailor them to the specific needs of the system which is being specified. These should then be defined in the system traceability manual (see **Guideline 9.4**).

Maintaining traceability information is expensive because it involves managing large volumes of information. Requirements changes may involve making changes to this traceability information in several places to record new or changed dependencies. You must be realistic in defining your traceability policies and you should not make them too bureaucratic. It is better to have lightweight policies which are followed rather than more comprehensive traceability policies which are ignored by project managers.

This guideline may be implemented by organisations at any level of requirements engineering process maturity. Simple traceability of requirements to their sources and other requirements may be implemented by organisations at the basic level in the requirements engineering process maturity model. As organisational maturity increases, more complex traceability policies may be introduced.

Traceability information

There are different types of traceability information which you might want to maintain. These are shown in Figure 9.1.

There are three basic techniques which may be used to maintain traceability information. These are as follows.

1 *Traceability tables.* A cross-reference matrix is produced where the entries in the table indicate some kind of trace-

Traceability type	Description
Requirements–sources traceability	Links the requirement and the people or documents which specified the requirement. See **Guideline 4.4**, *Record requirements sources*.
Requirements-rationale traceability	Links the requirement with a description of why that requirement has been specified. See **Guideline 4.7**, *Record requirements rationale*.
Requirements-requirements traceability	Links requirements with other requirements which are, in some way, dependent on them. You should always try to maintain this type of information.
Requirements-architecture traceability	Links requirements with the sub-systems where these requirements are implemented. This is particularly important where sub-systems are being developed by different sub-contractors.
Requirements-design traceability	Links requirements with specific components in the system which are used to implement the requirement. These may be hardware or software components. It is particularly important to maintain this type of information for critical systems.
Requirements-interface traceability	Links requirements with the interfaces of external systems which are used in the provision of the requirements. Should be maintained where there is a high dependency on other systems.

Figure 9.1 Types of traceability information

ability link between the items in the rows and the items in the columns.

2 *Traceability lists.* Each requirement has a list of associated traceability information

3 *Automated traceability links.* The requirements are maintained in a database and traceability links are included as fields in the database record. This is covered in **Guideline 9.5**.

Traceability tables

Traceability tables show the relationships between requirements or between requirements and design components. The requirements are listed along the horizontal and vertical axes and relationships between requirements are marked in the table cells. They can be implemented using word processor or spreadsheet tables; a requirements database is not necessary.

Traceability tables for showing requirements dependencies should be defined with requirement numbers used to label the rows and columns of the table. In the simplest form of traceability table, you simply put some mark such as a * in the table cell where there is some kind of dependency relationship between the requirements in the cell row and column. That is, if the requirement in row X

Depends-on

	R1	R2	R3	R4	R5	R6
R1			*	*		
R2					*	*
R3				*	*	
R4		*				
R5						*
R6						

Figure 9.2 A simple traceability table

(say) depends on the requirement in columns P, Q, and R, you should mark table cells (X, P), (X, Q), and (X, R). By reading down a column, you see all requirements which depend on a requirement; by reading across a row, you see all requirements which the requirement in that row depends on.

A very simple example of a traceability table is shown in Figure 9.2 for a system with six requirements.

Each row in the table shows dependencies so that R1 is dependent on R3 and R4, R2 is dependent on R5 and R6, etc. Therefore, if a change to R4 is proposed, we can see by reading down the R4 column that requirements R1 and R3 are dependent requirements. You should therefore assess the impact on R1 and R3 of the proposed change to R4.

You can extend the simple model of traceability tables by distinguishing between the types of relationship between requirements and by indicating each of these, using a different symbol, in each table cell. Possible relations between requirements which might exist are as follows.

1   specifies/is-specified-by. This relation indicates that some requirement B adds detail to another requirement A. For example, if A is a general security requirement which states that data should be encrypted, B might specify the characteristics of the encryption algorithm which should be used.

2   requires/is-required-by. This relation indicates that some requirement B requires the result provided by some other requirement A. For example, A might specify that the system should maintain a record of the current time and date in some specific format; B might specify that each transaction processed by the system should be date stamped.

3   constrains/is-constrained by. This relation indicates that some requirement B is constrained by some other requirement A. For example, B might specify that some real value should be displayed and A might state that all real numbers should be implemented as 12-digit fixed-point numbers.

If you have a relatively small number of requirements (up to 250, say), you can implement and manage traceability tables using a spreadsheet. Traceability tables become more of a problem when you have hundreds or thousands of requirements as you end up with very large and thinly populated tables. Sometimes, dependencies between requirements are confined to requirements groups and you can create separate traceability tables for these groups. Dependencies across groups can be specified separately. If this is not the case, we recommend that other traceability techniques such as traceability lists should be used.

A common error which arises with the use of traceability tables is confusion between the rows and columns. Therefore, rather than filling in Row R1 which shows that R1 depends on R3 and R3, column R1 is filled in showing that R3 and R4 are dependent on R1. Obviously, these do not mean the same thing and can cause problems to users of the traceability tables.

Traceability lists

Traceability lists are a simplified form of traceability table where, along with each requirement description, you keep one or more lists of the identifiers of related requirements. Traceability lists are more compact than traceability tables and do not become as unmanageable with large numbers of requirements. They are probably less prone to error than traceability tables.

Requirement	Depends-on
R1	R3, R4
R2	R5, R6
R3	R4, R5
R4	R2
R5	R6

Figure 9.3 A traceability list

Traceability lists are simple lists of relationships which can be implemented as text or as simple tables. Figure 9.3 shows a traceability list for the dependencies shown in Figure 9.2.

You may use several lists, one for each type of relationship such as *requires*, *is-required-by*, *specifies*, etc., or may simply keep a single list of related requirements. The disadvantage of these lists compared to traceability tables is that there is no easy way to assess the inverse of a relationship. We can easily see that R1 is dependent on R3 and R4 but, given R4, we must look through the whole table to see which requirements depend on it. If you wish to maintain this 'backward-to' information, you need to construct another table showing these relationships.

Traceability lists can either be maintained manually as word processor or spreadsheet tables or created from the requirements database. To create the list automatically, the database record for each requirement must include a link to a list of related requirements.

Costs and problems

The cost of introducing this guideline into your requirements engineering process are comparable with the costs of defining any other significant quality management procedure. Several months of calendar time may be needed for consultation, and significant effort is required to ensure that high-quality policies are defined and reviewed. Once these procedures have been agreed, there are some maintenance costs as you introduce changes based on experience with them. Making these changes should not normally be an expensive process.

The costs of implementing traceability depends on the specific traceability policies and on the number of requirements for your system. Unfortunately, the costs of traceability increase disproportionately as the number of requirements increase. Therefore, while the costs of implementing fairly comprehensive traceability policies may be moderate for a small system, the same policies may be impractically expensive for large systems. You need to derive specific traceability policies from your general policies, as discussed in Guideline 9.4.

The main problem that you are likely to encounter is doubts about the value of procedures which do not provide an immediate benefit (see the discussion in the introduction) and some resistance, perhaps, to implementing these procedures. People may have had previous experience with traceability problems and the difficulties posed by managing large volumes of traceability information. You must be realistic about what traceability information can be maintained; you should not ask analysts to record information which will never be used. You must also stress the long-term benefits of traceability and convince people (by example if possible) of the benefits of maintaining this information.

9.4   Maintain a Traceability Manual

Key benefit	Acts as a central record of all project-specific traceability information
Costs of introduction	Low
Costs of application	Moderate–high
Guideline type	Basic

A traceability manual is a supplement to the requirements document which includes the specific traceability policies used in a project and all requirements traceability information. This document is used by requirements engineers and system developers.

Benefits

- Team members can easily find the specific traceability policies for their project

- A traceability manual keeps all traceability information in one place and makes information (relatively) easy to find and update.

- The specific traceability policies used in a project are made available to all project members through the traceability manual.

- For systems where a safety or security case must be made a traceability manual may be used to show that components are independent or to argue that component failure cannot propagate in an uncontrolled way.

Implementation

The traceability manual is a central record of the traceability policies for a specific project and all of the relevant traceability information. Your general traceability policies should be specialised to take into account the characteristics of the project. This may involve leaving out some traceability information, deciding on exactly how traceability information should be represented, deciding on the responsibilities for traceability information collection, etc.

The specific traceability policies which should be used for a project depends on a number of factors. These factors include the following.

1 *Number of requirements.* The greater the number of requirements, the more the need for formal traceability policies. However, if there are a *very* large number of requirements, you have to be realistic about what traceability policies can be implemented in practice. Complete requirements-design traceability is impractical for most large systems.

2 *Estimated system lifetime.* More comprehensive traceability policies should be defined for systems which have a long lifetime.

3 *Level of organisational maturity.* Detailed traceability policies are most likely to be cost-effective in organisations which have a higher level of process maturity. Organisations at the basic maturity level should focus on simple requirements–requirements traceability.

4 *Project team size and composition.* With a small team, informal discussions between team members may be all that is required to assess the impact of proposed changes. With larger teams, however, you need more formal and detailed traceability policies. This is particularly true if all members of the team are not located together.

5 *Type of system.* Critical systems such as hard real-time control systems or safety-critical systems need more comprehensive traceability policies than non-critical systems.

The traceability manual should normally be developed incrementally as the system is specified, designed and implemented. The first chapter should always include the project traceability policies. Requirements dependencies can then be documented as soon as the requirements document is agreed but design traceability, documentation traceability, etc., must be added at later stages of the development process.

Traceability information must be regularly updated if it is to remain useful. If the document is maintained on paper, there will always be a lag between changes made to the paper document and the document which is used by the engineers maintaining the requirements and/or the system. Furthermore, if a document exists on paper, there is always a temptation to use this, even if it is out-of-date. This often results in errors or misunderstandings.

We strongly recommend that the traceability manual should be implemented as a networked electronic document rather than as a paper document. When traceability information is required, the document is either consulted on-screen or the relevant sections of the document are printed. Some kind of hypertext system (e.g. a WWW-based system) may be used to implement the manual or, alternatively, it may simply be maintained as word processor text. There will be a different version of the traceability manual for each different version of the system. The traceability manual, therefore, should be managed using your normal configuration management procedures.

To ensure that the traceability manual is kept up-to-date, you should assign someone to be the traceability manual manager. He or she should work with system developers to ensure that changes to the requirements/design, etc., have been incorporated in the manual and should review and update traceability policies. The traceability manual manager should also be responsible for following up deviations from traceability policies and ensuring that the required information is subsequently added to the traceability manual.

Costs and problems

If you have a set of organisational traceability policies as recommended in Guideline 9.3, there are relatively low costs involved in introducing this guideline. However, it can be expensive to maintain a traceability manual. For large systems, maintaining the traceability manual is likely to be a full-time job and, even for relatively small systems, you must allocate at least 25% of someone's time for traceability manual management. As discussed above, the costs of collecting the traceability information itself are obviously significant and dependent on the number of requirements.

The main problem you will find is keeping the traceability manual up to date. When people are working under pressure to make system changes, they will forget to make amendments to the traceability manual as these are not critical for the change to be made to the system. There is always a temptation to deviate from traceability policies because of the need to deliver on schedule. If this happens in an uncontrolled way, the traceability manual will, fairly rapidly, become useless.

9.5   Use a Database to Manage Requirements

Key benefit	Makes it easier to manage large numbers of requirements
Costs of introduction	Moderate–high
Costs of application	Moderate
Guideline type	Intermediate

Rather than maintaining requirements in text documents, establish a requirements database and store the individual requirements as entries in this database.

Benefits

- Managing requirements in a database makes it easier to maintain links between individual requirements and to search for and abstract related groups of requirements.

- If the database is a general-purpose repository for system information, links from the requirements to design and implementation information may be maintained.

- If the database supports concurrent working, it allows for different groups to work on the requirements specification at the same time without generating requirements inconsistencies. Database facilities for data backup, integrity and security mean that requirements engineers need not be concerned with these issues.

- The requirements may be automatically processed to extract particular types of information. For example, it may be possible to generate traceability tables and lists automatically from information in the requirements database.

Implementation

The most appropriate way to implement this guideline depends on the type and the number of requirements which must be managed and the particular ways of working in your organisation. Issues which influence design choices are as follows.

1   How are requirements expressed? Do you use natural language, graphical models, mathematical expressions, etc.? Do you need to store additional information such as photographs as part of the requirements rationale? If you need to store more than just simple text, you may need to use a database with multi-media capabilities.

2   How many requirements do you typically need to manage? Is it tens, hundreds, thousands or tens of thousands? The requirements for a small to medium sized system can be managed using commercial PC databases. Larger systems usually need a server-based system and a database, such as ORACLE, which is designed to manage a very large volume of data.

3   Are the requirements always developed and managed by teams which work together at the same site and which use the same types of computers or do you need to access the requirements database from different sites? If you need multi-site access from different types of equipment, you should using an Intranet-based solution which provides access to the requirements database through a WWW browsing system.

4   Do you already use a database for software engineering support? Do you have a company policy on database use? What types of computer do you use? These factors obviously constrain the type of database which you can use.

5   What in-house database expertise do you have available? Will requirements engineers be responsible for database administration or will this be a separate responsibility? Database management costs can be high and a solution which requires a specialist database administrator may not be cost-effective.

If you maintain your requirements in a database, you can design the requirements database to include traceability information. With each requirement in the database, you should include at least two fields for traceability information. These should be filled in with references to other requirements which the requirement depends on and with references to requirements which are dependent on that requirement. Obviously, if you wish to maintain other types of traceability information such as requirements-architecture links, you must include database fields to record information about each different type of relationship.

Using the database system has the advantage that the database itself usually includes facilities for browsing and report generation. You can browse the requirements in the database then move immediately to related requirements. You may also write simple scripts which scan the database and generate the specific traceability information which you require.

Relational databases are now the most commonly used type of database. Relational databases were designed for storing and managing large numbers of records which have the same structure and minimal links between them. A requirements database, however, may have relatively few records (hundreds rather than hundreds of thousands) each of which includes many links such as links to documents, text files and other requirements. Maintaining these links is possible with a relational database. However, it is inefficient as it requires operations on several different tables. For very large numbers of requirements, you may find that this type of database is too slow.

To use a relational database, you may have to keep the text of the requirements in a separate file or files and access these files through the database. The database tables (which use the requirements identifiers as keys) are used to index requirements and to store links between related requirements. You find linked requirements using the relational join operation.

Object-oriented databases have been developed relatively recently and are structurally more suited to requirements management. They allow different types of information to be maintained in different objects and managing links between objects is fairly straightforward. However, this type of database is still immature and low-cost object-oriented databases are not widely available.

They are also probably more expensive to manage than relational databases.

If you have a very large number of requirements, you will need to use a powerful database management system such as ORACLE. This might be organised as a database server on a workstation with access through other client workstations or PCs. This is an expensive approach but the power of these systems allows for fast database manipulation. They also usually have excellent report generation tools which can be used to create skeletal requirements documents from the requirements database. These databases can support many simultaneous users and provide good facilities for backup and recovery in the event of system failure.

Lower-cost approaches are possible using simpler PC database systems. Modern PC databases include facilities for managing multimedia information such as diagrams and photographs. Some of them can use object sharing facilities (such as OLE) to link directly to word processor files where the requirements text is stored. Their support for simultaneous access may be limited to locking the whole database when it is in use and they have limited facilities for error recovery. The requirements database must provide shared access and access control to the requirements.

Whatever database you use, some data administration will be required. The data administrator must set up and manage the database schema. He or she should also be responsible for executing backup and recovery procedures and providing support to database users. Database administration can take up quite a lot of time; a large requirements database may need several hours per week of a professional database administrator's time.

If you require access to your requirements database from remote sites and using a variety of different computers, you might consider using WWW-based information system as a front-end for a requirements database server. At the time of writing, various off-the-shelf solutions of this type have just become available. We do not know of any experience reports of using this type of information system for requirements management but it is an interesting development which has significant future potential.

A requirements database may be used in conjunction with special-purpose CASE tools for requirements management. There are now several of these tools on the market, ranging from simple PC systems to large and complex workstation-based tools intended to manage large requirements databases. These tools provide built-in traceability support and some of them support the automatic creation of requirements databases from a natural-language requirements document. We do not endorse any specific tool but include details of tool suppliers in the book's WWW pages.

Costs and problems

There is a significant cost involved in setting up a requirements database and putting procedures in place to ensure that it is used. Using special-purpose tools obviously incurs some capital costs and training costs to put these systems into use. It is unlikely that you will recover all of these costs from improved requirements management in a single project. The benefits of this guideline will only emerge after the database is used in several projects.

The costs of applying the guideline include the costs of database administration and, obviously, data entry costs for entering the requirements in the database. These costs are proportional to the number of requirements to be managed.

One of the major problems with a requirements database is linking the database to the requirements document. Readers of the requirements document will not be prepared to use the database directly so you must have procedures which will automatically create the requirements document from information in the database. This is becoming much easier as it is possible in some databases to link directly to word processor files. In other cases, the database information may be processed to generate the requirements in a standard word processor format such as Microsoft's RTF format or in HTML, the formatting language for WWW documents.

If you are planning to use a database for requirements management, adding traceability links is relatively inexpensive. If you already have a database and you have not designed these into the database schema, it may be very expensive to retrofit them. A problem which you may encounter is that many database systems do not allow you to create fields which include more than one reference to other database records. Most requirements, however, will include dependencies on several other requirements, so you must get round this limitation in some way.

9.6   Define Change Management Policies

Key benefit	Provides a framework for systematically assessing change proposals
Costs of introduction	Moderate–high
Costs of application	Low–moderate
Guideline type	Intermediate

You should define policies for managing changes to requirements which set out how changes are formally proposed, analysed, and reviewed. Accepted changes are then implemented to create a new version of the requirements document.

Benefits

- Change management policies allow overall costs to be controlled by ensuring that the whole life-cycle impact of requirements changes is taken into account.

- As requirements changes are proposed, there is a need to keep track of the status of these changes and to be able to produce reports on requirements evolution.

- Change management policies give stakeholders a formal mechanism for proposing changes to requirements which does not favour any specific group of stakeholders.

Implementation

Change management policies are concerned with the procedures, processes and standards which are used to manage changes to system requirements. Change management policies mean that similar information is collected for each proposed change and that overall judgements are made about the costs and benefits of proposed changes. Without change management policies, you cannot be sure that proposed changes to the requirements add to the general services provided by the system and help support business goals (see **Guideline 3.4**, *Make a business case for the system*).

The change management policies which you establish should define the following.

1 The change request process and the information required to process each change request.

2 The process used to analyse the impact and costs of change and the associated traceability information.

3 The membership of the body which formally considers change requests.

4 The software support (if any) for the change control process. We recommend that you develop a change management database where you store all change requests. Within this database, you should maintain information about the change request, its status and how it has been implemented.

Stakeholders should submit proposals for requirements changes using a pre-defined form. This should include fields to collect information about the change and the impact of the change on other requirements, the system implementation and other system documentation. After initial filtering to remove changes which are a result of stakeholder misunderstanding, the impact and the costs of the change are assessed. The change and its associated costs are then considered by some formal group (in military projects, this is called a change control board) who decide whether or not the change to the requirements should be accepted.

If possible, the change management process should be supported by software. There are now several systems available which claim to support change management. Most of these are oriented towards software change control and some are tightly integrated with commercial configuration management systems.

Of course, you can use a general-purpose database to store change requests, associated status information and links to the requirements themselves. You can also use e-mail for information distribution and circulation.

However, you have to transfer information manually from the e-mail system to the change management system and this is a potential source of error and delay.

Ideally, you should integrate a change control system with a requirements database (see **Guideline 9.5**). This should let you keep track of the different versions of requirements and link the proposed changes with the initial requirement and any revision of that requirement. Unfortunately, CASE tools for version and configuration management are mostly geared towards managing files of information (such as source programs) rather than relatively short, individual requirements in a database. To manage this information, you need a version management system which can deal with 'fine-grain' objects. However, you can certainly use a conventional version management system to manage revisions of the requirements document.

You can find out more about change management and more general aspects of configuration management in Chapter 33 of *Software Engineering* (Ian Sommerville, Addison Wesley, 1996). This includes an example of a change request form which may be used. We have also included information about some commercial configuration management systems on the book's WWW pages.

Costs and problems

Defining and implementing change control policies is fairly expensive. You must allow several months for the change management policies to be defined and brought into use. After it has been introduced, the costs of running the system are the costs of assessing the impact of changes and ensuring that this information is recorded in the change management system.

If you have managed requirements changes in an informal way where stakeholders discuss changes directly with requirements engineers and software developers, you may find resistance to the scheme from both of these groups. They may perceive change management policies as an unnecessary overhead which increases the time needed to implement changes. To counter this, you must make clear that, in the long-term, uncontrolled changes cost a great deal. They are likely to lead to a 'require-ments drift' where the system evolves towards the needs of those who are most able to influence the engineers responsible for system evolution.

If you don't automate the change management process, you will probably have information management problems. These are not just due to the volume of infor-mation which must be processed but also due to the fact that change proposals must be analysed by different people. It is very easy to lose track of where each change request is in the process.

9.7   Identify Global System Requirements

Key benefit	Finds the requirements which are likely to be most expensive to change
Costs of introduction	Low
Costs of application	Low
Guideline type	Intermediate

Global system requirements are requirements which set out desirable or essential properties of the system as a whole. They cannot be assigned to individual sub-systems or mapped onto parts of the system implementation. These requirements should be explicitly identified and documented as part of the requirements management process.

Benefits

- Global system requirements are very expensive to change. The costs of change are high because many different parts of the system may be affected by the change. If the requirements can be identified in advance, particular attention can be paid to their analysis and validation and so ensure that future requirements changes due to omissions and misunderstandings are minimised.

- The management of global system requirements is particularly complex as changes to these requirements may involve consultation with many different contractors who are developing different parts of the system. Knowing global requirements simplifies the planning of this change process.

Implementation

We recommend that you identify the global requirements during the requirements analysis and the requirements validation processes. During these activities, you are analysing all the requirements so very little additional effort is needed to discover global requirements. Alternatively, you can identify global requirements when you are creating your initial traceability information.

There is no easy way to identify global system requirements. You need to use your judgement and knowledge of the system. To help with this identification process, it is sometimes helpful to ask the following questions about each requirement.

1 Is the requirement expressed in a very general way (for example, 'the system must never corrupt data in the database')?

2 Does the requirement express some global, non-functional system characteristic (for example, 'the system must process N transactions per second')?

3 Is the requirement a general user interface requirement?

4 Does the requirement refer to specific system functionality or a specific system service which must be provided?

5 Can the requirement be mapped onto part of the system model?

6 Does the requirement refer to specific data or components of the system?

If the answers to the questions 1–3 are 'yes' or if the answers to questions 4–6 are 'no' then the requirement may be a global requirement. If possible, you should try to identify global system requirements during analysis and negotiation activities. Where this is impractical, they may be identified at requirements reviews during the validation process.

You will not get the identification of global system requirements right first time. Some requirements which appear to be sub-system requirements will emerge as global system requirements. You must therefore expect new global requirements to be discovered throughout the requirements analysis, negotiation and validation processes.

Global system requirements really require separate

traceability management. The normal approaches to traceability where you link specific requirements or requirements and system components do not apply to these requirements. You cannot map them onto a set of system components. You should therefore maintain a list of global requirements as a separate section in the traceability manual.

Costs and problems

There are no significant costs involved in introducing this guideline. If global requirements are identified as part of other processes such as analysis and requirements reviews, the additional costs of applying the guideline are minimal. Apart from the general difficulties of identifying global requirements, there should be no significant problems in applying this guideline.

9.8 Identify Volatile Requirements

Key benefit	Simplifies requirements change management
Costs of introduction	Low
Costs of application	Low
Guideline type	Advanced

You should maintain a list of the most volatile requirements, that is, those requirements which are most likely to change. If possible, you should predict likely changes to these requirements.

Benefits

- System developers may be able to design the system so that volatile requirements are implemented in modules which are loosely coupled to the rest of the system. This means that software changes to accommodate requirements change will be easier to implement.

- Planning for change is easier if likely changes are predicted. You will find it easier to manage the evolution of the requirements document and to plan the development of the system.

Implementation

All system requirements may change but it is generally the case that some requirements change more frequently than other, more stable, requirements. To implement this guideline, experienced requirements engineers should examine all of the system requirements and identify those which are likely to be particularly volatile. We recommend that you should identify these requirements during the requirements validation process or when your initial set of traceability information is created.

We have suggested that this guideline is an advanced guideline because you will not really get any benefits from it until you have requirements management and change management policies in place.

There are different types of volatile requirements.

1 *Mutable requirements.* These are requirements which change because of changes to the environment in which the system is operating. For example, the requirements for a system which computes tax deductions evolve as the tax laws are changed.

2 *Emergent requirements.* These are requirements which cannot be completely defined when the system is specified but which emerge as the system is designed and implemented. For example, it may not be possible to specify, in advance, the details of how information should be presented. As stakeholders see examples of possible presentations, they may think of new presentations that would be useful to them.

3 *Consequential requirements.* These are requirements which are based on assumptions on how the system will be used. When the system is put into use, you will find that some of these assumptions will be wrong. You will also find that users will adapt to the system and find new ways to use its functionality. This will result in demands from users for system changes and modifications.

4 *Compatibility requirements.* These are requirements which depend on other equipment or processes. As these change, these requirements also evolve. For example, an instrument control system may have to be modified when a new display is added.

To identify volatile requirements, you must involve application domain specialists who will know which domain information is fairly stable and which is variable. If you can assign requirements to one of the above classes, that is also an indicator of volatility. It may also be helpful to discuss possible organisational change with senior management. However, they may not be completely candid here as they do not want people to know of the organisational impact of planned changes.

You will not get change prediction 100% right and you will not be able to identify all volatile requirements.

Unexpected changes will always occur. You should update your list of volatile requirements as you gain experience; you may find that some of the requirements which you thought were volatile are fairly stable.

To identify volatile requirements in a database, you should add a field to the requirements record whose value indicates the estimated volatility of the requirement. We suggest a three-point volatility scale where 1 means fairly stable, 2 means subject to medium term change and 3 means that the requirement is likely to change in the short-term.

Costs and problems

There are no significant costs involved in introducing this guideline. Applying the guideline is not expensive if you have experienced engineers available who can make judgements about requirements volatility during the requirements validation process. At that stage, you should have a stable and complete set of requirements so it should be possible to identify those requirements which are likely to change.

Maintaining information about volatile requirements is a form of traceability information. As with all traceability information, the major problem with this guideline is ensuring that the information about volatility and predicted change is kept up-to-date as the requirements change.

9.9   Record Rejected Requirements

Key benefit	Saves re-analysis when rejected requirements are proposed again after the system is in use
Costs of introduction	Low
Costs of application	Low
Guideline type	Advanced

Keep a record of requirements which have been proposed and subsequently rejected after analysis or negotiation. Record why these requirements were rejected.

Benefits

- It is fairly common for rejected requirements to be proposed again after the system has gone into use because there was, presumably, a good reason for proposing them originally. It is easy to forget why requirements were rejected. If you maintain an explicit record of this, you can avoid some or all of the costs of repeating the requirements analysis.

Implementation

You need a requirements database to implement this guideline. As part of the record of each requirement, you include a status field where a requirement is marked as accepted, under consideration, rejected, etc., plus a link to the reasons why the requirement was originally rejected. This must be built into your database when it is originally implemented. You can then discover the rejected requirements by querying the database using the requirements status field.

It is very important to ensure that rejected requirements and the reasons for rejection are recorded immediately after analysis or negotiation. This must be entered in the database along with the requirement. Otherwise, the reasons for rejection will almost certainly be forgotten.

As part of the process of assessing new requirements, you should always consult the database of rejected requirements to see if similar requirements have been rejected. This should be done at an early stage of the analysis of the new requirement. If the proposal has been rejected in the past, the reasons for the rejection may still be valid. You may also find it helpful to trace the original source of the rejected requirement and involve them in the analysis of the proposed requirements changes.

It does not always follow that a rejected requirement should automatically be rejected again if it is re-proposed. Changing circumstances may mean that the requirement should be accepted and the system changed. The requirements rejection information is simply a guide to analysts who must consider whether or not the original reasons for rejection are still valid.

Costs and problems

If you have designed your requirements database so that you can include rejection information, this is not an expensive guideline to introduce or to implement. However, requirements engineers may consider that maintenance of rejected requirements is a low-priority task and argue that they should be paying attention of accepted requirements. You may therefore have difficulties in convincing them to apply the guideline. In particular, they are likely to forget to record the rationale for rejection or to record rationale using a short phrase (such as 'no use') which does not convey useful information.

10 Requirements Engineering for Critical Systems

Summary

Critical systems are systems which have stringent reliability, availability, maintainability, safety or security requirements. The costs of system failure are very high and the requirements engineering and system development processes must ensure that stakeholders have confidence in the system. In this chapter, we suggest a number of guidelines for process activities which we think are particularly important for the specification of critical systems. The guidelines which we suggest are:

Guidelines

10.1 Create Safety Requirement Checklists.

10.2 Involve External Reviewers in the Validation Process.

10.3 Identify and Analyse Hazards.

10.4 Derive Safety Requirements from Hazard Analysis.

10.5 Cross-check Operational and Functional Requirements Against Safety Requirements.

10.6 Specify Systems Using Formal Specifications.

10.7 Collect Incident Experience.

10.8 Learn from Incident Experience.

10.9 Establish an Organisational Safety Culture.

Critical systems are systems whose failure can threaten human life, cause damage to the system's environment or can significantly disrupt the running of an organisation. Examples of critical systems are avionics systems controlling aircraft, chemical process control systems, telephone switching systems, and bank communication systems. Until relatively recently, most of these systems did not rely exclusively on software control. They were either controlled by hardware or the control system had some form of hardware backup. However, more and more of these systems are now eliminating hardware control and becoming exclusively controlled by software. Software control leads to lower costs as the size and weight of the system is reduced. Software control also gives greater flexibility than is possible with hardware control systems.

Critical systems always have stringent non-functional requirements which must be satisfied if the system is to deliver the service required. These systems are sometimes called RAMSS systems, which reflects their critical attributes.

1 *Reliability.* The system's behaviour must be consistent and must conform to its specification.

2 *Availability.* The system must be available for service when required.

3 *Maintainability.* It must be possible to maintain and update the system, sometimes without taking it out of service.

4 *Safety.* The system's behaviour must never cause damage to people or the system's environment.

5 *Security.* The system and its data must be protected from unauthorised access.

These non-functional attributes are not independent. For example, in order to be safe, systems must be secure. Otherwise, unauthorised access could cause some damage to the system which results in a subsequent safety-related failure. Similarly, system maintenance must be possible without introducing faults which cause operational failures and therefore reduce system reliability.

The focus on this chapter is on safety-related systems.

However, many of the guidelines are also applicable to other critical systems attributes. Safety and security are particularly closely related. Potentially unsafe systems will not always result in an accident; if there are system insecurities, it does not mean that the system will be abused. There are degrees of severity of an accident and degrees of severity of a breach of security. It may be necessary to make a formal case justifying the safety or the security of a system. Techniques such as hazard analysis used in safety-related systems engineering are similar to threat analysis for secure systems. Therefore, although the guidelines focus on safety, they can be easily modified so that they apply to other critical system attributes.

Critical systems are very expensive to develop because of their stringent non-functional requirements. Their specification and development processes should be designed to avoid the introduction of errors and the systems must be carefully and thoroughly validated. This changes the economics of some process improvements. Techniques, such as the use of formal methods, which might normally be too expensive to use may be cost-effective for critical systems specification.

Another important factor which must be considered when deciding whether or not process changes are likely to be cost-effective is the need for external system certification. For example, systems on civil aircraft have to be certified as safe by national aviation authorities. System certification has two consequences for process improvement.

1 The revised process may have to be certified. This effectively rules out radical process changes. The evolutionary approach which we propose should not normally cause problems.

2 System contractors may have to produce a safety case for their systems which is a set of arguments justifying why they believe their system to be safe. Therefore, the introduction of guidelines such as **Guideline 4.8**, *Record requirements rationale*, may be justified because it reduces the costs of writing this safety case.

External certification and regulatory bodies are themselves sources of system requirements. Typically, these requirements are expressed as general, whole-system requirements such as 'the system must conform to health and safety legislation'. These general requirements must be translated to functional system requirements and the system safety case must demonstrate the correspondence between these functional requirements and the regulatory requirements.

These external requirements are volatile requirements. Legislation may change in response to accidents and social and political pressure. If an accident involving a similar system occurs while a system is being specified, the external requirements may change to ensure that the situation which caused the accident does not recur.

The emphasis in this chapter is on safety-related systems. This area uses some very specific terminology which we use in the guidelines.

1 *Accident.* An unplanned sequence of events which results in human death, injury or damage to the system's environment. Therefore, if a software system controlling a radiation therapy machine causes the machine to deliver an excessive dose of radiation and injures the patient, this is an accident.

2 *Incident.* Potentially dangerous system behaviour which does not result in an accident because of other factors external to the system. For example, the braking system of a car may fail on a straight empty road so the car can come to a halt without damage; a robot arm may swing into an occupied area but, by chance, may not actually hit anyone.

3 *Hazard.* A system state or condition which can, but need not, result in an incident. In a radiation therapy machine, a hazard arises when the software instructs the machine to deliver an excessive dose of radiation. This need not result in an incident as some other safety device may be installed which detects the problem and cuts off the radiation before any incident occurs.

4 *Safety and security requirement.* Any constraint which is associated with the system for reasons of safety or secur-

ity. Safety and security requirements should almost always take precedence over operational requirements when conflicts are detected. These requirements are often expressed as constraints which are then developed into operational requirements in a detailed system specification. For example, a safety requirement may state that the system must not allow an operator access to the components of a machine while it is in operation; this may result in a functional requirement stating that the control software must switch the machine off when the casing is opened.

Safety and security requirements are often 'do nots' whereas operational requirements are 'do's'. A safety requirement may therefore be phrased 'The system *shall not...*' whereas operational requirements are phrased 'The system *shall...*'. System developers should normally take more care over the implementation of the 'shall nots' rather than the 'shalls'.

All of the guidelines in this chapter are specific to critical systems specification but other guidelines in the book are also relevant. In particular, it is very important that a high-quality requirements management process is in place for critical systems development. When requirements changes are proposed, you must be able to assess the impact of these changes on the rest of the system and to assess whether or not the change is justified. If a change might compromise a critical system attribute such as reliability or security, it may have to be rejected, irrespective of its value in other respects. The top 10 guidelines from other chapters which are particularly important for critical systems requirements engineering are shown in Figure 10.1.

We normally recommend that you should introduce basic guidelines before intermediate guidelines. However, if you are developing safety-related applications, you may have to introduce intermediate level guidelines before you have completed your improvements using basic guidelines. For example, we have rated the introduction of systematic hazard analysis as an *intermediate* guideline as it involves new methods or technology. However, organisations who are involved in critical systems develop-

Guideline	Chapter
3.1 Define a standard document structure	The requirements document
5.1 Define system boundaries	Requirements analysis and negotiation
6.1 Define standard templates for describing requirements	Describing requirements
6.4 Supplement natural language with other descriptions of requirements	Describing requirements
7.2 Model the system's environment	System modelling
8.2 Organise formal requirements inspections	Requirements validation
8.4 Define validation checklists	Requirements validation
9.1 Uniquely identify each requirement	Requirements management
9.2 Define policies for requirements management	Requirements management
9.6 Define change management policies	Requirements management

Figure 10.1 Critical guidelines for critical systems

ment may have to implement this guideline because of government regulations or customer requirements for safety-critical systems development.

If you are involved in critical systems development, you must be conservative. You cannot afford to risk radical change to your process. If it goes wrong, your system may not be able to meet its critical requirements. We believe that it should be possible in most organisations to introduce all of the *basic* guidelines in this book without compromising system safety, reliability or security. The guidelines provide a sound framework for requirements engineering and are not concerned with the introduction of new methods or tools.

Intermediate and advanced guidelines mostly suggest the use of advanced methods for requirements engineering. Before introducing new methods for critical systems, we advise you to experiment with them in non-critical applications. This will let you check that these methods really contribute to your process improvement goals. If this is impossible (e.g. for hazard analysis), you should introduce these new techniques in parallel with your normal development process so that you have a fall-back position should the techniques go wrong.

We have already discussed the REAIMS project which was a research project concerned with requirements engineering process improvement in the critical systems domain. As part of that project, systematic methods called FRERE (for integrating formal specification and refinement into the system specification process), MERE (for gathering and learning from incident experience) and PERE (for analysing the dependability of processes) have been developed. These have been evaluated in REAIMS but have not yet been widely used. We therefore do not feel that we can suggest them as good practice. However, organisations which are at the 'defined' level of maturity may find them helpful. Information about these methods is available from the REAIMS project web page whose URL is given in the Preface.

10.1   Create Safety Requirement Checklists

Key benefit	Helps find missing requirements which may affect system safety
Costs of introduction	Low–moderate
Costs of application	Low
Guideline type	Basic

You should create a safety checklist, relevant to the type of applications which you develop, and use this to check the completeness of requirements specifications. If you are also concerned about security, reliability, etc., you should also create comparable checklists for these attributes.

Benefits

- A safety checklist is an encapsulation of experience which can help you to assess if important requirements have been left out of the specification. Missing requirements which are important to system safety are a common problem especially when the people involved in writing the specification have not been involved in specifying similar systems.

- A safety checklist gives people who are new to this type of system specification an overview of the type of requirements which should be included.

Implementation

The safety checklist must be created from experience and information which has been collected about problems in previous systems. It supplements any general requirements validation checklists which you have defined (**Guideline 8.4**, *Define validation checklists*). Starting with some generic checklist, such as that proposed below, you must interview application experts, system and software engineers and safety experts to discover the checklist items which are most relevant to the type of systems which you develop.

Nancy Leveson in her book *Safeware: System Safety and Computers* (Addison Wesley, 1995) suggests a requirements checklist for process control systems. We have adapted her suggestions to create a more general set of checklist items which you can used as a starting point for your own lists.

1 *Start the system in a safe state* Include requirements which define a safe start-up state.

2 *Define initial values of all critical system variables* Critical system variables are those which are defined in the external system interfaces. Include requirements which define the initial values of these variables.

3 *Cope with manual intervention* Include requirements which describe how the software knows about manual intervention in the system and how it should be re-initialised after automatic operation re-commences.

4 *Specify behaviour when the system is off-line* Include requirements which specify what happens to inputs received when the system is off-line.

5 *Include time-out requirements* Include requirements which specify what should happen when expected inputs are not received within the time slot allowed.

6 *Specify what happens when unexpected inputs are received* Sometimes, inputs arrive when the system is in some state where these inputs are not expected and cannot be processed. Include requirements which specify what the system should do with these inputs.

7 *All sensor information should be used* Check that the requirements specify how all inputs from sensors are processed. If some sensor inputs have been missed out, this implies that there are missing requirements.

8 *Check if all classes of output value are produced* If the system can generate different classes of output value, check that there are requirements which define how each output value class is produced.

9 *Check validity of all inputs and specify responses in the event of out-of-range values* Include requirements which define valid ranges for critical input values and which specify the action to be taken if an out-of-range input is processed.

10 *Check reasonableness of all outputs* Include requirements which define the range of 'reasonable' output values produced by the system and which specify the action to be taken if an 'unreasonable' output value is produced.

11 *Specify action to be taken in the event of timing delays* Include requirements which set out the action to be taken if expected inputs do not arrive in time or required outputs cannot be produced in time.

12 *Specify overload behaviour* Include requirements which specify the maximum load under which the system should behave 'correctly' and the actions which should be taken if this load is exceeded.

13 *Specify alarm management* Specify how multiple alarms should be queued and displayed on the user interface. A well-known problem is alarm overload when operators are confused by many different alarms and cannot find the real problem because they have to deal with these alarms.

14 *Specify data ageing* Include requirements which specify when received inputs become outdated and should be discarded

15 *Specify exceptional responses to inputs* For every input which might be received, the system response should be specified when the input has an unexpected value, when it is missing and when it arrives too late or too early.

16 *Specify how to reverse commands* If system outputs affect actuators, then for every command which causes some action, you should specify a reversing command which causes the opposite action. Therefore, if there is a system function to open a valve, there must also be a function to close that valve. For all user interface actions, there should (if possible) be a command which cancels that action.

17 *Specify the fail-safe system state* If the system has a safe state which should be entered in the event of failure, you should include requirements which specify this safe state and how to get to it. If there is no safe state, you should, if possible, specify a minimum risk state.

18 *Specify error detection and recovery* Operators will always make errors in using a system. You should specify how operator errors will be detected and notified and what system facilities should be provided to allow operators to recover from the errors which they have made.

We normally recommend that checklists should not have more than 10 items but this is impractical for safety checklists. Safety checklists may become quite long. This means that users cannot keep all checklist items in their head at the same time. To counteract this, you can ask different document reviewers to focus on different sets of checklist items or you might keep detailed, explicit records of how each requirement relates to each checklist item. This approach is effective but it is time-consuming and expensive to manage this information.

Costs and problems

If you have a number of experienced engineers available who have been involved in previous safety-related projects then the cost of creating a safety checklist should be relatively low. It can probably be created by experienced people in a few person-days. However, if you are new to the development of critical systems, then you will need to start with a generic checklist. As you gain experience with its use, you should tailor the checklist to your particular needs. In all cases, you should have a checklist review procedure which updates the checklist as new experience is gained.

The costs of applying the guideline are relatively low if you use the checklist as an informal reminder of what to look for when validating critical systems requirements. It costs more, of course, if you keep detailed records of how each requirement has been checked against the safety checklist.

A problem with checklists, in general, is that people think of them as a complete list of everything they have to do. If they manage to 'tick off' all checklist items, then there is no more work to be done. Of course, this is not true. Checklists are a tool which reduces the chances of people forgetting to make some checks. You must emphasise that the use of a safety checklist helps with the validation of safety-related system requirements but that it is not a substitute for informed thought and analysis.

10.2 Involve External Reviewers in the Validation Process

Key benefit	External reviewers will not pre-judge the requirements
Costs of introduction	Low
Costs of application	Low–moderate
Guideline type	Basic

You should always include external reviewers who have not been involved in the elicitation, analysis and negotiation of requirements in the validation process for safety-related systems.

Benefits

- External reviewers bring a fresh perspective to the validation of a system. They do not have preconceived notions about the system, and so may discover problems which have been missed by those more closely involved in its development.

Implementation

External reviewers find it easier to be objective about the requirements than those who have participated in requirements elicitation, analysis and negotiation. People who know the system requirements well are liable to read them as they believe they ought to be rather than as they are actually specified. They may therefore take things for granted and make unjustified assumptions about the system.

Ideally, you should select a review team which includes several external reviewers who can look at requirements from different viewpoints e.g. safety engineers, domain experts, system developers, etc. Their remit should be to look for any problems in the requirements which might affect critical system attributes such as reliability, safety, etc. This should be part of your formal requirements review.

In practice, it may be difficult to involve a team of external experts in the requirements validation process. It may only be possible to get a single external validator involved in the process. In these circumstances, the role of the external validator should be that of a 'devil's advocate'. He or she should ask difficult questions about the requirements, should invent sets of circumstances where problems might arise and should ask how the system would cope with these problems.

Costs and problems

If you already have a formal inspection process in place, the costs of introducing this requirement are low. The costs of applying it as part of the requirements engineering process are the effort costs for the external reviewers. As discussed in **Guideline 8.2**, *Organise formal requirements inspections,* these vary but can be moderately high for large requirements documents. However, they are likely to be lower than the costs of discovering and correcting requirements problems through system testing.

A problem in implementing this guideline is the time pressure on most organisations to complete the system specification. Organising meetings with external reviewers is likely to take some time so this will delay the requirements validation process.

Furthermore, small or medium-sized organisations may not have external experts who have not been involved in the specification development or the experts may not be available. In these circumstances, you may have to use external consultants in the process, which obviously adds to your overall costs.

10.3   Identify and Analyse Hazards

Key benefit	Provides a basis for checking the safety of the system
Costs of introduction	Moderate–high
Costs of application	Moderate–high
Guideline type	Intermediate

Hazards are states of the system which can lead to an accident. You should include an explicit process activity which identifies potential hazards and their possible causes. You should also assess the probability of these hazards and the consequences of an accident resulting from them.

Benefits

- Hazard identification and analysis is an essential first step for safety/security assurance. You need to know the potential hazards before you can write requirements which will avoid these hazards or minimise the consequences of any accident.

- Hazard identification helps when negotiating and prioritising requirements. If safety or security is a critical system attribute, essential requirements to protect against hazards should have a high priority.

Implementation

Hazard analysis is a well-established systems engineering technique which is relevant not only for safety-related systems. It may also be used where other attributes such as security or reliability are critical. In these situations, you should think of a hazardous state as any state which may result in a system failure.

Various hazard analysis methods such as fault-tree analysis, event-tree analysis, cause-consequence analysis and hazops have been developed. These techniques are too detailed to be described here. In her book *Safeware: System Safety and Computers*, Nancy Leveson gives a good summary of these hazard analysis techniques. However, these approaches to hazard analysis are mostly designed to cope with the hazards arising from design rather than specification problems. They are based on the assumption that safety-related system failures are mainly a consequence of design, implementation and manufacturing errors rather than specification errors or omissions. In fact, hazards are not just a result of system failure; they can also arise during the correct operation of a system. There must be system requirements which ensure that these do not result in safety-related incidents.

The key problem is anticipating hazards and understanding the circumstances in which these hazards are likely to arise. This requires deep knowledge of the application domain. For example, the performance of a driverless vehicle is affected by weather conditions such as wind speed, visibility, etc. You need a vehicle expert to suggest how the machine may be affected in different conditions and how hazards might be avoided.

Some hazards are a result of interactions between subsystems or between sub-systems and the environment. For example, a portable medical system for monitoring patients may include a facility to call a doctor using his or her mobile phone. However, there may be interference between the cellphone signals and the system's instruments which cause faulty data to be collected. Detecting this type of hazard means that the analysis team must have knowledge of the characteristics of the different technologies used in the system.

Consequently, hazard analysis at the requirements level must be based on the good sense and judgement of the people involved. Some general guidelines are as follows.

1 Always carry out hazard analysis using a team of people which includes end-users of the system, domain experts and engineers from different backgrounds who understand all of the technologies used in the system.

2 Do not reject, without analysis, any suggestions of possible hazards irrespective of how outlandish they may seem. Many accidents have occurred because of very

unlikely or strange circumstances. Neumann's book on computer-related risks* describes some weird and wonderful causes of accidents.

3 You may use 'brainstorming' techniques where people meet to discuss possible hazards; however, some studies have found that it is not necessary for all participants to be in the same room at the same time. You can get as good or better results by simply requesting input from participants and circulating these and comments to all involved. This makes it much easier to involve experts who may not be available for brainstorming sessions.

4 The use of question-based 'what–if' approaches such as hazops is more likely to be effective at this stage than techniques which are based on system failure analysis.

5 Knowledge gained from previous incidents is invaluable for hazard analysis. You can gain this knowledge either from experienced people who have seen previous incidents or more systematically by analysing incident records (see **Guideline 10.7**).

6 As the analysis is concerned with the normal operation of the system, you may be able to reuse the hazard analyses from previous systems which have been developed in the same application domain.

You may find it helpful to adopt a viewpoint-oriented approach for hazard analysis (see **Guideline 4.9**, *Collect requirements from multiple viewpoints*). You should identify viewpoints from which you carry out the analysis and develop questions which are relevant to these viewpoints. Possible examples of viewpoints and associated questions are as follows.

1 *Victims of an accident.* Questions which might be asked are 'who might the victims be', 'how might they be harmed by the system', 'how serious is the harm that might be caused', 'what might they be doing when a hazard/accident occurs', 'what protection might be put in place to avoid an accident', etc.

---

*Neumann, P. G. 1995, *Computer-related Risks*, Addison-Wesley.

2 *Other sub-systems which are part of the system.* Questions which might be asked are 'what sub-systems could cause damage to people or property', 'what would be the extent of that damage', 'what are the anticipated interactions between sub-systems, 'what would happen if these interactions go wrong', 'could unanticipated subsystem interactions arise because of system failures', etc.

3 *The computer and associated safety-related software.* Questions which might be asked are 'what inputs are expected and what happens if these do not arrive', 'what happens if complete information is not available', 'what would happen if the software simply stopped', etc.

If you have no previous experience of using hazard analysis, there are several stages involved in introducing it into your organisation.

1 *Assess your need for hazard analysis.* In some cases, this may be obvious; in others, you may find it helpful to involve external safety consultants to assess whether or not your systems are sufficiently safety-critical to justify the use of this technique.

2 *Develop a training example.* This should be based on the type of systems which you develop (ideally, on an existing system). Its function is to demonstrate the relevance of the technique to your engineers.

3 *Introduce training in the technique for selected engineers.* We recommend that you involve external safety consultants here with experience of hazard analysis training.

4 *Try out the technique on a pilot project.* This will reveal weaknesses in the approach which you use and will demonstrate whether or not you can apply it successfully.

5 *Introduce the technique incrementally.* Assuming that the pilot project is successful, introduce it more generally into all critical system projects.

6 *Standardise your approach.* Once you have gained extensive experience with hazard analysis in your application domain, develop a set of standards for the hazard analysis process and its associated documentation. You will need

experience on a number of projects before this standardisation is possible.

Costs and problems

As with any new method, there are dissemination and training costs involved in the introduction of systematic hazard analysis. We recommend that you use external consultants with experience of hazard analysis techniques in your application domain to take responsibility for introducing it into your organisation. You must allow several months to introduce these techniques and introduce hazard analysis initially in small or medium sized projects.

Hazard analysis itself is also costly (although usually *much* less costly than an accident) as it requires a significant amount of time from experienced staff and, perhaps, external consultants. Initially, of course, you are almost certain to make mistakes and to miss possible hazards but as you gain experience, these problems will diminish.

The problems which you may encounter in introducing this guideline stem from lack of experience in hazard and accident analysis. It is sometimes very difficult to decide exactly what constitutes a hazard, to assess the circumstances when this will result in an accident and to understand the possible consequences of any accident. These problems can only be resolved by gaining experience of this type of analysis.

10.4   Derive Safety Requirements from Hazard Analysis

Key benefit	Ensures coverage of all identified hazards
Costs of introduction	Low
Costs of application	Moderate
Guideline type	Intermediate

Using information collected during the hazard analysis process and previous experience, generate functional safety requirements from each hazard. In essence, for each hazard, you should either have a 'shall not' requirement or safety requirements specifying how the hazard or an associated incident can be avoided or how the consequences of an accident can be minimised.

Benefits

- If identified hazards are used to drive the requirements elicitation process, the system requirements will include a complete coverage of the identified hazards. There is a lower probability that critical requirements concerned with the safety of the system will be missed out or mis-specified.

- Traceability links can be established between hazards and requirements, which simplifies the process of assessing the safety implications of requirements changes.

Implementation

This process is a natural continuation of the hazard analysis process. In some cases, you can interleave hazard identification with the specification of the safety requirements associated with the hazards. The overall objective is to derive requirements for a safe system, as follows.

1   The system is specified so that identified hazards cannot occur during normal use of the system. For example, the

specification of a software-controlled paper guillotine might specify that the machine can only be operated when all operator guards are in place.

2 The system is specified so that hazards are detected before they result in an accident and action is taken to ensure that an accident is avoided. For example, the specification for a guillotine might include a requirement to include a sensing system which disables the system if an object is detected in the blade path.

3 The system is specified in such a way that, if an accident occurs, then the dangerous consequences of that accident are minimised. For example, in an automobile system, the airbag control system in a car might also cut electrical power to the fuel pump on the assumption that an accident has occurred and that a fire resulting from fuel leakage might occur.

You should tackle the problem of deriving safety requirements in a systematic way. You should identify generic and specific hazards and break these down (where appropriate) to discover circumstances where these can arise. For each hazard, you should then define a set of specific questions which should be used to elicit requirements to counter that hazard. The questions should relate to the hazard and its causes. They might be based on the following general questions.

1 Under what circumstances can the hazard occur? Can these circumstances be avoided by one or more specific system requirements? If not, can the circumstances where the hazard arises be predicted and notified to the system operator?

2 Is it possible to protect against the hazard or associated accidents? What are the requirements for protection systems which could avoid an accident if a hazardous state occurred?

3 How can the system detect and recover from a hazardous state? How can this information be made available to system operators and associated systems?

4 If an accident occurs, will the same hazard persist and/or

will new hazards arise? If so, what can be done to avoid or protect against these hazards?

5 What are the requirements for minimising the damage resulting from an accident?

The PREview method discussed in Chapter 13 has been designed to be used for question-driven elicitation. In PREview, requirements elicitation is driven by a set of concerns which are global objectives for the system. Concerns are broken down into sub-concerns and, ultimately, into a set of questions for requirements elicitation. When you use this approach for critical systems, you can identify safety as a concern with the identified hazards as the first-level sub-concerns. These are then broken down into questions to help elicit the system safety requirements.

Costs and problems

The cost of introducing this guideline is not high if it is introduced with other requirements elicitation guidelines discussed in Chapter 4 and if a hazard analysis has been carried out. In particular, it relates to Guideline 4.9, *Collect requirements from multiple viewpoints*, which suggests a concern-driven, viewpoint-oriented approach to elicitation. The concerns in this case are safety concerns derived from the identified hazards.

Applying the method involves moderate costs because of the time required to carry out the systematic elicitation of safety requirements. However, these costs should be lower, in the long term, than the costs of a less structured process of safety requirements derivation.

You may find it difficult to derive specific questions from some of the hazards which have been identified. The hazards may be expressed in a vague way (e.g. electric shock hazards) and may apply to the system in general rather than to specific parts of the system. It may not be possible to decompose these into useful elicitation questions. Rather, you may have to wait until you have a complete picture of the system requirements then analyse them, as a whole, against the hazard as discussed in the next guideline. You may also find that some

10.5 Cross-check Operational and Functional Requirements Against Safety Requirements

Key benefit	Increased probability of finding safety-related problems
Costs of introduction	Low
Costs of application	Moderate
Guideline type	Intermediate

Systematically cross-check all safety-related operational and functional requirements against safety requirements to assess if the requirement could contribute to a system hazard or to an accident resulting from the hazard. In short, you should cross-check the *dos* (the operational requirements) against the *don'ts* (the safety requirements).

Benefits

- Systematically checking all safety-related requirements against safety requirements increases the probability of finding requirements problems which affect the safety of the system. Discovering problems at this stage rather than during system testing reduces the amount of rework required to fix the identified problems.

Implementation

This guideline should be introduced in conjunction with the previous guidelines on hazard identification and the derivation of safety requirements. To check the operational and functional requirements against safety requirements, you can use a traceability matrix (see **Guideline 9.3**, *Define traceability policies*) with safety requirements represented as columns and operational/functional requirements as rows in the table. Each table element is filled in with the type of interaction between the safety requirement and the operational/functional requirement. There are three possible values which may be filled in.

1   There is no relationship between the requirements.

2   There is an indirect relationship between the safety requirement and the operational/functional requirement. This means that this requirement in combination with other requirements could result in the hazard arising or could affect an accident which occurred as a result of the hazard.

3   There is a direct relationship between the operational/functional requirement and the safety requirement. The requirement could lead to the hazard or could affect an accident resulting from the hazard.

Using a traceability table is a systematic approach which reveals combinations of requirements which may lead to hazards or accidents. By examining the table, you can immediately see all requirements which may be related to a hazard and can check for problems which may arise because of interactions between these requirements.

The checking of requirements against hazards may be carried out during the requirements elicitation, analysis and validation processes.

•   During elicitation, you may do a very quick check by considering the identified hazards when a requirement is suggested and pointing out possible problems immediately.

•   During analysis, a more systematic approach can provide input to the negotiation process. You may not have identified all safety-related requirements at this stage, however, so a complete check may be impossible.

•   A complete check of all safety-related requirements against identified hazards should be carried out at the validation stage.

In principle, you should check safety requirements against all other requirements. In practice, this is unnecessary for most systems. You only need to check hazards against safety-related requirements. Most critical systems have a number of requirements (often more than 50%)

which are not safety-related or which have only a minimal effect on system safety. For example, they may be concerned with management reporting or with keeping data on the patterns of system use. These do not have to be included in the traceability table.

We therefore recommend that you should make an initial pass through the requirements to identify those requirements which are not safety-related. This will reduce the size of your traceability table and make the information easier to understand and manage. You can do this quickly because it does not matter if you include a few requirements which are not safety-related. This will not compromise the safety of the system.

Costs and problems

The introduction costs for this guideline are low but it is fairly expensive to apply the guideline. A significant amount of time and effort is required for the analysis of safety-related requirements against the identified hazards. However, the benefits of introducing this systematic checking can be significant if the checks detect problems which would otherwise only be discovered during system testing or after the system has gone into operation.

As with all other validation approaches based on cross-checking, a major problem arises for large systems which have hundreds or thousands of safety-related requirements. It is impractical to apply this hazard/requirement cross-checking to all requirements in these cases. The more requirements that there are, the more sparsely populated the requirements/hazards matrix. This can make the matrix difficult to read and mistakes are more likely to occur.

10.6   Specify Systems Using Formal Specifications

Key benefit	Increased confidence in the completeness and consistency of the system specification
Costs of introduction	High
Costs of application	High
Guideline type	Advanced

A formal mathematical specification is a system model which is constructed using a notation which has formally defined syntax and semantics. You should specify the critical parts of a system by developing a formal description of their functionality or behaviour.

Benefits

- To develop a formal specification of a system, you must carry out a detailed analysis of the stakeholder specification. Because you have to analyse the requirements very deeply, you are likely to find errors and omissions.

- Because the notations are formally defined, readers of a formal specification should all interpret the specification in the same way. There is less chance of specification ambiguity.

- Formal specifications may be analysed using mathematical methods and shown to be complete and free from inconsistencies.

- Formal specifications may serve as a basis for the proof of correctness of a system implementation. Some formal methods (such as the B method) are specially designed to help refine a formal software specification to 'correct' code. You can therefore be more confident that the system software is a correct implementation of the specification.

- As formal specification is widely regarded as an advanced and rigorous technique, its effective use demonstrates a commitment to the use of 'best practice' in product development. This can help protect an organisation against litigation in the event of product failure and may be helpful if product certification is required.

Implementation

Formal methods of system specification have been the subject of more than 20 years of research. They are now sufficiently well-developed that they can be used to specify small and medium-sized critical systems. Support and training has improved to the point where many computer science graduates have some exposure to formal specification; there are several consultancy companies which specialise in support for formal methods and some CASE tools for formal methods support are available.

Broadly speaking, formal specification methods fall into three categories namely algebraic methods, model based methods and process algebra based methods. We discuss these in more detail in Chapter 12. The details of these methods are not important at this stage. We think that the use of these formal techniques is most likely to show positive returns when applied to the development of systems which have stringent safety, reliability and security requirements. The development of formal specifications of system interfaces is particularly worthwhile.

Introducing formal specification techniques into an organisation is a long-term process. You may involve external consultants with experience in this area. Alternatively, some companies have employed an 'evangelist' who has some formal methods training and who is enthusiastic about the potential of formal methods in critical systems development.

The steps involved in introducing formal specifications are as follows.

1   *Assess your requirements for formal specification.* Sometimes, system procurers mandate that formal specifications and proofs must be used for safety-related systems.

If you are interested in bidding for this type of contract, you clearly need to implement this guideline.

2 *Assess your capabilities for using mathematical techniques.* You need to assess whether or not the background of your engineers is such that they would be willing to accept these techniques. This is particularly important for small organisations who may not be able to identify or employ formal methods specialists who have previous experience with these techniques.

3 *Choose the technique which is appropriate for the type of application which you develop.* There are several different techniques of formal specification and it is important to chose the best technique for your application domain. For example, in a real-time system, you may wish to use a process algebra approach; for an information management system, a model-based approach will probably be more appropriate.

4 *Identify a pilot project where the techniques may be used.* This helps you to find the problems of using formal specifications and it serves as a showcase for formal specification. If successful, you can use the pilot project results to convince people of the value of the technology. The pilot project that you select should be sufficiently large to be realistic but sufficiently small that the formal specification can be developed by a small team. It is important that the project customer is convinced of the value of using formal specification and that you are careful that the customer can understand the specification.

5 *Decide on the scope of the work.* This means deciding whether you will develop a formal specification of all or part of the system, whether or not you will try to develop proofs of consistency from the formal specification, etc. It is usually most economic to restrict formal specification to the most critical components. You should not consider advanced proofs and formal refinement until you have had experience with formal specification in several projects.

6 *Select and train staff for the pilot project.* You need to find staff for the pilot project who are inherently sympathetic to the concept of using formal methods·and who have the right background to assimilate the knowledge required. You will probably have to use some external consultants to provide the initial training for these staff. In subsequent projects, the members of the original team may form the nucleus of a specialist support team.

7   *Define assessment criteria.* Before you start the pilot project, you should define how you will judge the value of developing formal specifications. This may be based on qualitative assessment from the people involved, reduction in time required for system validation, etc. Be careful if you try to define the benefits as lower costs. You may find that initial development costs are higher in pilot projects because it takes time to learn how to use the methods cost-effectively.

8   *Carry out the pilot project.* When you carry out the project, you should keep careful records of the problems encountered and how these were overcome. Important issues which you must assess are the effects of developing formal specifications on the development schedule, making the transition from formal specifications to less formal design notations, and the need to integrate non-functional requirements with the formal specification. You will probably find it helpful to employ external consultants with formal methods expertise to assist with the project.

9   *Formally review the project results and plan the next stage of the process.* After the pilot project has been completed, you should formally review the results and decide whether or not to continue with the introduction of formal specification techniques.

We discuss the use of formal methods in more detail in Chapter 12. For information about formal methods experience, we recommend the article by Hall in the March 1996 issue of *IEEE Software* (Using Formal Methods to Develop an ATC Information System). This is an objective discussion of the benefits and problems of specifying part of a large air traffic control system using a formal language. Information about the REAIMS FRERE method which is concerned with integrating formal specification into the systems engineering process can be accessed from the book's WWW page.

Costs and problems

Introducing formal methods of system specification and verification is expensive. Many engineers still have little or no training in these methods and a comprehensive training programme must be developed. You may need to employ people who are formal methods specialists or bring in consultants who have worked in this area. It can take several years for formal specification techniques to be accepted in an organisation.

Formal system specifications are expensive to apply but they have been cost-effective in a number of projects. Formal specification led to higher confidence in the system which was developed without an overall increase in software development costs. There is some evidence that overall costs can actually be reduced. Most organisations which have persevered with formal methods have found them to be valuable but you must make a long-term commitment to this approach.

A major problem with the use of formal specifications is the fact that they may not be understandable by application and safety engineering experts. This means that they cannot analyse the specification from a safety perspective. Some people have suggested that the way round this problem is for the analyst to paraphrase the requirements and present them to these experts (see **Guideline 8.8**, *Paraphrase system models*). This is not really satisfactory, as the analyst is likely to paraphrase what he or she thinks is specified and to automatically compensate for any mistakes in the specification.

Reading and writing a formal specification are not the same thing. Training should not concentrate on the specification writers to the exclusion of those who must be able to read and understand the specification. For this reason, the training costs of introducing formal specification may be higher than initially expected.

Finally, you must expect the introduction of formal specification to skew the amount of resources required at different phases of the life-cycle. A 20% increase in specification costs can reasonably be expected. If the use of formal specification is successful, these should be at least offset by fewer faults and reduced rework costs. Once confidence in your application of formal specification has been gained from a number of projects, you may be able to reduce the effort needed for system testing.

10.7   Collect Incident Experience

Key benefit	Serves as an organisational memory which can support learning from experience
Costs of introduction	High
Costs of application	High
Guideline type	Advanced

Establish a system for collecting and maintaining information about safety/security/reliability-related incidents which have occurred in systems which you have delivered to customers. As well as incident information, you should also maintain information about how these incidents may be avoided in future.

Benefits

- Learning from experience is very important, particularly for critical systems. A database of incident experience exposes the mistakes made in previous systems and may be used to help reduce the chances of these mistakes recurring.

- An incident database may serve as a means of assessing requirements engineering process improvements. As the process is improved, fewer incidents should occur.

- Browsing the incident database is a good means of education. Newcomers to a project can discover what has gone wrong and why problems have occurred.

Implementation

To implement this guideline you need to have a process for collecting information about incidents and recording this incident information in a database. This will involve defining incident record forms and ensuring that these are filled in after each incident. Many organisations will already have this information for safety-related incidents as they conduct formal enquiries into why these incidents occurred. If you do not investigate incidents, setting up this investigation process is the first step in implementing this guideline.

An incident database should contain information about failures of previous systems and the possible causes of these failures. It should not just contain accident information but should include information about any failure related to the critical attributes of the system.

An incident database can be used in a number of different ways.

1 For training people who are involved in system specification. You can show how a different system specification could have avoided the incident.

2 As a general information facility which is used as a source of information during the requirements elicitation process. Therefore, you may document the source of a requirement as the incident database. You may design your requirements elicitation process so that you include checks of the incident database to find relevant information.

3 As a basis for developing rules and guidelines for system designers. As you learn about incidents, you may abstract information from the incident database to create design guidelines which would avoid a recurrence of the incident. We discuss this in the following guideline.

The type of database which you need depends on the type of product which you produce and the type of incident in which they are involved. For example, you may need to collect photographs of failed parts of systems, records of system state before and after the incident, etc. so will need a multi-media database to store incident information. Alternatively, you might have a much simpler text-based system where you simply describe incidents and their possible causes. This could be implemented using a simple hypertext system.

For each incident, you should collect at least the following information.

1 A description of the incident and when it happened.

2 A description of the environment where the incident occurred and the mode of use of the system at that time.

3 Suggestions regarding the cause of the incident. This may not be clear so you should be able to record a number of possible suggestions along with the evidence for each of them.

4 Suggestions of how the incident might be avoided in future. This does not necessarily depend on the reasons why the incident occurred. For example, problems with a door locking system might be circumvented by converting to a dual-locking system using different technologies and separate lock controllers.

5 Information about the costs and constraints associated with possible solutions to the problem.

To support these different uses of the incident database, you need complementary-based methods of retrieval from the incident database.

1 *Query-based retrieval.* It should be possible to discover incidents based on specify queries such as incidents thought to be caused by a particular type of failure, incidents which occurred on a particular version of a system, incidents which occurred in particular environments, etc. It is unlikely that the people using the database will be professional database programmers so you need to present this query system through some easy-to-use interface.

2 *Information browsing.* It should be possible for users of the incident database simply to browse the database, moving from one related information item to another. This means that the database must include explicit links from one entry to related data items.

The causes of an incident are sometimes not obvious and different people may have different opinions why an incident occurred. Ideally, your database should be able to capture these different opinions and to present what is thought to be the most likely cause of the incident. You must provide facilities to update and add information after it has been entered into the system.

Costs and problems

Introducing this guideline and setting up an incident database is expensive. The principal costs are as follows.

1   The costs of defining a procedure for systematically collecting and analysing incident data and including this data in the database. These include the costs of abstracting incident information from formal incident reports and, where appropriate, relating this to system requirements.

2. The costs of establishing an incident database. These include hardware and software costs and the costs of defining the database schema and user interface procedures for information retrieval.

As the database is likely to have a lifetime of many years, you will need to establish formal procedures for database management and administration. We recommend that someone should take responsibility for managing the incident database and associated rules and recommendations (See **Guideline 10.8**).

Once an incident database has been established, you will then have further costs in introducing its use into your requirements engineering process. This will involve some training costs to show people how to use the database. Critically, however, it will also involve the development of case study material which will illustrate the value of the incident database to those involved in the requirements engineering process. These will involve detailed analyses of incidents and demonstrations of how problems could have been avoided by modifications to the system requirements.

The main problem that you are likely to encounter is to ensure that the incident database is used effectively to inform the requirements engineering process. You cannot just leave it to individual initiative to consult the incident database. Rather, you need to design your requirements engineering processes so that the incident database is checked during these processes for relevant information. One way of doing this is covered in the next guideline.

You may also find it difficult to make quantitative financial arguments for incident information collection. In

10.8   Learn from Incident Experience

Key benefit	Avoids recurrence of previous errors
Costs of introduction	High
Costs of application	High
Guideline type	Advanced

Using collected incident information, you should cross-check the requirements against incident experience and the lessons learned from that experience. This will ensure that the requirements are specified so that the incident is not repeated and that requirements related to the incident have not been left out of the specification.

Benefits

- Checking requirements against incidents reduces the chances that previous requirements errors or omissions will be repeated. A natural consequence of staff turnover and promotion in organisations is that many of the people involved in a project have had little or no previous experience of similar systems. They may not be aware of previous problems or may forget about these problems.

- Demonstrating that the requirements have taken previous incidents into account may be an important part of the safety case for a system.

Implementation

Obviously, you need to implement an incident database before you can implement this requirement. However, it is not usually possible to use this directly for requirements checking. Checking takes too long as the database will contain a large volume of information. Furthermore, incident information may not be described in a way that is directly usable to check the system requirements.

We recommend that the information about each incident should be analysed and a set of rules and recommendations derived from the incident. These should also be stored in the database and should be linked to the incident description. If possible, an analysis of the incident in terms of requirements problems in the system where the incident occurred should also be included.

The rules and recommendations associated with each incident may do one of the following.

1 Define explicit checks which should be carried out on a set of requirements to ensure that the incident does not recur. In some cases, these may be expressed very precisely (e.g. as a mathematical formula), in others they will be vaguer descriptions of what to look for in the requirements.

2 Specify general requirements which should be applied in all systems which are similar to the system where the incident occurred. Obviously, these must be specialised for each system.

3 Specify particular requirements which define solutions that have been successfully applied in other systems. This is related to **Guideline 4.13**, *Reuse requirements*.

To ensure that these rules and recommendations are actually used to check the system requirements, you must establish a process which, firstly makes it easy for people to find relevant rules and recommendations and, secondly, gives engineers confidence that the rules and recommendations are correct and relevant to the type of system which they are developing.

To establish the set of rules and recommendations you should design a process with the following activities.

1 An incident analysis activity which classifies incidents and decides which aspects of these incidents are relevant for generating rules and recommendations.

2 A formulation activity where specific rules and recommendations to avoid a recurrence of the incident are formulated.

3 A checking activity where domain and safety experts

check the rules and recommendations to ensure that they do not introduce problems.

4 An improvement activity where existing rules and recommendations are continually improved as you obtain new experience on incidents and the use of the rules/recommendations.

To use the rules and recommendations to cross-check requirements you should design a process which include the following.

1 A rule/recommendation selection activity where the rules and recommendations which are likely to be applicable to the type of system which you are developing should be chosen. This is a question of judgement and the incident database manager should normally be involved in making the selection. Rules and recommendations are likely to be applicable when systems of the same type are being developed, where systems use common equipment and when similar system development techniques are being used.

2 A checking activity which looks at the recommended requirements, and ensures that either they are included in the requirements specification or that an explanation is given of why they have not been used.

3 A further checking activity which checks that the set of requirements conforms to the defined rules. As with the checking activity, this is a matter of engineering judgement.

4 A validation procedure which checks that the rules/recommendations have been followed and that any deviations have been documented.

This approach to learning from experience has been the basis of the development, in a large civil aerospace company, of a method called MERE. The MERE method is a systematic approach to the creation of design rules and guidelines from incident information. You can find out more about the MERE method from the REAIMS web pages whose URL is given in the Preface.

Costs and problems

There are significant costs involved in both introducing and applying the guideline. To introduce the guideline you need an incident database and you need to generate an initial set of rules and recommendations from the information in that database. Several months of effort should be allowed for this after the incident data is made available.

Additional effort is required over and above the normal requirements validation effort when this guideline is applied. This includes the effort to select appropriate rules and recommendations and the effort to apply these systematically to the requirements specification. However, one of the companies that has experimented with this technique estimated that it would have a positive return on its investment if it avoided a single mistake which had been made in previous systems.

The principal problem in applying the guideline is the difficulty of establishing and validating a useful set of rules and recommendations from incident data. This is a difficult and specialised task. You need to involve specialists from different disciplines and have a very extensive analysis process when a rule or recommendation is formulated. This is important because the consequences of having the wrong rule are potentially worse than the consequences of not having any rule at all.

10.9   Establish an Organisational Safety Culture

Key benefit	Everyone takes responsibility for system safety
Costs of introduction	High
Costs of application	None
Guideline type	Advanced

An organisational safety culture means that everyone in the organisation is aware of the importance of safety and feels that they have a responsibility for ensuring that the systems which are developed are safe. The guideline is equally applicable if security is your main concern.

Benefits

- If an organisation has a strong safety/security culture, everyone takes responsibility for avoiding, finding and removing system faults. Checking the safety/security implications of requirements and design decisions becomes second nature.

- A strong safety culture makes it easier to introduce process improvements aimed at improving the dependability of processes or products produced by the organisation.

Implementation

Introducing a safety culture normally involves changing the priorities of an organisation. Making such cultural changes in an organisation is difficult but not impossible. Large sections of European and US manufacturing industry have developed a 'quality culture' in response to competition from Asian manufacturers and we can draw on this experience to help develop a safety/security culture. Essential factors for cultural change appear to be the following.

1   Clear and explicit management commitment from all levels of management in the organisation. Everyone, from the most senior managers downwards, must participate and must be publicly involved in developing a safety culture.

2   Reporting procedures to senior management must be established which cut across normal hierarchies in the organisation. Anyone should be able to use these to report safety concerns. It must be possible for safety/ security concerns to be reported in a way that is not confrontational. Reporting must not threaten, in any way, the position of the people making the report. When problems are reported, they must be investigated and the results of the investigation fed back to the people making the report. If the concern is valid, action should be taken to address the problem.

3   The management of safety/security should be a defined organisational responsibility and named individuals should be allocated to this role. However, it is important to emphasise that this is a management rather than a development role. People involved in systems specification and development must take responsibility for safety/ security and should not think that they can leave this to other people.

4   An 'egoless' style of working should be established where errors are seen as team rather than individual responsibilities. The team must be empowered to introduce new ways of working which help reduce the number of errors which are made and which simplify the discovery and correction of errors. Individual personnel assessments should never be based on errors made, as this will lead to a culture where errors are concealed.

5   Good safety practice rather than productivity should be rewarded. Therefore, if someone reports a potential safety problem, they should be recognised for this, even when it results in additional costs for the organisation.

You will probably need to appoint a safety 'evangelist' whose job is to spread the safety message throughout the organisation. He or she is responsible for auditing for safety, disseminating information relevant to safety and arranging training courses for everyone (not just requirements engineers) involved in the requirements engineering process. It must be completely clear that the safety evangelist has senior management support and must have the autonomy to criticise practices in the organisation which may lead to safety problems.

Costs and problems

This is an unusual guideline as it cannot be related to process activities. The usual discussion of costs is therefore not really applicable. It is practically impossible to estimate the costs of cultural change. In organisations which are new to the development of safety-related systems or application domains where safety is becoming increasingly important, it takes some time (maybe several years) to introduce this requirement and to establish a safety culture. It may mean breaking down departmental barriers and people may have to discard traditional ideas about their own and other people's responsibilities. However, the establishment of a 'quality culture' in many organisations has demonstrated that cultural change is possible and worthwhile.

The question which should be asked, perhaps, is not 'how much will cultural change cost' but 'how much will it cost if we do not make this change'. This depends on the current market (will market share be lost) and the consequences and costs of an avoidable accident. Where an accident could threaten the survival of a company, then developing a safety culture is almost always worthwhile.

A major problem may be convincing senior management of the need for cultural change. Unless the organisation has had to cope with the publicity and costs arising from some high-profile incident involving its products, senior management may not appreciate that safety problems can arise in even the best managed and most technically competent organisations. The establishment of a safety culture is the best way to discover and eliminate these problems.

11 System Modelling with Structured Methods

Summary

This chapter describes the use of structured methods for system modelling. This is an intermediate level practice so it will be of most interest if you already use basic requirements practices. The purpose of system modelling is reviewed and the role of modelling different aspects of your system is described. We describe the most common system modelling techniques and illustrate them with examples. We also summarise how structured methods support system modelling by augmenting system modelling notations with heuristics and guidelines to help guide their use.

Contents

11.1 Background and Motivations.

11.2 Choosing Models and Methods.

11.3 Models.

11.4 Methods.

11.5 Further Information.

We use the term 'structured methods' to describe methods which seek to help develop system models in a systematic way through the use of guidelines and notations. Structured methods provide a vehicle for the analyst to explore some system aspects in some detail and to add clarity to the fuzzy picture provided by the stakeholder requirements, domain constraints, etc.

Structured methods, therefore, are concerned not only with imposing a structure on a vague notion of a system, but also with structuring the activity of developing system models. Without a structured method, the analyst must select and apply a number of techniques and notations in an *ad hoc* way. With a structured method, the analyst is provided with guidance on what system aspects to model, how to model the system aspects and the steps

	Principal modelling notations	
	Behavioural models	**Structural models**
Classical methods		
SADT	Hybrid Data-flow diagrams with control flow	
Ward-Mellor	Data-flow diagrams Control-flow diagrams Finite-state models	Entity-relationship diagrams
SSADM	Data-flow diagrams	Entity-relationship diagrams
Object-oriented methods		
Booch	Finite-state models Interaction diagrams (similar to event traces in OMT)	Object modelling diagrams
OMT	Data-flow diagrams Finite-state models Scenarios Event traces	Object modelling diagrams
OOA	Message passing models	Object modelling diagrams

Figure 11.1   Characteristics of popular structured methods

used to develop the models. This is what makes them methods rather than simply notations or techniques.

It will usually be worth investing in a structured method because it helps make the requirements process more deterministic than if *ad hoc* techniques are employed. Hence, the requirements process should become more repeatable across different projects as you gain experience and as procedures for developing system models are honed on different systems. This is not to imply that structured analysis methods de-skill the requirements process or that they always provide an optimal mix of techniques and procedures for a particular application domain. However, they remove some of the uncertainty and help to achieve a reasonable level of quality with a predictable resource requirement.

A distinction is sometimes made between the well-established methods based on top-down analysis (which we will call 'classical' methods) and the more recent object-oriented analysis methods. We consider them both to be examples of structured methods since they seek to model broadly the same system aspects. Structured methods are sometimes called semi-formal methods to distinguish them from formal specification methods. Although formal specification methods are also about developing system models, the purpose of these models is normally different. Formal specification methods are treated in more detail in Chapter 12.

Figure 11.1 summarises the main characteristics of some representative structured methods. Models and notations are discussed in Section 11.2. The remainder of this chapter introduces the principal themes of structured methods, shows what system models they support and shows how they are applied.

11.1   Background and Motivations

Structured analysis methods emerged during the mid-1970s from a variety of domains and disciplines. However, several have their roots in techniques developed for software design and many methods can be used for both system modelling (analysis) and design. Hence, for example, the same techniques can be used to model and understand the 'real world' of railway signalling as can be used to design a computer-based solution to a railway signalling problem.

This close relationship between design and analysis methods is symptomatic of the absence of a clear boundary between design and specification. This is not helped by the ambiguity of the phrase 'system modelling'. If 'system' is taken to mean the hardware/software 'product' which provides a solution to some engineering or information systems problem then system modelling implies modelling the design of the product. However, in requirements engineering, the 'system' is considered at a higher level as the real world context in which a particular solution may be installed. Here, we are not modelling a pure hardware/software product but the problem for which such a solution may be designed. This system will have a particular purpose which is independent of its implementation. For example, a railway signalling system can be computer-based or entirely electo-mechanical. Such a system will typically comprise humans, organisations, operating regulations, etc. It will have interfaces to other systems. Such systems are sometimes called 'socio-technical systems' to distinguish them from purely hardware/software products.

Not everything will be automated in a computer-based system. There will still be users and the system will be constrained by business or operating rules. The roles of some of non-automated system components may be changed by the introduction of the computer-based system. This is as true of critical systems, even critical embedded systems, as it is of information systems.

In a perfect world it would be possible to make a clean separation between modelling the problem and modelling the solution, since it is undesirable to prejudice the results of a requirements analysis by incorporating premature design decisions. In practice, however, design features are often imposed on systems. For example, constraints arising from the system's environmental context may impose a particular architecture. Where the problem is part of a systems engineering project, the requirements process typically includes partitioning the

problem space into sub-problems to be solved by hardware and software. This helps the project's feasibility and
costs to be assessed. It is clearly the first level of architectural design.

Another problem derives from the fact that many
projects are intended to replace existing computer-based
systems. Here, it is tempting to derive understanding of
the wider system by analysing the existing computer
system. Indeed, some methods advocate this. Although
this has the attraction of speeding the development of a
workable model (unless the existing system was a
complete failure), it makes it hard to develop a system
model which does not embody the shortcomings and
assumptions of the existing system design. You should
not make assumptions about the adequacy of the existing
system but should dig down into the characteristics of the
underlying problem. Even if the existing system works,
there may be better ways of doing things if the real
problem is properly understood. There are many examples where networks and cheap desktop workstations
have empowered users to perform their jobs more efficiently than was possible using mainframe technology.
Yet to analyse their requirements using a previous main-
frame-based solution as a guide would result in a very
distorted model of their socio-technical system.

The system model should avoid assumptions about
design solutions wherever possible, although this cannot
always this be rigorously achieved. However, most
methods provide guidelines and rules of thumb on how
to identify what to model and how to avoid prematurely
developing the model into a design. Nevertheless, achiev-
ing this balance is far from foolproof and some methods
are better than others at helping analysts achieve it.

11.2 Choosing Models and Methods

The aim of system modelling is to increase understanding
of the system and to clarify the requirements. Section
11.3 describes the modelling techniques used by different
methods. Section 11.4 briefly describes why a method is
more than simply a collection of modelling techniques. In

this section, we present some generic guidelines for choosing a method and applying it to your system.

- Select a method which supports modelling of crucial system aspects. For example, a method oriented towards information systems such as SSADM (Structured Systems Analysis and Design Methodology) would not be appropriate for a critical embedded system. Ensure that the method is acceptable to the customer, and is understandable by other members of the development team and key members of the customer organisation.

- Do not adopt a new method if it only offers marginal benefits over one for which substantial experience already exists. It is better to exploit analysts' previous experience than adopt a method which necessitates a long learning period. Of course, a new method may offer tangible benefits in terms of modelling crucial aspects or integration with other methods, and so may justify a change. If possible, build up experience with the method on relatively small or straightforward projects. Better still, evaluate the new method by applying the existing method in parallel.

- Model the crucial aspects to a level of detail which permits as full an understanding of the system and its requirements as possible. For example, in an embedded or distributed system, exhaustive dynamic modelling should be performed to ensure that interactions between the system and its environment are fully understood.

- For each aspect, ensure that the critical components of the system are modelled adequately. Of course, the critical components may only emerge during the course of the modelling. This rule therefore implies that system modelling should be employed, at least in part, to help identify the critical components.

- Be prepared to adopt other modelling techniques outside of the method if the method cannot be used to adequately model some system aspect or component. Recognise that not all system aspects can be modelled effectively (for example, real time and human computer interaction aspects are difficult to model) and that the semantics of structured methods are not completely defined. It may therefore be useful to employ other techniques or methods to supplement the models developed using a structured method. For example, formal specification methods may be selectively employed to increase understanding of critical components.

- Verify that the system model is consistent, not only with the stakeholders' requirements, but also with the results of any special analysis which has been performed. For example, a hazard analysis might identify that operator overload as a hazard. You should ensure that the system model incorporates a means to regulate the flow of information.

11.3   Models

Before looking at individual structured methods it is useful to characterise the kinds of models which may be used for analysing systems. Whichever model are developed, their role is to clarify the system requirements by, for example, showing the system's context within its environment, how data is manipulated to satisfy functional requirements or how events from the environment control the processing of data.

These are all aspects which cannot be fully understood from the raw stakeholder requirements. In a typical system, most users are not outside the system boundary but are part of the system. Hence the system cannot be viewed as a black box which simply services their needs. To understand the stakeholders' requirements, you must understand their context within the whole system, their roles, the nature of the data they manipulate, and the organisational or environmental constraints which have shaped their requirements. This understanding can be helped by modelling the system to see how all the various requirements' sources fit within the grand scheme of things and to understand their underlying purpose.

Even where the analyst can apply previously acquired domain knowledge, the construction of a system model will not normally be possible from the basic customer requirements. There will be gaps in the information, domain context will be hidden or absent and development of the model may reveal poor or unrealisable requirements. Development of the system model is therefore an iterative process requiring the analyst to seek clarification from the stakeholders. System modelling is closely coupled to requirements elicitation. Typically, the overall system requirements or statement of need will be necessary for system modelling to begin. Once these have been established it can then proceed in parallel with elicitation of detailed requirements. This helps to stimulate the search for these requirements. For example, given a statement of overall needs by an organisation's management, the analyst will typically start to model the system while also conducting interviews with users, investigating the domain, etc. This will help to clarify unclear aspects of the system and to ensure that all stakeholders' requirements are consistent with the model.

The system model therefore has a dual role. Not only is it used to clarify the analyst's understanding of the problem, but it should also help verify this by making the analyst's assumptions understandable by the customer. If the system model reveals weaknesses in the real world system, or incompatibilities between requirements and the system, it can be used by the analyst to argue for changes to the requirements.

There is an overlap between system modelling and viewpoint analysis (see chapter 13). Some structured methods recommend the development of different system models from different users' viewpoints which are then integrated into an overall system model. In addition, the different system aspects which the models (functional, dynamic, structural, etc.) aim to clarify may also be considered as viewpoints. This is reflected in recent work such as the ISO* draft standard for developing open distributed processing (ODP) systems which recommends analysis from five viewpoints corresponding to crucial system aspects. Despite the overlap between viewpoint-based analysis and system modelling, few methods

---

*See the article Cross-viewpoint Consistency in Open Distributed Processing by Howard Bowman *et al.* in the January 1996 issue of the *Software Engineering Journal.*

provide explicit guidance on how the two techniques or different viewpoint models can be integrated and applied systematically. Only CORE (which combines viewpoints with the construction of data-flow models) currently provides this integration.

As the system model is developed, more requirements will be discovered. These are sometimes called 'emergent requirements' since their existence only emerges from analysis of the problem. Emergent requirements can be crucial and often reveal constraints which underlie the stakeholder requirements. For example, analysis of a train control system where there is a requirement for emergency braking to prevent overshooting a signal will reveal that train speed, location information and signal state data must all be available in real time. These requirements may themselves impose further requirements on the sampling rate, communication mechanisms used, etc.

Various models which can be constructed have varying levels of usefulness. For example, with an embedded real-time system it is important to model control aspects. In contrast, with a transaction management system this may be less important than modelling the structure of the data to be manipulated. Both systems may benefit from both types of model but the relative importance of the different aspects differs. Hence, for critical systems, it is essential to address those aspects which reflect the critical requirements by developing the models appropriate for the domain and to the appropriate level of detail. This implies the selection of a method which supports the most helpful modelling techniques.

However, we do not advocate selection of system modelling methods on a per-project basis according to which method offers marginal benefits over another. It is much better to acquire experience with one method which strikes a good balance for a particular domain. This will be cheaper, since a new method will be expensive to acquire and train staff for. Furthermore, experienced staff will produce results more quickly using a familiar method.

The kinds of models typically supported by structured methods fall into two broad categories: behavioural and

An en-route (i.e. no landing or take-off is involved) air traffic control (ATC) system is required.

S1 The ATC system shall control a single sector of airspace (the problems of transitions between the sector and adjacent sectors are ignored).
S2 Flight plans for aircraft shall be posted in advance of the aircraft arriving at the sector of airspace under the ATC system's control. These flight plans provide static information such as the aircraft's call sign and dynamic information such as the projected time of arrival/departure at/from the sector, the aircraft's expected altitude, speed and heading. These are dynamic because circumstances may cause these planned flight parameters to change: the aircraft may arrive late due to a strong head wind; the presence of other aircraft may necessitate a change of altitude; etc.
S3 The aircraft's actual position and altitude within the sector shall be provided by an existing radar system. This is a primitive radar system which cannot calculate speed or heading.
S4 The facility shall exist whereby an aircraft can be instructed to change one of its flight parameters in order to optimise management of the airspace.
S5 The facility shall exist whereby an aircraft can request permission to change one of its flight parameters (e.g. a request to fly higher to save fuel).
S6 When an aircraft exits the sector a record of the flight parameters shall be archived for audit purposes.
S6 The ATC system shall be under the overall control of a human air traffic controller.

Figure 11.2 ATC system requirements

structural models. In Sections 11.3.1 and 11.3.2 we look at these two types of model in turn. In Section 11.3.3 we describe the use of data dictionaries in developing the models.

To illustrate the models described in the following sections, we use a very simplified example of an air-traffic control system described in Figure 11.2.

Note that this summary of the basic user needs leaves scope for many different design solutions. For example, although under the overall control of an air traffic controller, some functions such as predicting conflicts from converging flight paths could be automated or left as manual tasks. Hence, when initially modelling the system, we should try to avoid making design assumptions about these functions. However, the model may be used to present such possible alternatives to the client to clarify the requirements.

11.3.1 Behavioural models

This is a broad category and the word 'behaviour' is heavily overloaded. We mean all process aspects of a system. This includes the functional transformation of data and models of system dynamic behaviour. We describe these below under the headings functional and dynamic models.

Functional models

In broad terms there are two commonly used means of modelling the functional transformation of data. In the first, the data is considered to flow between functional processing elements; this is the model supported by classical methods and is usually represented as a data-flow diagram (DFD). In the second which is usually adopted by object-oriented methods, an entity in the domain is modelled as an object which has functions (variously called operations or methods) associated which can be invoked to render services and manipulate the object.

Figure 11.3 illustrates a DFD diagram model of the ATC system. Figure 11.3 is derived from the context diagram in Figure 11.13 which we discuss later.

There are many flavours of DFDs and the notations vary. However, they all share the basic concepts. In Figure 11.3 the squares represent entities in the ATC system's environment and arrows entering the squares indicate data output from the ATC system to the environment and data leaving the squares indicates data input from the environment to the ATC system. These form the interface to the ATC system. Hence there are three elements modelled in the environment: *Planning* where flight plans are logged and agreed; *Radar* which passes the ATC system raw radar signals; and *Aircraft* representing any aircraft within the sector controlled by the ATC system.

Everything excluding the external entities in Figure 11.3 is part of the ATC system itself. The round nodes are functional transforms and represent logical processes within the problem domain. These may or may not have concrete design analogues in a design solution for the

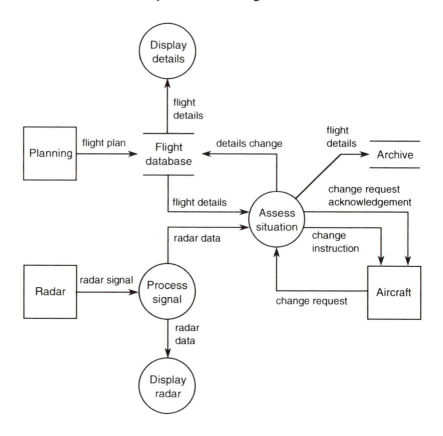

Figure 11.3 Data-flow diagram of ATC system

ATC system. In Figure 11.3 the ATC problem has been decomposed to four functional components: processing the radar signal, displaying the radar information,; displaying the flight details and assessing the general situation (the actual control of the airspace).

Data storage elements are represented as parallel horizontal lines. The need for two data stores has been identified: a flight database where information is held while it is 'current', and an archive where it is saved when it is no longer current. As with the functional transforms, data stores may or may not have design analogues. For example, the flight database and the archive might be a single component in a design solution but they have logically different roles in the problem. Note also that the name *flight database* implies nothing about the use of a particular database technology; it could even be a paper-based system. Data is exchanged internally by functional transforms and data stores just as it is between the ATC system and its environment.

The functional transforms could be further decomposed. For example, *Assess situation* could be decomposed into sub-processes including those for logging and assessing aircrafts' requests to change their flight parameters. The decomposition of a system into functional transforms, data flows and data stores reveals information about the nature of the problem. For example, Figure 11.3 corresponds to the first cut at analysing the system, but has already clarified that a flight database is needed to maintain the dynamic information about aircraft flight parameters. This is the real value of developing system models, because such emergent properties may otherwise remain implicit. Other models (see below) will reveal other useful information about different aspects of the system.

A functional system model can be decomposed to arbitrary depth. However, at some point, the model will cease to be a useful abstraction of the problem. Decomposition of a DFD should be performed only where it aids understanding to the problem and should stop before we have to start adding design detail. For example, after one or two further levels of decomposition of the *Assess situation* function, we might have to decide which control functions to automate and which to leave as manual tasks. Unless there were explicit requirements to automate some tasks, this would be the point where requirements become designs.

Top-down functional decomposition and DFDs form the core of all the classical structured methods. These were the first structured methods to be developed and are still widely used in industry. They are also used by some object-oriented methods; for example OMT (Object Modelling Technique) recommends the use of DFDs for constructing the functional model during the analysis process. In OMT, the data flows correspond to objects or object attributes and the functional entities are the operations bound to the objects. Other object-oriented methods such as OOA (Object-Oriented Analysis) dispense with

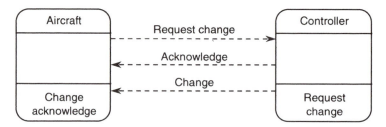

Figure 11.4 Message-passing between two objects in ATC System

DFDs and construct a functional model around a pattern of inter-object message-passing. Figure 11.4 illustrates two objects identified by an object-oriented analysis of the ATC problem (this is described further below): *controller* and *aircraft*. As with DFDs, the notation used by different methods differs. In Figure 11.4 objects are represented by round-edged rectangles and the functions which provide the objects' services are listed at the bottom of the rectangles. The fact that one object invokes a service offered by another is indicated by a dashed line connecting the two objects; the target of the arrow is the object which is having a function invoked by the source of the arrow.

Although the natures of their functional models differ, the various object-oriented methods suggest that the development of the functional model should follow development of models of the objects in the domain, their logical interrelationships, their classifications and their data attributes. Object-oriented methods orient the analysis around what is actually in the domain (the objects), whereas classical methods orient the analysis around the functions of the system.

Dynamic models

Early structured analysis techniques concentrated on developing functional and data models of the system. However, when they are applied to embedded systems it is obvious that the absence of a means to capture systems' dynamic aspects (such as the sequencing of events) is a serious weakness.

This shortcoming has been addressed by several structured methods including SADT (Structured Analysis and Design Technique) and Ward-Mellor. The essence of these methods is that data flows modelled by DFDs are augmented with control flows. These are modelled as control signals emanating from separate control transforms or from the functional transform of the DFD. They may appear on the DFD itself, or on a separate diagram which omits the data flows but preserves the functional transforms.

In the ATC system, for example, it is useful to model the approach towards, and exit from, the sector of airspace by aircraft. These are environmental events which determine when it is appropriate to display aircraft flight parameters and when it is appropriate to archive them. This is modelled in Figure 11.5 where the DFD from Figure 11.3 has been augmented with a control transform called *Sector status*. This represents a model of the state of the sector. Control signals (dashed arrows) from this indicate signals to the *Assess situation* function when an aircraft is approaching or exiting the sector. Similarly, a control signal indicates to the *Display details* function when an aircraft exits the sector. In addition, a control signal flows from *Assess situation* to *Display details* to permit the former to control when aircraft details are to be displayed.

Control flow diagrams like Figure 11.5 are insufficient in themselves to model control; they model the flow of control but not how the system reacts to the control. Several methods which support the modelling of control also recommend that a finite state model is developed. The finite state model describes the system's dynamic behaviour as a set of states and control event-driven transitions between states.

Figure 11.6 illustrates a simple state transition diagram used to model the control of an aircraft corresponding to the control flows in Figure 11.5. Where a control event is related to the activation of a function, the name of the functional transform from the DFD is listed beneath the label of the event. For example, the control event *aircraft approaching* enables the function *Assess situation*.

Taken together, Figures 11.5 and 11.6 specify that the decision when to display an aircraft is under the control

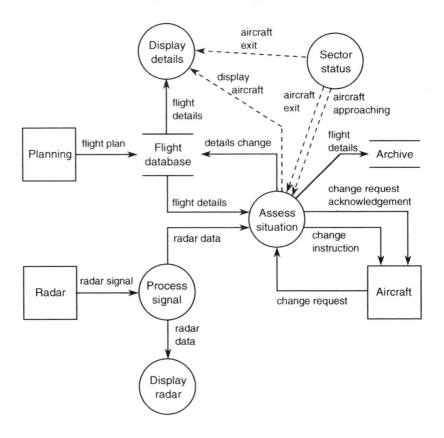

Figure 11.5 ATC DFD augmented with control flow information

of the controller (human or otherwise). This permits a range of options for aircraft display. We use an *aircraft approaching* control event rather than an *aircraft arrival* event to permit an aircraft to be displayed in advance of its arrival in the sector. This reflects the real world of air traffic control where controllers frequently need to plan the arrival of aircraft in advance of their actual arrival. Hence, we have taken care to model the air traffic control system rather than a possible air traffic control design product.

The same or similar techniques for developing dynamic models are commonly employed by object-oriented methods. For example, OMT recommends developing *scenarios* (**Guideline 4.11**, *Use scenarios to elicit require-*

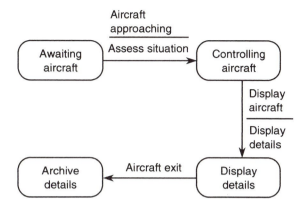

Figure 11.6 Simple state transition diagram model of state of aircraft control in the ATC system

ments) where events in the system's environment are mapped onto desired system behaviour. Inter-object events are identified to react to and process the environment events and traces of these are developed showing how the different objects in the system handle the sequence of events. These different scenarios and associated event traces are eventually fused and developed into finite state models. In OMT the functional model is developed after the dynamic model. Booch's method for object-oriented analysis and design employs similar models.

There is a variety of powerful notations for modelling system dynamic aspects. For example, Statecharts are more expressive than the various flavours of state transition diagrams and can be used for modelling systems with concurrent states, broadcast, events, etc. Similarly, Petri nets can be employed for systems where concurrency is a crucial aspect.

Finally, some methods advocate further refinement of the behavioural models by the development of *minispecs* or *process specifications*. These are often pseudo-code procedural descriptions of the functional behaviour. Each functional transform in a DFD has an algorithmic description of how events control the processing of data flows. These descriptions must be consistent with the other models and are couched in terms of the functions, control

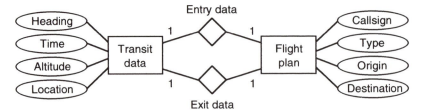

Figure 11.7   E-R model of flight plan data in ATC system

events, data objects, etc., already identified. It is also crucial that they do not introduce implementation constructs or otherwise influence design decisions. It is tempting to start writing code for clarity but to end up imposing a design model.

11.3.2 Structural models

Although behavioural models describe the process aspects of a system, structural models describe the structure of entities in the system. As described above, classical methods orient the analysis around the functional model. This means that structural models are typically developed following the functional decomposition of the system into functional transforms and data flows. The structural model is then confined to modelling the structure of the data manipulated by the functional transforms.

The most common way to model data is to use the Entity-Relationship (E-R) approach usually associated with logical database design. A simple example of data modelling is shown in Figure 11.7 where the flight plan data from Figure 11.3 is modelled using an E-R diagram. This shows that a flight plan is modelled as the entity *flight plan*. It is composed of four primitive attributes: *callsign* (e.g. BA1234) and *type* (e.g. Airbus A319), *origin* (e.g. Toulouse) and *destination* (e.g. Manchester). In addition, eight other components comprise the flight plan data which are modelled using the relationships *entry data* and *exit data*. These are both one to one relationships with instances of the entity *transit data*. One models the aircraft's predicted altitude, heading, location and time on entry to the sector, and one models the same attributes on exit from the sector.

In contrast to classical methods where the data model is an adjunct to the functional model, development of the structural model is the central activity with object-oriented methods. In this case, the structural model is the object model. Here, the system and its environment are analysed to identify the real-world entities or actors in the domain. These are the objects. For example, in the ATC system we might identify aircraft, radar, the controller and the sector.

In addition, it is useful to identify logical entities which do not necessarily have a physical analogue but which nevertheless exist as part of the problem. For example, flight plans are identified in the statement of user requirements so this is also a candidate for being modelled as an object. As with identifying functional transforms in a DFD, there is no way to guarantee the identification of the correct set of objects. An object model normally undergoes a number of iterations until a satisfactory model is derived.

Object modelling contrasts with the DFD-based model. In a DFD model we do not attempt to model the entities in the real world directly, but model the logical functions and their data inputs and outputs. An object model is an explicit description of the real entities in the domain. Development of a DFD is a top-down activity where the system's overall function is iteratively decomposed into sub-functions and their interfaces. Object modelling is bottom-up where objects are described and then composed into systems.

Once the objects have been identified, they are classified into object classes. An object class is essentially an object template. It is easier to deal with classes than objects because, for example, it saves having to worry about whether there is one or several similar objects. In addition, many methods support inheritance to permit specialisation/generalisation relationships between object classes which share characteristics. For example, if in the ATC problem there was a variation in the way that civil and military aircraft were handled, then it could be useful to model a generic class *aircraft* with two specialisations; *military* and *civil* aircraft. The jury is still out on the practical utility of inheritance for system modelling

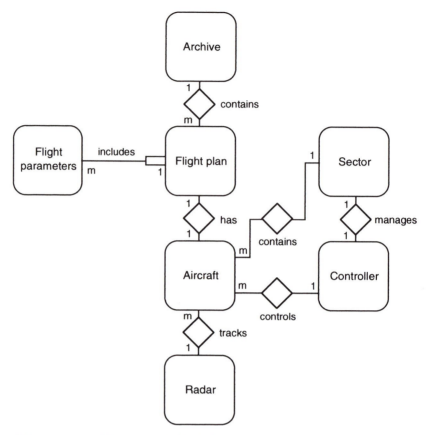

Figure 11.8   Object model of ATC system

but it is supported by most of the commercially successful methods.

Once the object classes have been identified, they are
analysed to identify logical relationships between them.
For example, in the ATC system, there is a one to one relationship between aircraft and flight plans. Similarly, there
is a one to many relationship between the sector and
aircraft. Figure 11.8 illustrates an object model of the ATC
system. As usual, methods differ and there are many
variants on notations used to describe object models. The
one used in Figure 11.8 is an amalgam of some of the most
popular. The object classes in the system are represented
by named rounded rectangles (as in Figure 11.4) and they
are connected to other classes with which they have a
logical relationship. For example, *Archive* has a one to

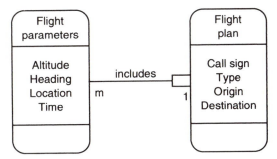

Figure 11.9   Attributes for Flight parameters and Flight plan

many *contains* association with *Flight plan*. *Flight plan* itself is a composite class and has a one to many aggregation relationship with *Flight parameters* called *includes*.

Following identification of the object classes and their relationships, further detail is fleshed out by identifying the attributes which constitute the state of the objects. Figure 11.9 lists the attributes of the classes *Flight plan* and *Flight parameters*.

The object model partially described in Figures 11.8 and 11.9 is a model of the actual and logical objects in the ATC system in the same way that Figure 11.3 is a model of its actual and logical functions. The object model, however, is only loosely related to the data models used to model the structure of the data forming the input and outputs to functions in the DFD. This is because of the fundamental differences in the basis of abstraction employed by the different schools of system modelling. The object model does not explicitly distinguish between the ATC system itself and its environment. Although the DFD in Figure 11.3 makes explicit that some things are fixed and part of the environment, the object model includes these in the general model. This necessitates the definition of the system boundary at a later stage in the analysis. This contrasts with classical methods where the system context is one of the first things to be defined.

11.3.3 Data dictionaries and other modelling techniques

When developing system models it is good practice to follow a number of common-sense rules to help their consistency and clarity. An obvious one is that the models should be reviewed to ensure their mutual consistency. The likelihood is that the models will undergo a number of iterations as:

- the analyst's understanding of the system evolves

- the customer's understanding changes in the light of what the analyst discovers from the models

- the models undergo a process of 'normalisation' (to eliminate redundant components, for example).

Other important rules are that meaningful names should be given to entities in the models and that the names should be unique. However, these measures alone are not enough to make the model understandable. The models may also grow so large that analysts are unable to maintain a complete mental picture of the system. To alleviate this problem, you need a key to the purpose and meanings of all the principal entities in the models. Data dictionaries are used to provide such a key. It is obviously necessary to maintain consistency between the

Name	Data flows Generated by	Used by	Description
flight details	Flight database	Display details Assess situation Archive	Flight parameters for an aircraft. Initialised as flight plan data but updated to reflect the actual status of the aircraft during its passage through the sector. In addition to the parameters relating to the aircraft's arrival and exit at/from the sector, another set of parameters is used to represent its real-time status when within the sector.
flight plan	Planning	Flight database	Flight parameters for an aircraft's expected passage through the sector as planned in advance of take-off.

Figure 11.10 Data dictionary for DFD model of ATC system

Requirement	Requirement source	Allocated to	Verification method
S1	Top-level statement of requirements (document XYZ)	Display details (Dd1) Flight database (Fd1) Assess situation (As1) Process signal (Ps1) Display radar (Dr1) Archive (A1)	Test (Test plan T1)
S2	Top-level statement of requirements (document XYZ)	Flight database (Fd1) Assess situation (As1)	Test (Test plan T1)

Figure 11.11 Tracing requirements and model components

models and model components, between the models and the data dictionary and between the models and the user requirements.

A data dictionary (**Guideline 7.5**, *Use a data dictionary*) is an ordered list of all the data items or objects used in a model with a textual description of their type and purpose. The aim is that, together, the data dictionary and system models should help readers to understand the system, and verify that the system models are consistent with the user requirements. Data dictionaries are used by both classical and object-oriented methods. Figure 11.10 illustrates a portion of a data dictionary for the DFD-based model of the ATC system.

Similar tabular techniques can also be used to manage traceability (**Guideline 9.3**, *Define traceability policies*). For example, the identifiers of requirements can be tabulated against the individual model components which address them. Other information such as requirement sources and specifications of their means of verification can also be provided. Figure 11.11 illustrates a portion of a requirements traceability table where the requirements S1 and S2 correspond to those numbered and listed at the end of Section 11.2. The table shows how the requirements 'flow down' to the DFD model components in Figure 11.3 which address them. We have numbered the latter so that for every level to which the DFD is decom-

Model type or technique	System aspect mainly addressed	Description
Data-flow diagrams	Behavioural	Model system as a directed graph of functional transformations of data.
Message passing	Behavioural	Functional models of how objects exchange messages to invoke services.
Control-flow diagrams	Behavioural	Model relationships between environmental events and flow of control.
Finite state models	Behavioural	Model system states and functional processing in response to events.
Mini specs/process specs.	Behavioural	Algorithmic descriptions of functional and dynamic behaviour.
Entity-relationship diagrams	Structural	Models of the data manipulated by functional transformations.
Object models	Structural	Models of the real entities in the domain in terms of their classification, structural relationships, state properties and functional properties.
Scenarios and event traces	Behavioural	Models of events and their processing by system objects.
Data dictionaries	–	Natural language descriptions of the components of all the models.
Tracing tables	–	Map requirements to model components in order to allow requirements to be traced to the functions or objects, etc. which address them.

Figure 11.12   Summary of modelling techniques

posed, corresponding entries can be made in the traceability table.

The system modelling techniques described in this section represent only a subset of those employed for requirements engineering. They are summarised in Figure 11.12. We have described them because they are representative of the two dominant system modelling paradigms: the classical functional decomposition approach based on DFDs and the object-oriented approach.

11.4 Methods

The previous section described the modelling techniques used by the most popular types of structured method. In this section we shift our attention from models to methods. First we examine methods' 'added value'; the additional guidelines and heuristics which make it worth employing a defined method rather than simply an *ad-hoc* collection of modelling techniques. We then look at the rationale for the various types of structured method, concentrating on the relative merits of classical and object-oriented methods.

11.4.1 Method added value

As different methods are similar and as their modelling techniques are well known, why should an organisation invest in adopting a particular method? There are several reasons.

- An established method has a considerable body of experience available through text-books, training courses, tool vendors, user groups and consultancies. Although the method may not be optimal for a particular application, this will be offset by the reduction of risk and uncertainty.

- CASE tools will be available which are tailored to the method. Tool support is essential for managing large system models. A tool should provide graphical editors for the method's modelling notations, on-line data dictionaries and report generators. In addition, they may include on-line help, version management, interfaces to other (e.g. design) tools and even animation facilities.

- The method will include a set of rules and heuristics to guide the application of these notations. This is the essence of the difference between a method and a collection of modelling techniques. These guidelines provide practical advice on (e.g.) what models to develop, the procedure for developing the models, guidance on how to identify the model components, how to refine a model, to what level of detail a model should be developed and how different models should be integrated. Effective application of modelling techniques will be much harder and more error-prone without these guidelines.

Many structured methods also support other life-cycle phases such as specification and design. Hence, guidelines for system modelling may form only a small component of the overall method. This has the advantage that the transition from analysis to design can be easier if the method supports both activities. Where this is supported, the method should provide clear guidelines on how to separate the two activities.

Many rules and guidelines are common to several methods. Probably the most universal one is the need to model the system's environment (**Guideline 7.2**, *Model the system's environment*). This is to partition what constitutes the system – and hence the problem for which a solution product is required – from everything else which is fixed but with which the system has an interface.

Classical methods advocate the development of a *context diagram*. This is a DFD where the system is represented as a single functional transform intended to represent the top-level, overall function of the system. Surrounding this are the fixed entities in the environment, the system's context. Data inputs and outputs to/from the system are represented as data-flows between the system and the environment entities. Figure 11.13 illustrates the context diagram for the ATC system.

Figure 11.13 is the same as Figure 11.3 except that all the system components have been collapsed into the

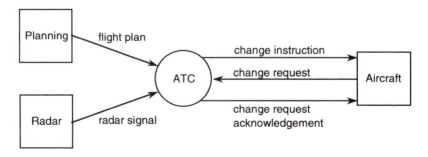

Figure 11.13   Context diagram for ATC system

single functional transform labelled *ATC*. The environment entities and, most importantly, the data flows into
and out of the system are exactly the same. The context
diagram is hence the most abstract view of the functional
model of the system. The system functional transform
forms the starting point of the top-down analysis; it is the
root of a hierarchy of DFDs each preserving the input and
output data flows from the level above.

Figure 11.3 illustrates the second stage; the explosion
of ATC into the component functions and data stores and
the data flows between them with the system inputs and
outputs are preserved. Each of the functional transforms
in Figure 11.3 may themselves be exploded into a new
DFD to reveal more detail. The level to which this iterative decomposition of the system should be performed
varies according to the complexity of the system. It
should always be constrained by the need for the model
to remain an objective abstraction of the system rather
than a design.

Partitioning of the system and its environment is also
necessary for object-oriented analysis. All the objects in
the domain and their relationships are explicitly identified as illustrated in Figure 11.8. The system partition
may only emerge once the object model is complete.
Objects are not usually iteratively decomposed in the
same way as functional transforms. Instead, you refine
the structure of the model by identifying new logical
objects, eliminating objects which have no role relevant to
the system or by fusing redundant objects into inheritance
hierarchies. It is normal for an object model to require
several iterations to achieve a satisfactory structure. This
should capture the nature of the problem domain and
permit a clean partitioning of the system from the environment. For example, the object model in Figure 11.8
requires further refinement before this partition is as clear
as it is in Figure 11.3.

Besides requiring a clear definition of the system
boundary, the rules which apply to classical and object-
oriented methods vary significantly. Even methods of the
same school vary. This is particularly true of object-
oriented methods where there is still no consensus on
object model components such as inheritance.

All methods, however will provide a process guide to applying the method. For example, OMT divides system modelling into 3 steps: object modelling; dynamic modelling; and functional modelling. Each of these steps is composed of a number of detailed steps. For example the first five steps recommended for object modelling are:

- object identification

- preparation of data dictionary

- identification of object relationships

- identification of attributes

- structuring object classes with inheritance

Within each of these activities, advice is provided on how to perform them and how to apply the various notations comprising the method. OMT provides advice on how to collate an initial list of candidate object classes and a set of rules on how to remove classes which are inappropriate or which are not true object classes at all. OMT is a design method as well as a requirements method and the guidance for system modelling is just one part of the method.

Structured methods are not fool-proof and skill and experience are needed to apply them successfully. The documentation on a particular method may run into many volumes. Many training and consultancy companies make a living by providing pathways through structured methods and their layers of rules, advice and recommendations. It is expensive for an organisation to acquire expertise with a structured method. The choice of which method to invest in should be considered carefully according to the method's domain suitability, its maturity, the availability of trained staff and the preferences or requirements imposed by customers.

11.4.2 Models and methods

As described in Section 11.3, most of the mature, commonly applied structured methods can be characterised as either 'classical', based on top-down functional decomposition, or object-oriented. Of these, the classical methods have the longest history. These are very widely employed in industry for all kinds of application domains. Recently, however, object-oriented methods have started to make inroads into the structured methods market.

As noted in Chapter 7, we have doubts about some of the claims made for object-oriented methods over others. Proponents of object-oriented analysis claim that it is closer to natural human problem-solving techniques. These can be crudely characterised by the three steps identify, classify and refine. It is unclear, however, whether this is actually true or whether the top-down decomposition 'divide and conquer' approach is not equally natural. The top-down approach evolved from proven techniques used in systems engineering, while object-oriented methods seem to have followed the rise of object-oriented programming languages. We are suspicious that some of the stimulus for object-oriented methods is driven by implementation issues rather than by the problems of understanding complex systems.

This does not mean that object-oriented methods may not genuinely prove better in practice. It is undoubtedly true that they build upon what has proven to be good practice in design and implementation. In contrast to classical methods' basis in procedural abstraction, object-oriented methods are based on data abstraction, which has proven to be a powerful weapon for managing program complexity. In applying data abstraction to system modelling, objects in the domain are treated as opaque entities with state, relationships to other objects and behaviour. Building the functional model follows building the object model. The functions form the interfaces between different objects which permit and control access to the attributes. This makes object-oriented models resilient to changing requirements, because the fundamental objects comprising the problem space are less likely to change. Changing functional requirements cause greater disruption to a DFD-based model than to an object-oriented model where they can be localised to a small number of object classes. This is an important consideration given the normal volatility of user requirements.

This view is reinforced by respected industry observers such as Ed Yourdon (who has been influential in the development of both classical and object-oriented methods). They see object-orientation as a 'killer technology' which will pervade the entire systems life-cycle. The transition from analysis to design to implementation is certainly likely to benefit if a coherent object-oriented strategy using (say) OMT and C++ is adopted. This does not, however, answer the question of whether object-oriented methods help construct system models.

At the time of writing object-oriented methods are still evolving. Some of the industry's major players are attempting to develop a coherent method based on a fusion of several different methods. However, classical methods will be here for many years yet, not least because of their large user base. They should not be dismissed simply because of the publicity surrounding object-oriented methods.

Most of the methods or method types described so far, while perhaps not being universally applicable, are broadly general-purpose in that they can be effectively used in a variety of domains. There are also a number of methods oriented towards specialist domains. For example, SDL is widely used in the telecommunications domain.

Finally, there are a number of methods which have emerged from outside the systems, software and requirements engineering communities. Systems science is a discipline in its own right and it has fostered a number of methods (e.g. Soft Systems Methodology) which can be applied to computer-based systems. These generally take the view that most non-trivial systems are too complex to be adequately understood by decomposing them into their constituent parts such as functions or objects. Describing the modelling techniques adopted by such methods is beyond the scope of this book. However, in some domains, neither classical nor object-oriented methods have a particularly good record of success. A characteristic of such domains seems to be that the human, organisational and social aspects are particularly crucial to an understanding of the system. It may be worthwhile investigating the use of methods with a more human/organisa-

	Typical application domain
Classical methods	
SADT	Embedded systems
Ward-Mellor	Embedded systems
SSADM	Information systems
Object-oriented methods	
Booch	Embedded systems
OMT	Embedded systems Information systems
OOA	Information systems

Figure 11.14 Summary of methods and their main application domains

tional orientation if the domain is one with a history of failed attempts at automation.

Typical application domains for the methods summarised at the start of this Chapter are listed in Figure 11.14. We characterise these as either embedded systems or information systems. Embedded systems are characterised by the need to react to events in their environment. Methods which can model these and their effect on system states explicitly are of most help here. With information systems, the structure of the system and the data it manipulates are typically the crucial aspects to model. Note, however, that methods are often used in for which they were not designed. In general, methods can be used outside their intended application domains. However, the user of the method should be prepared to augment the models supported by the method by others appropriate to the application.

11.5   Further Information

Good overviews of the use of structured methods and system modelling are provided by the books by Davis and Wieringa listed at the end of Chapter 1.

For a good description of a data-flow diagram based method, we recommend

Yourdon, E., 1989, *Modern Structured Analysis.* Prentice-Hall.

For a good description of an object-oriented method, we recommend

Rumbaugh, J., Blaha, M., Premerlani, W., Eddy, F., Lorensen, W., 1991, *Object-Orinted Modelling and Design.* Prentice-Hall.

Finally, an important contribution to modelling systems with a human and organisational perspective is provided by

Checkland, P., 1981, *System Thinking, Systems Practice.* Wiley.

12 Formal Specification

Summary

This chapter discusses the pros and cons of formal specification techniques. It should be read if you are considering adopting this approach for critical systems specification. This is an advanced practice, so as a minimum you should already be using intermediate level practices. The chapter is designed to clarify the current arguments for and against formal specification by helping you assess whether it offers significant advantages. This is dependent not only on technical issues such as provability or expressiveness but also on economic, standards and procurement issues. All these issues are discussed and a brief example in Z is provided at the end to illustrate the role of formal reasoning.

Contents

12.1   Why Formalise?

12.2   Definitions and life-cycle Issues.

12.3   Formal Specification Issues.

12.4   Motivations and Potential Benefits.

12.5   Problems, Pitfalls and Lessons Learned.

12.6   Costs.

12.7   Reasoning About a Specification.

12.8   Further Reading.

Formal specification means the use of mathematics to construct models of systems. These models serve as specifications of system behaviour which, thanks to the use of mathematics, are unambiguous and tractable to reasoning. In principle, this should permit us to write a specification which has only one interpretation and which is provably complete and consistent. This is a seductive promise but how realistic is it?

This chapter is designed to help answer this question. It is motivated by the real problems which organisations have in assessing the industrial applicability of formal specification. There is a perceived mismatch between the claims of formal specification's proponents and the reality faced by industrial practitioners. The simplistic appeal of the opening paragraph is easy to debunk yet there are organisations that use formal specification successfully. For other less committed organisations, it straddles the boundary between theoretical toy and practical technique. There are indications that it is finally about to make the breakthrough into routine applicability in certain domains. This is causing many organisations to re-appraise their attitude to formal specification. We are concerned here with helping you decide which side of the boundary it occupies for your problem domain.

There is no easy answer to this and the answer depends on many factors. There is much misleading information about formal specification and the chapter will try to dispel some of the myths. The factors which have to be weighed when assessing formal specification's utility are a complex mixture of (among other things) business area, customer (process) requirements, technological limitations and staff training.

Note that this is not intended as a tutorial on formal specification as there are many existing sources of information on the various methods and how to apply them (see the section on further reading at the end of this chapter). Rather, we aim to give you an overview of the state of the art in the application of formal methods without having to understand any formal techniques. However, for the interested reader, section 12.7 provides a simple example using the formal specification language Z. The formal parts can be skipped without affecting the essential points about the role and costs of formal reasoning.

12.1   Why Formalise?

Parallels are often drawn between software engineering and other engineering disciplines where mathematics is the fundamental tool used to analyse and describe artefacts. For example, a structural engineer uses mathematics to calculate the loads which must be supported. From this, he or she derives a design based on the known properties of the materials of the structure and the deployment of loads throughout the structure.

This is analogous to analysing the requirements on a system to derive a requirements specification. However, while the structural engineer deals with forces, moments of inertia, etc., the analyst deals with functional transformations, timing constraints, reliability, usability and other requirements. These are usually modelled using a variety of techniques of varying precision and expressiveness. Formal specification is the use of mathematically-based techniques for the same purpose. It is formal in the sense that the semantics of what is specified (assuming that the method has been correctly applied) is fully defined. It exploits the properties of the underlying mathematics. Properties can be expressed in a precise, unambiguous manner which is tractable to mathematical reasoning. This does not make formal specification fool-proof; it is merely one approach to reducing errors.

The mathematics which has proved most useful for this is set theory, logic and algebra. This is different from the mathematics used by other engineering disciplines. There has been much debate over the utility of mathematics for modelling these properties, much of which has been of a philosophical nature of little practical relevance. Arguments along the lines of *it can only be proper engineering if it is founded on mathematics* are silly; engineering is about pragmatic issues. However, while the technology transfer of formal specification from laboratory to industry is far from complete, the answer to the question *are formal methods practically useful?* seems to be emerging as a qualified 'yes'. For example, they may often be justi-fied, if used selectively, on critical system components. Even here there will be several ways of applying formal specification, each with its own advantages and costs, so the issue is seldom simple.

12.2 Definitions and Life-cycle Issues

Formal specification methods are different from struc-tured analysis methods. Structured methods are used primarily to develop system models to help the analyst understand the system and its context within its environ-ment. This is usually done by using a variety of tabular and graphical notations to model different system aspects and to document the models (see Chapter 11). Formal specification is about modelling the system behaviour; usually functional or concurrent behaviour but nearly always a model of a single system aspect. The depth of understanding gained by formal modelling is far greater than that afforded by structured methods. However, formal modelling is not effective to present an overall picture of the system. Formal specification methods, therefore, are *not* in competition with structured methods but are complementary to them.

Another term which causes confusion is 'formal methods' which is sometimes used synonymously with formal specification methods but actually has a wider scope. Formal methods is the generic term used to describe any technique based on the use of mathematics for software development. Formal specification methods are formal methods which are specialised for writing specifications.

Formal methods have been developed to support differ-ent stages of the life-cycle but the economics of their use vary widely. The first technique for which the term was used is what is more precisely described as formal verifi-cation (sometimes called 'program proving'). Here, the source code of a program is analysed using the known properties of programming constructs to 'prove' its compliance to a specification. This approach has received a great deal of investment but has proven in practice to be very expensive. It has recently received a boost from the development of the SPARK annotated subset of Ada and its associated toolset (see the book's Web pages for more information). Nevertheless its practical utility will continue to be very restricted. Moreover, since its successful application depends on a precise specification against which to prove the implementation, it needs to be used in conjunction with formal specification techniques.

Formal specification, by contrast, is oriented towards the mathematical expression of a specification. It is intended to permit the specifier to describe the system without implementation constraints. Of course, implementation constraints are sometimes unavoidable (if the system must have an interface to an existing device, for example), but these can generally be accommodated. The overall philosophy is that you can model the essential properties of a system at a level which allows analysis of its externally observable behaviour. Because of the potential to eliminate errors earlier in the life-cycle, formal specification is far more economically viable than formal verification.

As all subsequent stages of the life-cycle follow from specification it is useful to consider how these are impacted by formal specification. Ideally, we want to have confidence that we have got the requirements specification right and that our resulting software is a faithful implementation of it. One way to do this is to use formal specification to ensure that the requirements specification is complete and consistent and to formally verify the subsequent implementation. As stated above, the economics of formal verification precludes this for most applications.

An alternative approach, and one which is just beginning to make the transition to industry is to use a process of iterative refinement where a formal specification undergoes a series of small refinement steps (Figure 12.1). Each step results in a specification which is more implementation-oriented than its predecessor but which is formally equivalent. Eventually, a low-level specification is derived which can be directly implemented. The motivation for this approach is that it is much simpler to verify each small iteration (a 'proof obligation') than it is

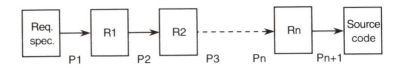

R = refinement of the requirements specification
P = proof obligation

Figure 12.1 Formal iterative refinement

to verify that an implementation is faithful to an abstract specification. It is still expensive, however, and requires a far greater level of skill and training than the writing of a formal specification alone. Moreover, it does not guarantee correctness, since proofs can contain errors, particularly as proofs are usually large. Anecdotal reports of experience with this technique include a pilot project where the size of the implementation measured in lines of Ada was exceeded by the number of lines of proof by a factor of three!

Fortunately, good tool support is becoming available (for example, Digilog's Atelier B system). Heuristically-based theorem provers can now be used to automate much of the proving process and to generate source code. The levels of skill and training required are still very high. This is because manual intervention is required where the tools lack rules and axioms to guide complex proofs. The tools work by automating 'routine' proofs, so the proving process becomes shorter and less error-prone. Because of this, formal iterative refinement is becoming industrially viable for developing highly critical system components. For the immediate future, however, its use is feasible only for organisations who already have substantial existing experience with formal specification.

The greatest economic pay-offs accrue from getting the specification right. For this reason, most practical applications of formal specification concentrate exclusively on specification. Formal specification of all or part of a system, used in conjunction with conventional good practice such as design and code reviews, test planning, etc., offers a good cost/confidence compromise for most critical applications. This pragmatic approach is an order of magnitude less expensive than the fully formal approaches described above. It requires less training and, crucially, has a lower impact on established development processes. It is the only viable option for an organisation new to formal methods, because competence with formal specification is a pre-condition for the effective deployment of any other formal technique.

12.3   Formal Specification Methods

Formal specification is not a homogeneous technology but a collection of different techniques. What unites them is their use of mathematics to specify system behaviour. Just as conventional analysis and design methods may be classified as being data-flow based, object-oriented, etc., formal methods can be classified according to their different underpinnings and the system aspects which they are designed to model. In many cases the term 'method' is itself misleading. Few formal methods are 'methods' in the sense that the better-developed structured methods provide notations and process guidelines for their systematic application. Most formal methods are simply notations which permit requirements to be encoded and reasoned about. In general, little systematic guidance is available to help the analyst develop a specification from an informal set of requirements, manage their integration, develop and structure a system model and handle change. This implies that substantial expertise in developing abstractions and system models is necessary for the effective use of formal specification. Such expertise can only be gained by previous experience of developing informal specifications and system models.

Formal specification methods vary in the system aspects which they model. The largest group (e.g. Z and VDM) are oriented towards the modelling of functionality. The increasing use of communications and distributed systems has also stimulated the development of methods focusing on concurrent properties (e.g. CSP and Lotos). There are also a number of methods which seek to model timing, although there are fundamental problems with modelling discrete time events. In scientific terms, the techniques for modelling functional and concurrent behaviour are fairly mature. It is the engineering issue of how to exploit these in practice which is still crystallising. The modelling of real-time behaviour is less mature and a far more specialised domain. This is unfortunate, as many critical applications are real-time systems. Nevertheless, even real-time systems can benefit from the formal specification of their functional or concurrent properties.

The costs and benefits of formal specification also vary depending on its mode of use. The simplest mode of use is to use a formal specification notation as a vehicle for documenting and communicating requirements. Writing a specification in a formal notation can bring substantial benefits in terms of understanding the application, the absence of ambiguity and the identification of useful abstractions. It is important to realise, however, that a specification written in a formal notation can contain errors.

In order to counter this and increase confidence in a formal specification's correctness the specification should be verified. In many applications this is done informally by inspection and review meetings. However, most formal specification methods are designed to permit correctness properties to be formally proven. A simple example of the use of such formal reasoning is given in Section 12.7. Much of the original motivation for formal specification was predicated on the assumption that specification proof was essential for the development of correct systems. More recently, this has been called into question due to the high costs involved. Proof is expensive and to prove a large specification will require substantial resources. A pragmatic solution is to use proof selectively and concentrate resources on proving only the most critical properties of the specification. In a train control system, for example, effort may be best spent on proving the specification of the application of emergency braking.

What is commonly termed 'proof' covers a range of reasoning techniques from fully formal mathematical proof to semi-formal (but easier) rigorous argument. Hence, it may be possible to achieve a high level of confidence in a specification by using shortcuts and making reasonable assertions.

Another approach to verification is to simulate the state-space from the specification and test this across a range of values. This suffers from the disadvantage that formal notations are usually undecidable. A typical abstract specification will generate a very large state space with a potentially infinite range of values. A specification cannot be exhaustively tested so some errors may remain undetected. Nevertheless, testing to demonstrate the presence (if not the absence) of errors under certain conditions often instils greater confidence than the development of a long and possibly error-prone proof which is opaque to all but a handful of personnel.

Whichever way a method is used, it will require tool support for non-trivial applications. Until recently, many tools were of poor quality and were little more than editors. The situation is improving however with increasing numbers of commercial tools appearing which support syntax and type checking, verification and even refinement. Section 12.8 describes how to find information on formal specification tools.

In terms of the methods themselves, the most widely known and applied can be classified using three categories.

- *Algebraic specification methods.* Here, a system is modelled using multi-sorted algebras, essentially, as a set of types and operations on those types. Each type (or 'sort') is considered to be a set of values and the operations are modelled as functions over those sets of values. The operations are defined by axioms – equations specifying constraints which the operations must satisfy. Because of their orientation towards types and operations which manipulate them, algebraic methods lend themselves to modelling abstract data types. They are particularly useful for specifying the interfaces between system components, where the system is considered at an abstract level to be composed of abstract data types.

  To help address the pragmatic problems of scaling up and reuse, most algebraic methods permit already defined sorts to be imported into other sorts' specifications, sorts to be enriched to derive new more specialised sorts, renaming and parameterisation of sorts. There are complex problems with formally reasoning about algebraic specifications to prove (e.g.) completeness. Nevertheless, they provide an approach which permits critical component interfaces to be specified with precision. Example methods include Larch and OBJ, both of which have been in use for several years. Several algebraic methods are supported by tool such as LP (for Larch) and 2OBJ for OBJ.

- *Model based methods*. The methods which fall into this category are perhaps the best known, and they include Z, VDM and B. These methods are based on set theory and first-order logic. A system's state-space is modelled in terms of its components which are themselves modelled as sets, functions, etc. Invariant conditions on the state space are modelled as predicates over the components. Operations which manipulate the state space are specified as predicates relating different states of the components. This explicit specification of state and the effects of operations on the state contrasts with algebraic methods' 'stateless' modelling of abstract types and their operations.

  The individual methods vary in the semantics which they layer on top of their basic underpinnings – the framework provided by the method. All provide a means to build modular specifications by naming collections of components and associated predicates. However, the calculi used for manipulating these named entities for (e.g.) proving compliance with pre and post conditions varies. Opinions vary on the relative merits of the different methods. Broadly, however, Z is perhaps the easiest to learn and is relatively strong on structuring specifications. However, unlike the other two methods it is purely a specification method. VDM and B, by contrast, support subsequent design and development using refinement. Tool support is available for all three. For example: Z/Eves, Mural and Atelier B.

- *Process algebra based methods*. The methods mentioned above are concerned mainly with functional properties and sequential behaviour. This limits their applicability for applications where functional properties are not the most critical. Process algebras are concerned with modelling the interactions between concurrent processes. Here, for example, properties such as liveness ('something will eventually happen') are important. Process algebras represent process behaviour using constraints on allowable communications between processes.

They have been most widely used in the telecommunications field for (e.g.) protocol specification but are becoming more widely applied to distributed and concurrent systems. Among the original methods in this field were CSP and CCS. Subsequently, the Lotos method has emerged which is adapted from both of these and from algebraic methods. Lotos' development has been sponsored by the International Standards Organisation (ISO). This has given the method substantial impetus and is partly responsible for the widespread interest in the method and the maturity of Lotos support tools such as the CADP toolset.

We have not mentioned techniques for modelling real-time events such as temporal logic-based methods. In general, they are less mature in terms of supporting tools and availability of training. Consequently, good examples of their industrial application are hard to find. This is not to imply that they are inherently unusable, merely that assessment of the costs and risks involved in their adoption is difficult.

Methods can be extended to widen their expressiveness. For example, there are examples of adding temporal logic operators to Z to help specify timing constraints. However, this risks making the method still harder to apply and there is little industrial experience from which to learn. Similarly, attempts have been made to address the problems of scaling apparent in some methods. For example, object-oriented features have been grafted on to Z and VDM to enhance their ability to structure large specifications. A beneficial side-effect of this may be to ease their integration with object-oriented structured methods. At the time of writing, however, standard definitions of these extensions are absent and examples of their use in industrial applications are hard to find.

It is important to realise that no single method is likely to be perfectly adapted to a particular application due to limitations in expressiveness, the ability to handle large specifications, the availability of tool support and other restrictions. The choice of which method to adopt should depend on what are the critical properties to model and the practicalities of deploying the method. In any case it will need the commitment of resources to investigating the appropriate method. As a general rule of thumb, however, the more mature and better supported (by tools, training and consultancy) the method, the lower the risk.

12.4   Motivations and Potential Benefits

Before you can assess the benefits of adopting formal specification, you should be clear about why it should even be considered as an option. This section examines some of the typical stimuli and motivations acting upon organisations which can lead to consideration being given to formal specification.

One of the most important external stimuli to the adoption of formal specification is mandate by clients. Several powerful customer organisations have been instrumental in the development of standards which enforce the use of formal specification. Notable among these have been UK Defence Standard 00-55 and the European Harmonised Security Evaluation Criteria (ITSEC). In the UK for example, a result of 00-55 is that some developers bidding for Ministry of Defence work have been forced to invest in training, pilot projects, etc. This has led to opportunities for niche companies specialising in formal specification, not only as a direct result of 00-55 being applied to particular MoD projects but also as a result of the change in culture which it has signalled.

A similar effect can be seen in the railway domain, caused in part by public concern over increasing automation, privatisation-induced fragmentation, and recent accidents. Some operators have encouraged the use of formal methods to make the development of safety-critical components more rigorous while being publicly seen to be taking steps to increase safety.

Another motivation for embracing formal specification might be described as the 'halo effect' which it can confer on an organisation and its products. The use of what is perceived to be an advanced technique can bring kudos from the high level of organisational competence and product quality which it implicitly demonstrates. It may help an organisation's ability to attain quality or process maturity accreditation. It may also strengthen the case for external regulators' approval for critical products. Finally, it may help demonstrate an organisation's commitment to best professional practice as a defence in litigation resulting from product failure.

In addition to contractual or PR-related stimuli, the use of formal specification can contribute to improved quality and lower life-cycle costs. We need to reduce rework costs, because these provide tangible evidence of shortcomings in the requirements process. Of course, rework may be due to incorrect requirements being elicited or because the customer changes his or her mind. Formal specification can do little to reduce these costs. However, some errors are introduced at the specification stage. For example:

1 where correct requirements are ambiguously documented

2 where inconsistencies between requirements have not been detected

3 where essential requirements are left unspecified.

Formal specification offers potential advantages here. When writing a formal specification, awkward questions cannot easily be side-stepped. The analyst is forced to establish a sound understanding of the application domain otherwise the specification will be impossible to develop. This fact alone can eliminate many errors. Errors of type 1 should be eliminated by the inherent lack of ambiguity of the mathematics used to express the requirements. In principle, savings on this type of error come for free simply by writing the specification.

Verification of the specification is necessary to detect errors of types 2 and 3. A specification can only be guaranteed to be free errors of type 2 or 3 if the specification is proven, and if the proof is free of errors. In practice, however, no specification can be guaranteed to be error-free but a very high level of confidence can be established by proving critical parts of it or by simulation testing. The level of confidence required and the techniques chosen depend on both the nature of the application itself and on the quality of tools and expertise available.

The limits imposed by methods' expressiveness restrict the potential benefits for many classes of system. However, the fact that some properties cannot be modelled formally, does not mean that those which can should not be specified as precisely as possible. For example, in a real-time system, it may be worth-while to formally specify the functional behaviour of the critical tasks even if the behaviour of the real-time executive which schedules and dispatches the tasks is specified informally. If this leads to increased confidence in the individual tasks, resources may be diverted from module testing to integration testing.

Even greater confidence in the developed product may be gained if formal iterative refinement of a specification is used to generate 'proven' source code. As noted above, this requires still greater skill than proving a specification, even where it is tool supported. In at least one industrial application, however, the additional costs involved in this have been offset by savings from the complete elimination of unit testing.

One of the frequently cited advantages of formal specification is increased communication between developer and customer; all that is required is for both parties to accept a particular formal notation as the *lingua franca* for the specification. We have purposely not listed this above since, in practice, it needs qualification. We return to the subject of customer-developer communication below. Here, however, we merely note that in particular circumstances, such as at review meetings, benefits come from the elimination of the need to resolve differing interpretations. Needless to say, this requires that all participants can understand the specification.

12.5   Problems, Pitfalls and Lessons Learned

The potential advantages of formal specification are offset by a number of disadvantages and problems. Perhaps the biggest impediment to formal specification has been lack of evidence that they are cost-effective. Developers have been rightly suspicious of an apparently esoteric technique with little track-record of industrial use. A related problem has been that unrealistic claims for their efficacy have been made and have led some organisations to invest heavily for little return.

Fortunately, discussion of formal specification has become more balanced in recent years, and good quality advice, training and consultancy is more readily available. Similarly, a body of experience of their industrial use is slowly building up. These should help to prevent organisations from adopting inappropriate formalisms such as unsupported methods, methods whose expressiveness is poorly matched to the application domain, or even from investing in formal specification at all if other good practices offer a better alternative. They should also help prepare organisations to assess the effects of adopting formal specification.

Just as it is crucial to choose an appropriate method, it is also important to choose a tool appropriate to the method and the purpose to which it will be put. For example, there is little point in investing in a sophisticated theorem prover if you do not intend to use formal refinement. Ideally, it would be possible to integrate a tool with other analysis and design tools and be able to import requirements information and trace requirements between tools. This would ease the task of integrating formal specification with existing practices. We do not know of any commercial tools which support this.

Training is a crucial issue for formal specification. There are hopeful signs that personnel are becoming better prepared for the use of formal specification. In Europe at least, most Computer Science and related undergraduate programmes include courses on formal specification. It is often claimed that the skills required to write a specification and perform basic reasoning are

straightforward and well within the grasp of most prac-
tising engineers and analysts. This is certainly true of
the syntax and semantics of most of the methods
described above. What is less often admitted is that
these skills alone are not enough to make someone
competent at writing formal specifications. The ability to
derive appropriate abstractions is a crucial skill for a
formal specifier to acquire. This is very difficult to
teach. There is a strong contrast between formal specification and structured methods which generally provide
much more support for developing models and abstractions.

It is necessary to be realistic about the lead time
before trained personnel will be able to develop good
quality formal specifications. As with any other complex
skill, its effective use requires practice. When personnel
have gained experience and the necessary skills, it may
help organisational integration to harness their skills as
internal consultants or trouble-shooters. In the absence of
in-house expertise of this nature, you will need to use
external consultants to accelerate the acquisition of
skills.

One of the most frequently cited advantages of formal
specifications is that they provide a means for communicating the requirements. Unfortunately, this is only true
in the unlikely event that all the stakeholders in a
project (customers and users as well as developers and
members of other engineering disciplines) are familiar
with the notation. It is crucial to recognise that the
specification must be made accessible to those who must
agree, validate and use it as the basis for subsequent
development or for defining interfaces to other components. This means that training should not be restricted
to those who must write the specification. However,
although the level of training needed to read a specification is lower than that needed to write one, the provision of training will probably not be feasible for all
stakeholders.

Because of this, a good formal specification document
should clearly describe the structure and meaning of the
formal specification in natural language and any other
notation useful for clarity. The formal parts of the specifi-

cation should be paraphrased so that the essential points can be understood without close reading of the mathematics (**Guideline 8.8**, *Paraphrase system models*). This enhances readability for readers trained to read the formal notation as well as making the specification accessible to those who lack training. The document must make explicit the relationship between the stakeholders' requirements and what is expressed formally by the specification. This is needed for validation of the specification and for requirements traceability.

Formal specification methods, with their concentration on precision and the banishment of ambiguity, are often regarded as being the antithesis of a prototype-evaluate-modify development cycle. However, because even a formal specification can embody errors of interpretation of stakeholders' requirements, it is sometimes useful to develop a prototype from the specification to validate its assumptions. Some tools even permit a specification to be animated by generating an executable program from the specification. This constrains the specifier to use a machine-processable subset of the notation which risks compromising the separation of concerns between specification and implementation issues.

Perhaps the fundamental problem with the adoption of formal specification derives from the fact that it must be integrated within an overall development process. Organisations cannot afford to throw their current methods and processes away in order to adopt formal specification. Hence, if an organisation has invested heavily in SADT, it would be foolish to simply replace it with Z. Rather, formal specification should be used to augment existing techniques. This is particularly true where, as with SADT and Z, the formal and non-formal techniques address different issues. Similarly, formal specification is not a substitute for safety or security analysis techniques.

Integration is a particular problem where, as will often be the case, only part of the system is specified formally. The formal specification of these parts must be consistent with the other parts' non-formal specification so that interfaces can be defined and requirements can be traced between the subsystems and notations. The integration of formal specification with other techniques is addressed by FRERE*.

Unless the entire system is to be specified formally, you must define the critical components of the system. These may be the safety or security-critical components. However, non safety- or security-critical systems may also benefit from formal specification, particularly if they are mission- or business-critical. Regardless of the application, a preceding analysis of the requirements should be performed to determine the critical requirements. The insights afforded by a range of techniques such as hazard analysis or viewpoint analysis may be helpful here (**Guideline 10.4**, *Derive safety requirements from hazard analysis*).

12.6   Costs

A quality management system should be in place before a formal specification method is adopted. The resources consumed by different stages of the life-cycle should be measured to establish how the effort is distributed and identify where the bottlenecks are. Similarly, the size of the specification and any proofs should be recorded in the same way as lines of source code are routinely measured. This can help correlate effort and productivity and give a measure of the efficacy of tools, evaluate proof against other verification techniques, etc. An organisation should also be clear about the benefits that they expect to obtain from formal specification such as improvement in product quality or development cost savings.

Formal specification has a skew effect on development effort and an organisation must be prepared for this. Depending on how it is adopted, the requirements phase (including specification) can be expected to require between 10 and 20% more time than a conventional approach. The pay-off comes later when the code should exhibit fewer specification errors. If applied successfully,

---

*FRERE has been developed as part of the REAIMS project. REAIMS is introduced in the Preface to this book.

overall costs and time-to-market should not increase and confidence in the product should increase. However a programme of phased introduction using, for example, pilot projects, will help ensure that this is the case before commitment is made to a large project.

There is now sufficient industrial experience with formal specification (see further reading) to indicate that, as predicted, overall productivity should benefit from formal specification. Figures available suggest that productivity can actually be improved by a factor of anything from a few to four hundred percent! The latter figure represents an extreme case where the formal specification was formally refined to code (6000 lines of Ada). This negated the need for unit testing and persuaded the customer to accept fewer validation tests. Formal refinement is currently a highly specialised activity so most organisations should not expect productivity increases of more than a few percent. Experience suggests that the occurrence of faults in the developed source code can decrease at a more dramatic rate, however. As confidence in a formal specification process improves over time it is possible that this higher product quality may translate into more significant cost savings.

Training costs vary according to the level of formalisation used. For formal specification with basic reasoning, approximately ten days' training per person will typically be required. However, another six months of practical application will usually be needed before personnel become productive. In some cases, training will also need to be provided for non-development personnel such as customer representatives.

Tools and training in how to use them have to be purchased. In addition, the changes to the development process implied by the introduction of formal specification may also cause hidden costs. For example, your quality plan will need to be adapted.

12.7   Reasoning About a Specification

This section is included to illustrate the use of formal reasoning to prove properties of a specification. The example is trivial, a common criticism of illustrations of the use of formal specification. However, as this is not intended to be a tutorial and as we wish only to illustrate the difference between writing a specification and reasoning about it, we make no apologies. In a 'real' application the specification would obviously be much larger and more complex. Hence, the likelihood of errors being identified informally would be lower and the advantage gained by being able to reason about the specification would be correspondingly higher.

The example is based around an abstract specification of a simple microwave oven. The oven is considered to emit microwave radiation at a given level for a given period of time. For example, different power levels would be used to defrost, reheat or cook a turkey. Similarly, a turkey would be cooked for longer than a small chicken. The purpose of the specification is to ensure that food is not cooked for longer than required and that the oven cannot emit microwaves if the door is open.

The formal specification of this is written in Z. Z is a model-based formal specification notation developed by the University of Oxford's Programming Research Group from the work of Jean-Raymond Abrial in the late 1970s. It has become one of the most widely used formal specification methods. The section on further reading at the end of this chapter includes several references to information on Z.

The main unit of structure in Z is the schema. Schemas are a good example of the added value which a formal method brings to the underpinning mathematics. In Z, they permit the named association of logically related components and predicates. These can then be manipulated using a schema calculus which builds upon the semantics of set theory and predicate calculus. The schema calculus permits the modular construction of specifications and reasoning about the relationships between different parts of a specification. For example, it is possible to test theories about how operations interact or to establish whether 'loose ends' exist.

In a Z specification, the state space of the system must be specified before any functional behaviour is specified. This defines any of the variables needed to represent the state of the system and any constraints on, or inter-relationships between, the values of these variables. The microwave oven's state space is specified by the schema Microwave_oven shown in Figure 12.2.

The schema models the oven in terms of three variables declared in the top (declaration) part.

- power represents the power emitted by the oven. This will normally stay constant while the food is cooking. The type POWER is a discrete type with four possible values: OFF, DEFROST, REHEAT or COOK.

- timer represents the time for which the food is to be cooked. This will 'count down' to zero while the food is cooking. TIME is a non-negative integer type.

- door models the state of the door to the oven. Its type DOOR_STATUS is a Boolean type with the values 'OPEN' or 'SHUT'.

The bottom (predicate) part of the schema contains a predicate which specifies the constraint that the microwave emitter must be off if the timer has counted down to zero or if the door is open. The schema Microwave_oven is used to model the state of the oven at all times and the predicate must always be true. Because of this, it is known as the 'state invariant'. We cannot specify an operation which leaves the oven in a state which conflicts with the state invariant.

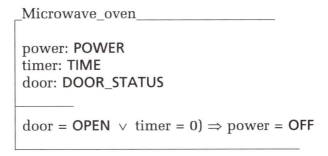

Figure 12.2   Microwave_oven

```
_Monitor_oven_____

power, power': POWER
timer, timer': TIME
door, door': DOOR_STATUS

time_since_last?: TIME
door_state?: DOOR_STATUS
_____

(door = OPEN ∨ timer = 0) ⇒ power = OFF
(door' = OPEN ∨ timer' = 0) ⇒ power' = OFF
door' = door_state?
timer' = timer - time_since_last?
power' = power
```

Figure 12.3   Monitor_oven

The embedded control software for the oven is required to monitor the state of the oven every n clock cycles. We do not attempt to model this temporal requirement. However, the schema Monitor_oven (Figure 12.3) models the behaviour of the scheduled monitoring task as an operation on Microwave_oven. This illustrates a limitation imposed by the expressiveness of the method (at least in the way we have deployed it here). Even if we could prove that our specification of the monitoring task was correct, our confidence in the correctness of the scheduler might be low and would need to be verified carefully. Failure to assure this could lead to an unacceptable delay between opening the door and switching the microwave emitter off.

The Monitor_oven operation's job is to evaluate the state of the oven by decrementing the timer and by checking the state of the door. To do this, the current state of the door and the time since the operation was last invoked must be known. It is assumed that these are supplied by the run-time environment. The operation must comply with the state invariant by ensuring that the power is switched off if the door is open or if the timer has counted down to zero.

In Z, the effect of an operation on the system is indicated by changes to values of the variables defined in the state-space. To model change to a state variable's value, the state before the operation is invoked and the state after the operation has taken effect are represented explicitly. The state before is indicated by the variable's name as given in the state schema (e.g. door). The state after the operation is indicated by the same name but with a prime suffix (e.g. door').

As the effect of the operation on the state variables must be specified, both the 'before' (unprimed) and 'after' (primed) state variables are included. The declaration part of Monitor_oven therefore lists all the variables from Microwave_oven and their primed counterparts*. The state invariant from Microwave_oven is also included in the operation's predicate part. As this must be true both before and after the effect of the operation, a duplicate of the state invariant but using the 'after' state variables is also included. Where predicates occur on separate lines, they are implicitly AND-ed (unless another logical operator is explicitly overrides this). The first two lines of predicates in Monitor_oven are the 'before' and 'after' state invariant from Microwave_oven.

In addition to the variables from Microwave_oven, Monitor_oven includes two variables of its own: time_since_last? and door_state? By convention, a '?' suffix indicates that these are input values to the operation. The first variable is a measure of the time since the operation was last invoked. The second is an indicator of whether the door has been opened.

The effect of the operation is specified by the three predicates at the bottom of the schema. This is that:

- The new state of the door (door') is set to the value of the input variable door_state?

- The new value of timer (timer') is calculated from the old value and the value of time_since_last?

- The power setting (power') retains its previous value.

---

*Z provides a shorthand notation for this but we have ignored it for clarity.

These are implicitly AND-ed to the state invariant from Monitor_oven. This ensures that whatever is specified by the schema, the state invariant must still be true.

As written, the intention of the operation is to ensure that the timer is correctly decremented and that the power setting remains constant until either the door is opened or the timer reaches zero. We must satisfy ourselves that this is what it *actually* specifies. We may do this informally by inspection or we can invest more resources into the specification by attempting to prove it. As a specification increases in size and complexity the likelihood of subtle errors being detected by inspection decreases. Of course, a large, unproven or informally verified formal specification is no more error-prone than a large informal specification. Indeed, it should be less error-prone. Nevertheless, for a highly critical system or component, the level of confidence afforded by the specification may still be lower than required. The additional cost of proving properties of the specification is justified, as this will be offset by fewer errors and increased confidence.

To illustrate one small aspect of what proving a specification means, we will perform a formal precondition investigation on Monitor_oven. Precondition investigation is defined as part of the Z schema calculus. It is intended to reveal the preconditions on an operation to determine whether the operation specifies the behaviour of the system under all conditions. It is a useful mechanistic means of establishing whether we have forgotten anything. If we have, it is better to discover it and amend the specification rather than leave it to surface later in the life-cycle. Clearly, an operation should have defined behaviour for any possible state of the system. However, it is common to overlook certain boundary states. Precondition investigation provides a means to identify when this is the case.

In a precondition investigation, we are only interested in the specification of the state of the 'before' variables. To do this we need to discard the 'after' state variables: power', timer' and door'. However, to ensure that the meaning of the schema is not distorted, these can only be discarded if we follow the rules of formal reasoning and substitute an expression for them which is formally equivalent. The first step in doing this is to move their declarations to the predicate part. Here, they are by convention existentially quantified (preceded by the '∃' quantifier). This is shown by the schema pre_Monitor_oven in Figure 12.4.

Once the 'after' state variables are in the predicate part, we try to re-write the predicates in a way which means that they are no longer needed, while being careful not to alter the meaning of any predicates specifying the state of the 'before' variables. In programming terms, this is analogous to re-writing the body of a procedure to eliminate the use of a redundant variable. However, in a complex schema, it is usually the most difficult part.

In Monitor_oven, it is possible to eliminate all three 'after' state variables. This is done simply by substituting them wherever they occur for the right hand sides of the last three predicates (note that it is seldom this easy!). Once this is done the last three predicates and the

```
┌─pre_ Monitor_oven─────────────────────────────
│
│  power: POWER
│  timer: TIME
│  door: DOOR_STATUS
│
│  time_since_last?: TIME
│  door_state?: DOOR_STATUS
│├───────────────────
│
│  ∃ power': POWER; timer': TIME; door': DOOR_STATUS ·
│
│  (door = OPEN ∨ timer = 0) ⇒ power = OFF
│  (door' = OPEN ∨ timer' = 0) ⇒ power' = OFF
│  door' = door_state?
│  timer' = timer - time_since_last?
│  power' = power
│
└───────────────────────────────────────────────
```

Figure 12.4   pre_Monitor_oven

declarations of the 'after' state variables can be discarded. This is shown in Figure 12.5.

We are left with a schema which models the required state of the oven at the point when the operation is invoked. It contains two predicates. The first is the unchanged state invariant. The second represents the preconditions on the operation:

(door_state? = OPEN ∨ timer - time_since_last? = 0) ⇒ power = OFF

If, when the operation is invoked, the oven is in a state which conflicts with this, the behaviour of the operation is undefined. The precondition can be re-written as:

(door_state? = CLOSED ∧ timer > time_since_last?) ∨ power = OFF

This can be paraphrased as:

Either: The power is already off

Or: The door is closed and the time is not yet up

The result of our formal precondition investigation is to reveal that the operation only works for a subset of the

```
 ┌─ pre_ Monitor_oven ─────────────────────────────
 │
 │  power: POWER
 │  timer: TIME
 │  door: DOOR_STATUS
 │
 │  time_since_last?: TIME
 │  door_state?: DOOR_STATUS
 │ _____
 │
 │  (door = OPEN ∨ timer = 0) ⇒ power = OFF
 │  (door_state? = OPEN ∨ timer - time_since_last? = 0) ⇒
 │                     power = OFF
 │
 └──────────────────────────────────────────────────
```

Figure 12.5 Simplified pre_Monitor_oven

possible states which the oven could be in. The problem is that if the door is open or the time is up, the power must already be turned off. If the power is on and either the time runs out or the door is opened, then the behaviour is unspecified. Formally, the problem can be solved by negating the precondition above and using this as a precondition on a new operation schema. This can then be OR-ed with the schema Monitor_oven to yield a new, complete operation. Informally, the problem can be solved by replacing the predicate

power' = power

in Monitor_oven with the following predicate which qualifies when the power level can retain its former value:

(door' = CLOSED ∧ timer' > 0) ⇒ power' = power

The example has illustrated the role of formal reasoning about specifications. In principle, formal reasoning can guarantee to detect errors of incompleteness or inconsistency which may otherwise remain undiscovered. The example has not illustrated the level of effort required to perform formal reasoning. The full precondition investigation for the above occupies two pages of A4 paper. Had the schemas been more complex, as would normally be the case in an industrial application, the proof would have been much longer and more complex. In general, proving a specification requires substantially greater resources than are required simply to write an unproven specification.

The example has not touched upon formal iterative refinement. If the microwave oven was to be developed in this way, the specification would have to undergo a number of stages in which it became successively less abstract and closer to a machine representation. The derived algorithms and data structures would need to be proven to be semantically equivalent to the specification. This is far more costly than merely proving a specification but it potentially furnishes the highest degree of confidence in an implementation's compliance with its specification.

12.8   Further Reading

There is an enormous amount of information on formal specification. Most is in the form of textbooks and tutorials. There is relatively little public information on implementing formal specification methods.

For a wider perspective, we recommend the April 1996 edition of *IEEE Computer* which has a special issue of formal methods with contributions from practitioners in both industry and academia. This provides a good snapshot of the current arguments for and against formal specification. In addition, the following paper describes the use of formal methods in an industrial application.

Hall, A., 1996, Using formal methods to develop an ATC system. *IEEE Software* **13**(1)

Most of the popular formal specification methods are now served by a range of textbooks. This is particularly true of Z, for which the following book is probably the most comprehensive:

Woodcock, J., and Davies, J., 1996, *Using Z Specification, Refinement and Proof.* Prentice-Hall

Finally, for up-to-the-minute news on developments in formal specification methods and tools, Oxford University maintains an excellent set of resources on the World-Wide-Web at:

http://www.comlab.ox.ac.uk/archive/formal-methods.html

Information on all the methods and tools mentioned in this Chapter are available from this site.

13 Viewpoints

Summary

This chapter describes the use of viewpoints for requirements engineering. It covers, in more detail **Guideline 4.9**, *Collect requirements from multiple viewpoints*. This chapter should be read if you have problems with requirements elicitation due to a failure to identify all the major system stakeholders. Viewpoints are designed to reduce the risk of overlooking stakeholders and their requirements. They can help to manage and analyse the requirements once they have been elicited. We discuss the basic principles underpinning viewpoints and how they can be used informally. We also describe a systematic approach, called PREview, to the use of viewpoints and illustrate this with an example of a safety-related system.

Contents

13.1 Why Viewpoints?

13.2 PREview: A Pragmatic Viewpoints Approach.

13.3 Further Reading.

In this chapter we suggest that viewpoint identification should be one of the first steps of a requirements analysis because it helps the elicitation and management of requirements. **Guideline 4.9**, *Collect requirements from multiple·viewpoints*, introduced viewpoints as an intermediate level technique. In this chapter, we review the benefits which can be gained by using viewpoints, and suggest how viewpoints can be used by introducing the PREview* approach.

The term 'viewpoint' is broadly synonymous with a perspective on a system (Figure 13.1). As a simple example, consider a proposal to commission and install traffic lights at the intersection of two roads. There is a wide range of configurations which such a traffic light system may have and a corresponding set of requirements which an analyst must collect and make sense of. For example, should the system have left/right turn filters? Should pedestrian crossings be provided? Should the period between changes of the lights be dynamically configurable? The answers to these questions depend on the domain problems which the system seeks to solve. However, there are several people or roles who, because they will use, operate, or pay for the system, have a stake in it. Each of these has a perspective on the system and analysts cannot be confident about developing an adequate specification unless they have collected and analysed all their requirements. Those which might be identified here include:

1 drivers

2 cyclists

3 pedestrians

4 emergency services

5 the highway authority

Each of these viewpoints represents the perspective of a particular stakeholder on the traffic management problem

---

*PREview has been developed as part of the REAIMS project. REAIMS is introduced in the Preface to this book.

where each stakeholder imposes requirements on the solution to the problem. As explained below, there are often other useful viewpoints on a system which represent requirements with no human or organisational source.

Viewpoints focus primarily on the early elicitation stages of the requirements process. Systematic support has always been harder to provide here than for system modelling or specification. Hence, practitioners looking for a method capable of solving their elicitation problems, in the way that (for example) SADT solves their modelling problems, will be disappointed. However, using viewpoints can help structure the elicitation process. Viewpoints can also help prioritise and manage requirements.

Another way of thinking of viewpoints is that they:

- focus the analyst's attention on the parts of the problem which affect stakeholders, and

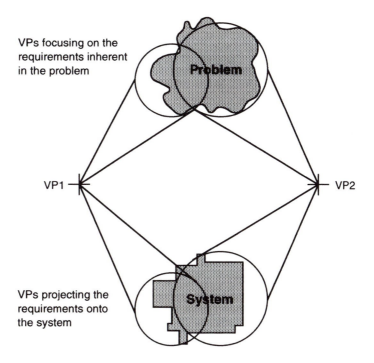

Figure 13.1 Viewpoints on the problem and the system

- project the discovered requirements onto the system to be developed.

This is illustrated in Figure 13.1. Here, two viewpoints focus on the hazy and ill-formed proposed system and project their requirements discovered by these foci onto an emerging system specification. Elicitation of the two viewpoints' requirements take place without regard to each other in order to explicitly separate elicitation from distracting issues such as conflict resolution. Overlaps between the viewpoints' foci indicate that the viewpoints' domains of interest are not disjoint. This may result in duplicated requirements. There may also be incompatible requirements. The fact that the requirements are explicitly associated with an identified viewpoint helps to inform the resolution of inconsistencies and duplications.

If you are working in a familiar domain where systems are highly constrained (e.g. the architecture of the systems is fixed) then viewpoints probably do not offer significant advantages. Similarly, if you are involved with developing systems where there are few or homogeneous sources of requirements, viewpoints may offer little advantage. If, however, you frequently perform require-ments rework, experience incompleteness-derived quality problems, or have problems with managing requirements from different sources, then viewpoints may offer signifi-cant advantages.

If incompleteness in your elicitation process is your principal problem, then it may be most cost-effective to apply viewpoints informally. Viewpoint identification based on a checklist of viewpoints 'classes' (i.e. view-points likely to occur in the domain) can be used to guide the search for viewpoints. Elicitation of each view-point's requirements then contributes to system modelling and specification with no intermediate inconsistency handling step. Instead, inconsistencies are identified and rectified in an *ad hoc* manner as they emerge during system modelling and specification. The viewpoints and associated information are discarded.

This approach is broadly compatible with the use of viewpoints as informally practised in many development projects. However, many users experience difficulty using viewpoints like this. Without a good definition of viewpoint, viewpoint identification is hard. There are also problems in integrating viewpoints' requirements and handling inconsistency in large projects. In any project where there are more than a handful of viewpoints, these problems may nullify the advantages of viewpoints. In this case, a systematic approach to the use of viewpoints may be helpful.

Although the viewpoints concept has been around for many years, there are very few methods which are viewpoint-oriented and which are in widespread industrial use (and therefore properly validated). Although a few structured methods such as SADT support the general notion of viewpoints, perhaps only CORE* can be truly described as an industrial viewpoints-oriented method. We therefore prefer to refer to viewpoints 'approaches' rather than 'methods'. Later in this chapter, we suggest an approach to the use of viewpoints called PREview. This provides guidelines on the fundamentals of using viewpoints such as how to identify and manage viewpoints.

13.1   Why Viewpoints?

A viewpoint-based approach to requirements analysis recognises that all information about the system requirements cannot be discovered by considering the system from a single perspective. Any single perspective inevitably emphasises the requirements of one stakeholder at the expense of other viewpoints. Developing a solution to a traffic management problem based only on drivers' requirements would be unsatisfactory for pedestrians and cyclists. Similarly, analysis of the problem from a single synthetic perspective which attempted to represent every stakeholder would be very difficult.

The principal advantages offered by viewpoints are as follows.

---

*CORE (COntrolled REquirements specification) was developed in the late 1970s and has been used in aerospace and defence applications in the UK

- The requirements are likely to be more complete than if viewpoints are not explicitly identified. In the latter case, important requirements may be easily overlooked because their viewpoints were never recognised.

- A separation of concerns is provided which permits the development of a set of 'partial specifications' in isolation from other viewpoints. This avoids having to confront conflicts with other viewpoints' requirements during elicitation. A result of this is that, when they prove necessary, the trade-offs between requirements can be better informed.

- Traceability is enhanced by the explicit association of requirements with the viewpoints from which they are derived.

  Viewpoints are complementary to a number of other requirements engineering practices. In particular, they can help inform the development of system models (System modelling is described in Chapters 7 and 11). Similarly, system models can be developed for each viewpoint to help clarify their requirements.

13.1.1 What is a Viewpoint?

A viewpoint represents an encapsulation of partial information about a system's requirements from a particular perspective. The information is *partial* because it is restricted to one perspective on the system and therefore omits other perspectives' requirements. A viewpoint should not only contain requirements. It is good practice to associate additional information with requirements to help with assessing requirements' mutability and with tracing. A viewpoint provides a convenient structuring mechanism with which to associate requirements with this other information. Hence, a viewpoint may contain a set of requirements as well as a definition of the viewpoint's perspective, a list of the sources from which the requirements were elicited and a rationale for each requirement.

Viewpoints are not only concerned with human perspectives. Viewpoints can be associated with:

- the system's stakeholders

- the system's operating environment

- the system's domain

A stakeholder is a human, role, or organisation with an interest in the system. This can include both the customer's and developer's organisations. For the traffic light problem, the customer's viewpoints might be those identified at the start of this chapter. For an MIS application by contrast, the customer's viewpoints might be those of users such as sales staff and systems administrators as well as those with a more strategic interest in the system such as finance and logistics managers. Developers' viewpoints may include those of the analyst(s) and other disciplines involved in the system development.

Stakeholders are not the only sources of requirements. A system is always installed in an environment. Where the environment includes other systems/components with which it must exchange data or control, these impose requirements. An interfaced system/component has a perspective on the system just as a stakeholder does. Hence it makes sense to use a viewpoint to model that perspective.

In addition, many applications are constrained by phenomena inherent in their domain. Signal propagation errors occur in communications media; government information systems are the target of unauthorised users; and traffic lights are constrained by vehicle braking and acceleration capabilities. The latter might be represented by a 'safety' viewpoint because this may be useful as a means to isolate and explicitly represent the safety requirements on the system. Similarly, we might have signal processing and security viewpoints in other domains. The domain imposes requirements just as stakeholders and the environment do. These tend to act as constraints on the system.

In some applications the domain-imposed requirements are trivially obvious. In others, they are implicit in the principal stakeholders' requirements. Unfortunately, in some applications neither of these are true and the domain requirements are obscure and hard to elicit. They may have no stakeholder to articulate them, they may remain implicit features of the domain culture; evident to experts but obscure to others. Their discovery depends on the availability of domain expertise. If the analyst is not a domain expert, they must be sensitised to the need to explicitly seek expertise. Explicitly identifying a domain viewpoint can help raise the profile of the domain requirements.

13.2 PREview: A Pragmatic Viewpoints Approach

In this section we introduce the use of the PREview viewpoint-oriented approach. PREview helps to avoid the problems of identifying and managing viewpoints. It has been developed from experience of large systems engineering projects and is rooted in pragmatic issues such as the need for flexibility. In particular, PREview seeks to support the management and analysis of viewpoints without introducing specialist notations. Checklists and tables are used where some other viewpoints approaches use more formal notations. Although these approaches hold long-term promise we think that they are currently impractical for industrial applications.

To be usable, a viewpoint-oriented approach should integrate with an existing requirements process. This reduces both the costs and risks of applying the approach. Although there is no universal requirements process, most processes broadly conform to the spiral model illustrated in Figure 13.2.

The key point about the spiral model in Figure 13.2 is that requirements engineering is iterative rather than linear. Requirements information emerges spasmodically and is poorly formed. To make sense of this, three basic activities have to be repeatedly applied until order emerges. These activities are represented by the three segments of the spiral. The radial arms of the spiral represent both increasing cost and the generation of information by all three phases. The more times we go round the spiral, the better the quality of our requirements information should be. However, we consume more resources in doing so.

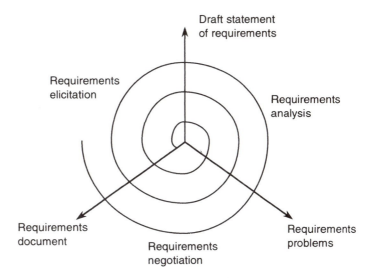

Figure 13.2 A spiral model of the requirements engineering process

The discovery/analysis/negotiation cycle is iterated a number of times. During each iteration, new information emerges which may necessitate the modification of already acquired information. Eventually, the requirements information meets an acceptable level of completeness and consistency. The requirements definition information emerges from each cycle and forms the basis of a requirements document.

In more detail, the three basic activities performed each cycle are as follows.

1 *Requirements elicitation.* Given a statement of organisational needs and other inputs, various different sources are consulted to understand the problem and the application domain and to establish their requirements. These requirements may not be complete and may be expressed in a vague and unstructured way.

2 *Requirements analysis.* The requirements collected during the elicitation phase are integrated and analysed. Usually, this will result in the identification of missing requirements, inconsistencies and requirements conflicts.

3 *Requirements negotiation.* Inconsistencies and conflicts discovered during analysis need to be resolved. The ana-

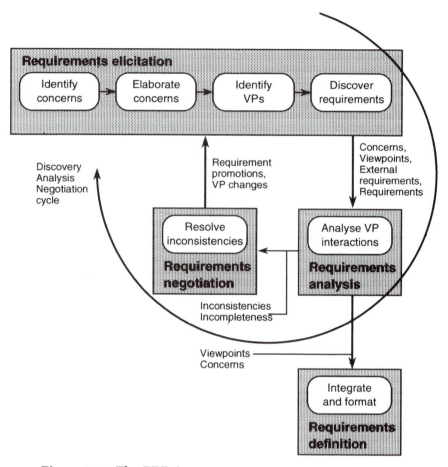

Figure 13.3 The PREview process

lysts and stakeholders consider the problematic requirements to try to reach a consensus about their resolution.
This typically requires negotiations to establish the necessary trade-offs. These trade-offs may necessitate the elicitation of further requirement information.

The viewpoint-oriented approach which we suggest
(PREview) is compatible with this general model. PREview
maps onto the model as illustrated in Figure 13.3.

The shaded boxes correspond to each of the segments
of the spiral model except the box labelled requirements
definition. This corresponds to the axes in the spiral
model. In PREview, the main activities are as follows.

- Requirements elicitation involves identification of the system's viewpoints and elicitation of the requirements information from the stakeholders/documents/etc. These are the 'sources' of the viewpoints' requirements. Before viewpoint identification, however, the system concerns are identified and elaborated. Concerns are discussed below.

- Requirements analysis involves analysing the viewpoints to discover inconsistent and redundant requirements. The task here is limited to their identification by analysing how different viewpoints' requirements interact. For this activity, viewpoints' foci can be used as a guide. Requirements belonging to viewpoints with overlapping foci are more likely to have potential for inconsistencies. Requirements belonging to disjoint viewpoints, by contrast, are less likely to conflict. Resolution of the conflicting requirements is performed by the next activity.

- In requirements negotiation, the conflicting and redundant requirements are resolved. The resolution of inconsistencies normally involves assessment of competing requirements' relative importance, feasibility, cost, etc., in order to inform the necessary trade-offs. These trade-offs may be localised to the requirements concerned. However, they may have side-effects which necessitate the reformulation of other requirements or stimulate the elicitation of new requirements. This implies a further iteration of the discovery-analysis-negotiation cycle.

This cycle is usually iterated a number of times until the set of viewpoints and their requirements is stable and redundancy has been reduced. Once this state of equilibrium is reached, the requirements can be integrated into a cohesive requirements document (see Chapter 3).

It is useful to distinguish two types of requirement: those which are specific to particular viewpoints and those which are global to the whole system (**Guideline 9.7**, *Identify global system requirements*). We use the term 'external requirements' for global requirements to distinguish them from requirements discovered from particular viewpoints. External requirements derive from 'concerns'. Concerns are the top-level, overriding goals of the system and are usually derived from the customer's critical business objectives. Typical examples include reliability, safety, cost and maintainability. Concerns are characterised by being crucial to the success of the project and by being non-negotiable. Concerns exist for most systems but are often subverted by the sheer difficulty of handling large volumes of volatile and non-complementary requirements. This can result in systems which fail to meet the most basic needs. It is therefore useful to carefully distinguish between concerns and other requirements.

Concerns are frequently vaguely defined and express concepts rather than detailed system properties. To be satisfied, they must be converted into specific, verifiable requirements. They can then serve as constraints on the other system requirements. To achieve this, concerns are converted into external requirements which must be explicitly satisfied. In addition, they are converted into 'concern questions'. These provide a quick and easy check on requirements' compliance with concerns. PREview therefore provides two levels of protection from requirements which have the potential to compromise concerns.

- Concern questions are applied when requirements are first discovered in order to quickly eliminate grossly incompatible requirements.

- External requirements are checked more systematically during analysis of each viewpoint's requirements in order to identify more subtle conflicts.

To illustrate the PREview viewpoints approach we use an example taken from the railway domain; the specification of an on-board train protection system called TCS (Train Control System). In this application, the train is controlled by a human driver. TCS is a safety-related system whose job is one of monitoring the train and intervening if an unsafe state is detected. This is done by ensuring that the driver respects the operational rules in force on the track and takes corrective action when the driver breaks these rules. Operational rules include speed limits and protocols for passing signals. Some rules are constant while others may vary according to track conditions. Data is collected in real-time from track-side equipment to monitor speed restrictions and to detect signals. Essentially, if the driver allows the train to go too fast or to illegally cross a 'stopping point' (such as a signal at stop), TCS will cause the emergency brakes to be applied.

TCS must be integrated with an existing execution environment and other on-board systems. A module called Hardware Systems Interface (HSI) exists, through which the TCS software communicates with all the hardware interfaces. This provides:

- an interface of functions permitting (for example) emergency braking to be invoked, and
- data permitting TCS to poll for train speed, distance to next stopping point, etc.

13.2.1 Requirements elicitation in PREview

Before viewpoint identification can begin, an understanding of the system's technical and organisational environment must be gained. The analyst needs to understand the organisational environment. This will allow him or her to identify the correct mix of technical and managerial personnel in the customer's organisation to discover their (and, by implication, their organisation's) concerns.

Concern identification

Concerns are identified at the outset of a project. In the TCS application, the customer's concerns are: *'Safety'* and *'Compatibility'*. 'Safety' is a concern because although TCS does not control the train it does contribute to train safety. 'Compatibility' is a concern because TCS must be integrated with the existing systems' execution cycle and because the HSI module provides the interface to all other modules.

Concern elaboration

Once identified, concerns must be elaborated into external requirements and concern questions. Concern questions act as the conscience of the analyst who should apply them as a test for compliance when a viewpoint's requirements are first discovered. They therefore serve as a first defence against non-compliant requirements. The following concern question can be derived for 'Compatibility':

Q1: Is the requirement consistent with the interface provided by the HSI module?

Consider the case where a stakeholder sets out a requirement to calculate a minimum braking distance to a degree of accuracy which requires as parameters the train speed, mass, line gradient and track surface conditions. Applying the concern question to this requirement would prompt checking that these parameter values were indeed available through the HSI interface. In the TCS, track surface conditions are not monitored via the HSI module so the requirement would be shown to be infeasible.

Of course, sufficient information will not always be available to demonstrate compatibility at the elicitation stage and incompatible requirements will inevitably escape detection. For this reason, every concern is developed into one or more requirements. These are the external requirements with which every viewpoint's requirements must be compliant. Tests for compliance are performed within the requirements analysis phase (Figure 13.3).

For example, the external requirements derived for the 'Compatibility' concern are as follows.

ER4: The TCS software shall be executed in the Ada safety environment of the coded processor.

ER5: The TCS software shall execute within the application cycle of the existing on-board software.

ER6: The reaction time of the TCS software to the change of state of one bit in the variants table shall be 280ms.

ER7: The real-time performance of the existing on-board software shall be maintained.

Concern elaboration must be performed carefully. By investing resources at this very early stage, the elaborated concerns will serve to guard against incompatibilities which may be introduced later. Some classes of concern may employ other techniques to assist with their elaboration. For example, a safety concern may exploit hazard analysis techniques to identify the specific hazards against which the system must provide a defence (**Guideline 10.4**, *Derive critical requirements from hazard analysis*). Here, a specific external requirement and concern question might be developed for each hazard.

For example, in the 'Safety' concern, the specific hazards against which TCS must protect are excess speed and overshooting a stopping point. These can be elaborated into the following three external requirements:

ER1: The system shall detect the occurrence of excess speed

ER2: The system shall detect the occurrence of overshoot

ER3: The system shall apply emergency braking when either excess speed or overshoot are detected.

Note the wide variance in the level of detail expressed by these external requirements. They range from low-level implementation constraints (280 ms) to abstract concepts (overshoot). This illustrates the naivety of the view of requirements engineering as dealing only with the 'what', with all 'how' decisions being conveniently deferred. In reality, and especially for systems installed in an existing technical environment, it is not such a clean process. It also illustrates that in analysing requirements for inconsistencies, the analyst must be prepared to handle requirements at many different levels.

Viewpoint identification

Viewpoint identification is difficult but crucial to the effective use of a viewpoint-oriented approach. Failure to identify an appropriate set of viewpoints implies that some, possibly important, perspectives on the system are omitted, leading in turn to an incomplete and unrepresentative requirements specification. The analyst must find a balance between ensuring that all the viewpoints are represented and deriving an unmanageably large set of

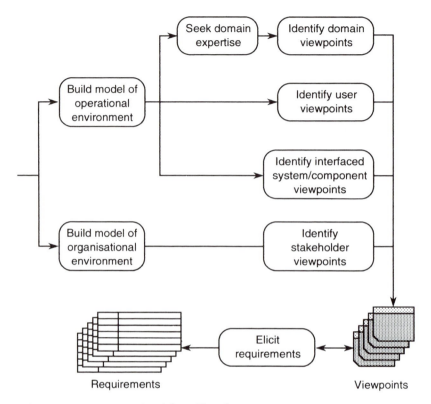

Figure 13.4 Viewpoint identification

viewpoints. Too many viewpoints will hinder integration of their requirements and lead to excessive duplication. To help this balancing act, viewpoint identification must be supported by guidelines. However, much viewpoint information can be reused between projects in the same domain, so their application becomes easier as experience is gained.

To identify viewpoints, the analyst must develop a good understanding of the system's operational and organisational environments. The operational environment will reveal the users and other systems/components with which the system will interact. It also embodies any inherent domain phenomena. The organisational environment will reveal the indirect stakeholders such as managers and regulators. This is illustrated in Figure 13.4.

In order make them manageable, viewpoints have a structure. They consist of the follows.

- The viewpoint *name*. This should reflect the perspective adopted by the viewpoint.

- The viewpoint *focus*. This defines the perspective taken by the viewpoint.

- The *concerns* applicable to the viewpoint. By default, this is the set of all system concerns. Concerns may be eliminated from the viewpoint if it can be demonstrated that they have no constraining effect on the viewpoint.

- The viewpoint *sources*. These explicitly identify the sources of the requirements associated with the requirement. They may be individuals, roles, groups or documents.

- The viewpoint *requirements*. This is the set of requirements discovered by analysing the system from the viewpoint's perspective and by consultation with the sources.

- The viewpoint *history*. This records changes to the information recorded in the viewpoint over time. For example, a rationale for why a particular concern need not be considered by the viewpoint should appear here.

The name, focus and sources must be formulated before the requirements can be elicited. All three of these properties contribute to the viewpoint's identification. Focus defines the scope of the viewpoint's requirements as a function of the problem domain and the components influenced in the system. This is indicated in Figure 13.1 by each viewpoint focusing on a portion of the system. In a typical application, focus will initially be defined in terms of the application domain but as analysis proceeds and a system architecture emerges, focus will become more specific.

Sources may be human or documentary. Examples include system users for a user viewpoint, existing specification documentation for an interfaced system/component viewpoint, and domain experts for a domain viewpoint.

Several sources may contribute requirements to a viewpoint. Similarly, a single stakeholder may contribute requirements to more than one viewpoint. For example, a manager may have one perspective as a user and another concerned with the system's affect on the company's business. In these cases it is common for the stakeholders requirements to be contradictory across different viewpoints. To cope with this you must be able to recognise when a stakeholder has different viewpoints. You can then use this to help the stakeholders set out their requirements by inviting them to adopt different viewpoints.

In some applications, the viewpoints are obvious but in others, the viewpoints will need to be actively sought. In this case, it may be helpful to decompose from the three categories of viewpoint identified above, namely: 'stakeholder' viewpoints, 'operating environment' viewpoints and 'domain' viewpoints. Figure 13.5 illustrates such a decomposition for TCS where the viewpoints are identified in a top-down manner. Here, the leaf nodes are the actual viewpoints identified for the application. Examples include:

Driver: The driver is a stakeholder whose requirements should be identified. This is implicit from both the operational and organisational environment.

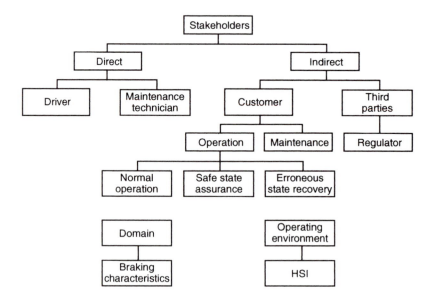

Figure 13.5   TCS viewpoint hierarchy

HSI: The HSI viewpoint represents a subsystem/component from TCS's environment. This is implicit from the operational environment.

These correspond to identifiable perspectives on the system and cohesive sets of requirement sources. For example, drivers are a homogeneous group whereas HSI's requirements can be derived from its existing specification documentation. The non-leaf nodes represent more general viewpoint classifications. They represent stages in the process of identifying the appropriate viewpoints.

For example, stakeholders can be characterised as either direct (i.e. users or operators) or indirect (i.e. they will not interact directly with the system). In the railway domain, indirect stakeholders can be further classified according to whether they represent the customer who commissions the train or third parties. In TCS, the latter are represented by a regulator responsible for assuring safety, compliance with standards, etc. 'Regulator' is a leaf because there is only one regulator. 'Customer', however, can be decomposed to greater depth. The customer will have to maintain the train systems and operate the train. There are three additional viewpoints related to train operation. The 'Normal operation' viewpoint is that of operating the train in the absence of driver errors which necessitate the emergency intervention of the TCS software. The 'Safe state assurance' viewpoint is where the circumstances under which the TCS software intervenes are defined. Finally, the 'Erroneous state recovery' viewpoint is that of how the train can return to normal operation following emergency intervention of the TCS software.

A viewpoint hierarchy may be reusable by similar systems to guide the search for viewpoints. Note, however, that decomposition of viewpoints is primarily a tool to aid identification of viewpoints and their sources. This must be balanced against the need to minimise the number of viewpoints. Following the elicitation of their requirements, it may be useful to collapse viewpoints with common roots back into a single viewpoint. This will make management of the viewpoints easier later on. The leaves of the hierarchy form the starting point for requirements elicitation, because they should correspond closely to actual stakeholders, etc., in the system. However, the set of viewpoints actually used in subsequent analysis may be a smaller number of more general viewpoints.

Below, we give two examples of viewpoints on TCS. 'Safe state assurance' is illustrated in Figure 13.6 and represents requirements for maintaining the train in a safe state. The definition of its focus serves to describe the extent of the requirements' influence on the system. At a later stage of the analysis this could be augmented with a list of the components to which the requirements had been allocated.

Both concerns are considered to constrain the viewpoint:

- 'Safety' is used because incorrect requirements may compromise safety

- 'Compatibility' is used because performance and interface issues are affected by the viewpoint's requirements.

When the viewpoint's requirements are elicited from the sources, they must all be checked to ensure that they satisfy each of the concern questions elaborated from the

Name	Safe state assurance
Focus	Detection of dangerous conditions and application of emergency braking
Concerns	Safety Compatibility
Source	Customer procurement executive TCS preliminary hazard analysis
Requirements	• SS1 (Detection of excess speed) • SS2 (Detection of overshooting) • SS3 (Frequency of invocation)
Change history	

Figure 13.6 The Safe State Assurance viewpoint

Name	Erroneous state recovery
Focus	Return of train to normal operation following emergency braking
Concerns	Safety Compatibility
Source	Customer procurement executive
Requirements	• ESR1 (Recovery following excess speed) • ESR2 (Recovery following overshooting)
Change history	

Figure 13.7 The Erroneous State Recovery viewpoint

'Safety' and 'Compatibility' concerns. In addition, at the requirements analysis stage they must be analysed to verify that they do not conflict with any of the concerns' external requirements.

We have added the three requirements elicited from the viewpoint's sources, although these would normally be elicited only after the viewpoint's identification. These are described below.

Figure 13.7 illustrates the 'Erroneous state recovery viewpoint'. Again, both concerns are applicable.

Sometimes it can be demonstrated that a viewpoint cannot affect a concern. In this case, the concern can be omitted from the concern field and the viewpoint requirements need not be checked against the concern questions or external requirements. However, you should record the justification for ignoring the concern in the change history.

Requirements discovery

Once a viewpoint has been identified, the requirements arising from that viewpoint can be discovered from the viewpoint's source(s). For each requirement, the concern questions should be asked to discover if it is likely to conflict with the concern.

Identifier	SS1 (Detection of excess speed)
Description	If the speed of the train is excessive, emergency braking shall be applied.
Rationale	The train must be forced to comply with the speed limits in force on the track.
Change history	

Identifier	SS2 (Detection of overshooting)
Description	If the front of the train has passed a stopping point, emergency braking shall be applied.
Rationale	The train must be prevented from penetrating occupied or otherwise hazardous sections of track.
Change history	

Identifier	SS3 (Frequency of invocation)
Description	Detection of excess speed, detection of overshooting and determining the necessity of emergency brake application shall be performed once every iteration of the on-board software application cycle.
Rationale	Delays in detection of illegal train states must be minimal.
Change history	

Figure 13.8 Example requirements discovered from the Safe Sate Assurance viewpoint

The examples in Figure 13.8 are those elicited as part of the Safe state assurance viewpoint. Note that each requirement is uniquely identified, has a rationale to help inform any subsequent trade-offs, and includes provision for recording the history of any changes to the requirement.

The following concern question must be applied to each requirement.

Q1: Is the requirement consistent with the interface provided by the HSI module?

This raises the question of whether the requirements are feasible within the limits imposed by the interface provided by the HSI module and the train's on-board execution environment. In the case of SS2, for example, the analyst must ensure that information about the train's relationship to stopping points is available from the HSI interface, and that emergency braking can be invoked through the HSI interface.

In principle, all of a viewpoint's requirements should be mutually consistent but this is not always the case. Some contradictions are natural. For example, a 'user' viewpoint may represent many users, each with the same task to perform but each with different preferences. In this case, it is best to try to resolve the inconsistencies without reference to other viewpoints. Developing a system model for the viewpoint may help to clarify how to reconcile competing requirements.

In other cases, the viewpoint will less homogeneous. For example, another viewpoint may include operators and managers. In this case, the conflicts will be more fundamental due to their different tasks and interests in the system. Occasionally it may be impossible to resolve these inconsistencies without reference to the wider system. In such cases the viewpoint should be decomposed into two new viewpoints, each reflecting the divergent requirements. This does not mean that the contradictions are never resolved. Rather, resolution is deferred until the requirements negotiation stage when the viewpoints' requirements can be looked at in the context of the wider system rather than in isolation. It will then be easier to assess the competing requirements' wider implications. This will help identify the most appropriate trade-offs.

It is important that the viewpoints which emerge from requirements elicitation are internally consistent. Only then can they be analysed for consistency with other viewpoints at the requirements analysis stage. However, this must be tempered by the need to minimise the number of viewpoints.

In practical terms, the number of leaf viewpoints identified in Figure 13.5 is about the maximum which is manageable. Five viewpoints are probably ideal, but when more than this are used, it can become difficult to manage them and identify inconsistencies and redundant requirements. It is reasonable to have more than this to aid requirements discovery, however. If there are more than five viewpoints you should try to collapse some viewpoints back to more general viewpoints once their requirements have been discovered. This can only be done where their requirements are mutually compatible and must therefore follow requirements discovery. If this was the case for the 'Driver' and 'Maintenance technician' viewpoints, for example, they could be collapsed back into a 'Direct' viewpoint. The Direct viewpoint would then contain the union of both viewpoints' requirements, concerns, foci, sources and history.

Eventually, the viewpoints' sets of requirements will be complete. The next task is to integrate them.

13.2.2   Requirements analysis in PREview

The first task in integrating the viewpoints' requirements is to ensure that they each conform to the external requirements derived from the concerns applicable to their viewpoint. Hence, all of 'Safe state assurance' requirements need to be checked for consistency with the external requirements for 'Safety' and 'Compatibility'. Interaction matrices (**Guideline 5.7**, *Use Interaction matrices to find conflicts and overlaps*) are used to support this checking.

The viewpoint's requirements are tabulated against the external requirements as shown in Figure 13.9. Where they intersect, an assessment of whether they are mutually reinforcing (1), do not effect each other (0), or conflict (1000) is performed and entered in the table. A 0 means that no action need be taken. A 1 means that the requirement may be redundant and consideration should be given to eliminating or simplifying it. A 1000 means that the requirement needs to be changed to make it consistent with the external requirement.

		Safety ER1	ER2	ER3	Compatibility ER4	ER5	ER6	ER7
Safe	SS1	1	0	1	0	0	0	0
state	SS2	0	1	1	0	0	0	0
assurance	SS3	0	0	0	0	1000	1000	1000

Figure 13.9 Interaction matrix for checking compliance with concerns

Note that for the 'Safe state assurance' viewpoint, SS1 reinforces external requirements ER1 and ER3. These are all concerned with detection and correction of excess speed. A similar situation exists for SS2. SS3, however, has a potential conflict with ER5, 6 and 7.

The potential conflict arises because of the need to integrate TCS into the existing on-board execution cycle and the consequent need to meet performance constraints. This raises the question of whether requirement SS3 is feasible under these constraints.

The result of the analysis is that all 3 of the 'Safe state assurance' viewpoint's requirements go forward to the requirements negotiation stage: SS1 and SS2 to see if they are redundant and could be simplified; and SS3 to investigate whether it needs to be modified or if a further constraint needs to added. Hence we have detected potential conflicts with the compatibility concern and raised the need for further analysis.

Interaction matrices are also used to focus the analysis on inconsistencies between different viewpoints' requirements. Analysing and checking each requirement against every other requirement quickly becomes infeasible as the number of requirements increases. To counter this, viewpoints' foci can be used as a guide to whether two viewpoints' requirements are likely to interact. If their foci intersect (i.e. impose requirements which influence the same parts of the system or its environment), then they should be tabulated and checked for consistency. For example, the foci of the two viewpoints 'Safe state assurance' and 'Erroneous state recovery' imply that there may

		Erroneous state recovery	
		ESR1	ESR2
Safe	SS1	0	0
state	SS2	0	1000
assurance	SS3	0	0

Figure 13.10 Cross-checking viewpoints for consistency

be some overlap. They share a common state of the train, namely the state following emergency braking. This is the state which 'Safe state assurance' should cause the train to be in and the state which 'Erroneous state recovery' should cause the train to recover from.

The two potentially interacting viewpoints should be tabulated against each other as shown in Figure 13.10. Here, there is a potential inconsistency between SS2 and ESR2. ESR2 is as illustrated in Figure 13.11.

Identifier	ESR2 (Recovery following overshooting)
Description	When the train has stopped following the application of emergency braking caused by overshooting a stopping point, the train shall be permitted to proceed with caution.
Rationale	The train must be able to clear the section of track into which it overshot but must only be permitted to do so at low speed. This is because it is unknown whether access to the section of track was barred because of a genuine hazard or because of an error from the track status data. If the latter, the train must be able to proceed, but only with caution.
Change history	

Figure 13.11 Requirement discovered from the Erroneous State Recovery viewpoint

There is an inconsistency with SS2 (if the front of the train has passed a stopping point, emergency braking shall be applied) which implies that, because the train has crossed a stopping point, emergency braking should be applied immediately the train tried to move off under caution. Clearly, some form of clarification is needed to specify that emergency braking is applied only once when the train passes a stopping point. The two conflicting requirements must go forward to requirements negotiation for resolution.

Redundant requirements should also go forward to requirements negotiation.

13.2.3   Requirements negotiation

PREview does not define how the inconsistencies and redundancies identified by the requirements analysis phase are resolved. How this is done must be left to the judgement of the analyst and the various requirements' sources. However, the lists of inconsistent and potentially redundant requirements provide an agenda for any requirements negotiations between the analyst and conflicting stakeholders.

Note that the existence of redundant requirements is useful information. A requirement originating from several viewpoints may be taken to suggest that the requirement is of relatively high priority. By contrast, a requirement originating from only one viewpoint suggests that it may be likely to change. For this reason, no attempt to eliminate redundancies between viewpoint requirements should be made. However, it may be useful to try to harmonise the requirements if they do not express exactly the same requirement.

After recommendations have been made for resolving redundancies and inconsistencies, the changed requirements are fed back into the requirements elicitation phase. This is to ensure that any changes are themselves compliant with concerns and are mutually consistent. An application of PREview will typically result in several iterations of the discovery/analysis/negotiation cycle. Each cycle should require diminishing effort. Eventually,

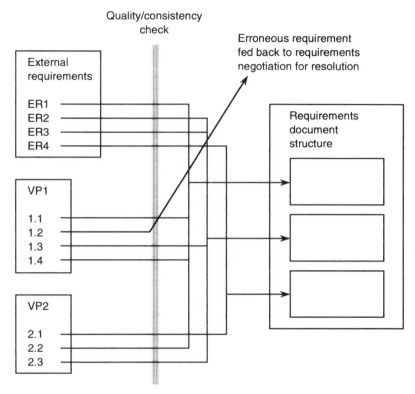

Figure 13.12 Mapping requirements to an requirements document

the viewpoints and their requirements should be sufficiently stable to integrate into a requirements document.

13.2.4 Requirements definition

Once a stable set of viewpoints and requirements has been achieved, the requirements must be integrated into a usable form. To most practical purposes, this means a requirements document. Typically, the organisation of a requirements document is not viewpoint-oriented. This means that the requirements information must be mapped onto the form defined for the document. Chapter 3 describes the requirements document. Mapping viewpoints onto a requirements document is illustrated by Figure 13.12. Note that it is essential to preserve the viewpoint information so that requirements can be traced back from the requirements document to their viewpoints and their sources.

There are six activities involved in this mapping.

1 Identify the required structure of the requirements document and divide it into the main sections. For example, it may be structured into sections on: system constraints, functional requirements, performance requirements, interface requirements and usability requirements.

2 Identify a set of quality, consistency or other standards which the document should meet and formulate these as a checklist against which any requirement can be evaluated.

3 For each external requirement, allocate it to one of the sections according to whether it expresses a system constraint, functional requirement, etc.

4 Repeat activity 3 for each viewpoint requirement.

5 For each requirement (external or viewpoint) apply the checklist defined in activity 2 and adapt requirements which fail to satisfy the checks.

6 Review each section and eliminate redundancy.

Activity 2 is designed to ensure that requirements use consistent terminology (a glossary may be a useful byproduct of this activity) and are formulated at a level of detail which is acceptable. Where requirements fail these checks, they should either be reformulated or flagged as needing more detailed attention at a later stage.

It is also possible that other more serious errors will be identified here. This will require a feedback of the erroneous requirement(s) to the requirements negotiation phase and at least one more iteration of the discovery-analysis-negotiation cycle until the error is resolved (e.g. requirement 1.2 in Figure 13.12).

Activity 6 will be needed as any viewpoint-oriented requirements elicitation method inevitably results in redundant requirements. This is the price paid for increasing the likelihood of completeness. Even with the requirements analysis and negotiation phases, it is unlikely that all redundancy in the requirements set will have been detected and resolved.

13.2.5 Tools issues

Dedicated tool support for viewpoint-oriented analysis is not currently available. However, PREview is designed so that all the information can be collected and analysed using forms or check-lists. This makes it relatively easy to adapt a requirements management tool such as DOORS (see the book's web page) to support the approach. In addition, interaction matrices can be readily implemented using a spreadsheet.

13.3   Further Reading

The January 1996 edition of the *Software Engineering Journal* carried a special issue on Viewpoints in Requirements Engineering. This included a useful set of 'FAQ's in the editorial. It also included the following two descriptions of recent viewpoint approaches:

Easterbrook, S., and Nuseibeh, B., 1996. Using ViewPoints for inconsistency management. *Software Engineering Journal*, **11**(1)

Kotonya, G., and Sommerville, I., 1996. Requirements engineering with viewpoints. *Software Engineering Journal*, **11**(1)

Another important contribution to viewpoints is described in:

Leite, J. C. S. P., and Freeman, P. A., 1991. Requirements Validation through Viewpoint Resolution. *IEEE Transactions on Software Engineering*, **17**(12)

Finally, the first true viewpoint-oriented method was CORE, which has been used in defence and aerospace projects in the UK. Unfortunately, published information is hard to find, but Mullery's original paper still makes interesting reading.

Mullery, G., 1979, *CORE: A Method for Controlled Requirements Specification*. Proc. 4th Int. Conf. on Software Engineering, Munich.

Index

accident 258
air-traffic-control system 307–8, 357
architectural design 39, 302
  model 162, 173–6
availability 256

behavioural model 164, 308–15
Bootstrap 20
bulletin boards 122
business concerns 49, 66, 81–3
  process 170

Capability Maturity Model 19
CASE 16, 29–30, 166, 167, 175, 177–9, 181, 187, 239, 244, 282, 213, 323
change management 222, 242–5
checklist 117–120, 126, 200–2, 262–6
  items 120, 201, 263
  size 119
client-server systems 174
concerns 368–72, 374, 378–9, 385
configuration management 234, 244
control-flow diagram 313
CORE 306, 363, 388
critical systems 256, 260, 331

data dictionary 148, 181–4, 319–21
data-flow diagram 155, 212–3, 309–15, 317, 319, 329
decision tables 155
diagrams – use of 151–3
documentation 207

domain constraints 84–6, 302, 365
  handbook 86, 87

electronic information exchange 121–4
end-users 45
entity-relationship model 316
environmental model 79, 162, 169–72, 324–5

faceted classification 130
feasibility study 66–8
finite-state model 314
formal specification 167, 213, 281–6, 304, 331–58
  methods
    B 339–40
    CCS 340
    CSP 337, 340
    Larch 339
    Lotos 337, 340
    OBJ 339
    VDM 337, 339–41
    Z 331–2, 337, 339–41, 347, 349–58
  refinement 335–6, 344, 348
  verification 281, 285, 334–6, 338, 343, 349–57
fourth generation languages 95
functional requirements 7, 42
  specification 6, 38

global requirements 246–8, 369–71, 382, 387
glossary 51–3, 387
guideline classification 18
  implementation priority 27

lists 30–5
top ten 31

hazard 258
identification and analysis
269–73, 274, 304, 347,
372
hypertext 88, 234

IEEE standard 42
improvement costs 28
incident 258
database 287–91, 292
experience 287–91, 292–5
interaction matrix 134–6,
382–84
Intranet 86, 123
ISO 9000 12

Java 96

layout guidelines 54–5

maintainability 256
measurement programme 29
mathematical model 7
natural language 6, 142, 147–50,
154–6, 212, 214
non-functional requirements 7,
42, 43, 158

object-oriented database 238
methods 178, 301, 309, 311,
314, 326–8
Booch 300, 315, 329
OMT 300, 311, 314–5,
325–6, 328–30
OOA 300, 311, 329
modelling 163, 316–9
operating environment 78–80,
365, 373–4
operational processes 102–5,
114–5, 170
organisational factors 64, 69–71,
113

petri nets 315
pipeline systems 174
political factors 64, 69–71, 113

PREview 91, 104, 135, 359, 363,
365–87
procedural methods 178, 315
process assessment 23–6
improvement 2, 15, 26–30
goals 16
group 17
management 17
maturity 18–23
re-engineering 2
prototype 94–8, 203–5, 207,
346

QFD 135
quality management 221, 348
quantitative specification 157–60

railway signalling system 8,
301–2
REAIMS 18, 261, 359
relational database 238
reliability 256
repository-based systems 174
requirements – definition 4–5
expression 6
analysis and negotiation 11,
367–9, 381–5, 387
classification 130–3
conflicts 112, 125–7, 195,
361–3, 372, 381–3, 385
database 75, 123, 132, 210,
236–41, 252
document 9, 23, 38, 369,
385–6
definition 5–6
layout 54–6
modifiability 61–2
standards 41–4, 192
usability 57–9
elicitation 11, 64, 360–2,
367–8, 371–82, 385
engineering – definition 5
problems 23
process 9, 11
maturity levels 21
problems 10
identification 117, 134, 145,
210, 218–20
inspection 195–7, 198–9, 268

management 216, 360, 366
  policies 221–3
priority 128–9
problems 2, 191, 209
rationale 87–9, 145, 364, 380
reuse 106–9
review 267
risk 128, 106, 137–9
sources 75–7, 145, 364, 367–8,
    374–5, 378–9
standards 144–6, 222
summary 47–8
testing 209–11
validation 11, 190

safety 256
  case 257
  culture 296–8
  requirements 258, 274–7,
      278–80
safety–critical systems 82
scenarios 99–101, 107, 112, 205,
    315
security 256
Smalltalk 96
socio-technical systems 301, 303
soft systems methodology 328,
    330
software requirements
    specification 6, 38
stakeholder 7, 8, 64, 72–4, 82,
    99, 102, 125, 129, 164, 170,
    198, 203
  requirements 39, 143, 185–7,
      305–6, 364, 368, 375, 377

statecharts 315
structural model 165, 315
structured methods 177–80,
    299–330, 333
  SADT 300, 312, 329, 347, 360,
      362
  SSADM 300, 303, 329
  Ward–Mellor 300, 312, 329
system boundaries 114–6, 170
  model 7, 155, 162, 185–7,
      212–4, 219, 285, 324–5
  properties 43
  requirements 39, 246–8

traceability 181, 185, 217, 274,
    321, 363
  information 226–7
  lists 229–30, 236
  manual 232–5
  policies 222, 224–31, 233,
      278
tables 227–9, 236, 279

use-case (see scenarios)
user manual 206–8

viewpoints 73, 76, 82, 90–3,
    271, 276, 306, 347, 359–88
Visual Basic 96
volatile requirements 249–51,
    258

workflow 104
writing style guidelines 148–9